Louise de Marillac
A Light
in the Darkness

Kathryn B. LaFleur, S.P.

Louise de Marillac
A Light
in the Darkness

A Woman of Yesteryear,
A Saint and Model for Today

New City Press

DEDICATION
For
The Sisters of Providence of St. Vincent de Paul, Kingston, Canada

My Sisters, M. Joan and Marie
and
To the Memory of Our Parents
George and Evelyn LaFleur

Published in the United States by New City Press
202 Cardinal Rd., Hyde Park, NY 12538
©1996 Kathryn B. LaFleur, S. P.

Cover photo: Louise de Marillac
©1992 Christine Brandt, D. C. Window located in the Basilica
of the National Shrine of St. Elizabeth Ann Seton, Emmitsburg, Maryland.

Library of Congress Cataloging-in-Publication Data:

LaFleur, Kathryn.
    Louise de Marillac : a light in the darkness / Kathryn LaFleur.
        p.   cm.
    Includes bibliographical references and index.
    ISBN 1-56548-075-9
    1. Louise de Marillac, Saint, 1591-1660.   2. Daughters of Charity of St. Vincent de Paul.
3. Christian saints—Francis—Biography.   I. Title.
BX4700.L5L34 1996
282'.092—dc20
[B]   96-6432

Printed in the United States of America

Table Of Contents

Foreword

Sr. Kathryn LaFleur, S.P., who labored very hard and well during these past years to capture the inner spiritual and dynamic life of Louise de Marillac, has put into this book the inner and outer account of someone relatively unknown to the Western world, although held lovingly in memory by the Church, especially when Pope John XXIII declared her the patroness of all Christian Social Workers. The community she founded, the Daughters of Charity, is much more known, however. Moreover, hers was the very last statue to be placed in the circles of heroes and heroines around Saint Peter's Basilica in Rome, which prompted an Italian newspaper headline to say at the time: "The Saint of Charity Enters The Vatican Basilica."

Louise's faith journey, for the first time in a systematic way theologically exposed for the English-speaking world, is the story of an inner theological encounter of human toil with the hidden power of grace, as she deals with seemingly insurmountable obstacles from within and without. Louise is yet another proof of the strength of grace over human frailty and difficulty, as the doctor of grace, Augustine, has demonstrated so well. As we go through her life and mull over the many principles Louise had learned from her mentor, Vincent de Paul and *the* mentor, the Holy Spirit, we become struck by the necessary sense of hope that must pervade all human endeavor, especially in new creative adventures for the sake of the kingdom. Louise is rightly called by Sr. Kathryn "a pioneer and a prophetic witness," to which I would add a prophetess whose message not only preaches but will gather more momentum during the third millennium.

Louise de Marillac, as Sr. Kathryn weaves carefully throughout her book, was a married woman, mother, widow, and foundress of an apostolic congregation of Sisters. Each stage produced its character of virtue and paved the way for newer challenges. She did not lose the virtuous results of her earlier years as she faced new challenges later on. If someone enters the chapel of the Daughters of Charity located on rue du Bac in Paris, he or she will find the tomb of Saint Louise and nearby the reliquary containing the heart of Saint Vincent, which indicates how close their friendship was. Yet, Louise was not in utter dependence upon Vincent as a daughter, but hewed out for herself some important principles of action that make her a model for women (and I would add men as well) of today, as we approach the new millennium with a sense of regenerating Western civilization with a "gospel of life."

To be a foundress in seventeenth-century France of a group of women dedicated to serving the poor in many different ways required a very indomitable spirit to overcome the many obstacles facing any foundress. It had been tried before by Jane Frances de Chantal, and her community was now cloistered. Women had not dared to give retreats; but here was Louise giving conferences to women and men sneaking away to come and listen to her enchanting wisdom. Here was a woman concerned with deep emotion about the life of her son, struggling with the beginnings of her first community of Sisters and yet able to put it all into perspective and be absorbed by God's plans and will for her, subordinating all to her greatest love. Her "Only Hope," she learned by experience, was the "Only Cross."

Louise's faith development feasted upon a spiritual climate in France that was dominated theologically by Bérullian principles. Tempered and assisted by her dearest friend, mentor and spiritual father, Vincent de Paul, she faced and overcame many an obstacle within her mission. However, without Bérulle's articulation of Christ's states being still in existence, much like sacraments which give grace to those who ponder these states, Vincent might not have been able to see, much less "obey" the Lord Jesus in the poor that literally came upon him. Had he not been able to see in the weakest human person an image of Jesus, Louise might not have labored with the dregs of French society to the degree that she did, nor spent much time before the tabernacle with her eucharistic Lord so highly spoken of by the same Bérulle. For Louise and for Vincent, the mystical body of Jesus is but the extension of Christ in people, especially the poor. Before we heard or read about liberation theology and the phrase, "preferential option for the poor," Louise and Vincent were living it.

Again, from the Bérullian patrimony of theological principles and persons pervading the Church during her time, Louise's mysticism became at once Trinitarian, Christocentric, Marian, ecclesial and pastoral with a special focus on Christ. It was not by accident that the eldest daughter of the Church, France, would also generate in this seventeenth-century explosion of saints much reflection and devotion to the Sacred Heart of Jesus, beginning from the pens of St. John Eudes and Francis de Sales, who in turn inspired the work of Margaret Mary Alacoque. It is of note that fifty to sixty years prior to Margaret Mary Alacoque, Louise de Marillac is reputed to have painted the first known picture of the Sacred Heart of Jesus, which she called "The Lord of Charity."

Spirituality has once been described as the cream of theology, taking in and synthesizing elements of moral, dogmatic, ascetical and mystical theology. You will see this at work as you begin this book, which you should not hurry to finish but linger over, as other thoughts suggest themselves to you. Louise still loves her poor ones and wants all of us to prolong her mission in the state of life we live in. Now my dear reader, let us begin to fathom Louise's depths wherein you will find some echoes of what it means to be a friend and servant of God.

Basil Cole, O.P.

Introduction

"O Lord, it is thy will that we should speak of thy servant, for she is the work of thy hands."[1]

Background

This study is, I believe, the result of the inspiration of Vincent de Paul. When I began to study in earnest the spirituality of Vincent de Paul and his spiritual legacy to the Daughters of Charity particularly through his Conferences to them, I became truly immersed in Vincent's spirituality and grew to love him deeply; yet, there was always a question hovering in the back of my mind: "What about Louise?" As I continued to study, the question continued to emerge. I began to pray that the Spirit would show me the direction for my study and in the course of time, providence seemed to point the way. After having made a weekend retreat, I was walking down from the University when I met the former Dean who began to question me about my research. When I answered that I was researching Vincent de Paul and his spirituality, he countered with: "Why are you not doing the woman?" After five months of research and a profound affection for Vincent de Paul, I felt somewhat stunned. Was this a direct answer to prayer or was it a sidetrack? My reaction was so strong that I had to begin some study of Louise's personal spirituality to see if indeed this was the way I was supposed to follow. The next day, Father Robert Maloney who is now the Superior General of the Congregation of the Mission (Vincentians), kindly lent me his copy of the newly-published English edition of the *Spiritual Writings of Louise de Marillac* and thus began my study of the spirituality of Louise de Marillac in May of 1992. At that point I was still seeking confirmation as to changing my topic from Vincent to Louise. I continued to pray for guidance as did my friends and members of my prayer group, Lumen Christi. Then, on Pentecost Sunday, June 7, 1992 I picked up a small book by J.P. Sheedy, C.M. entitled *Untrodden Paths* and there on the first page read the following words of Vincent de Paul to Louise de Marillac:

> I have omitted many things I might have said about yourself. Let us leave it to Our Lord to say it to the whole world some day, and let us hide ourselves in the meantime.[2]

Hidden in the meantime Louise has certainly been as it has taken nearly three hundred years for her to be duly recognized within the Church and even now her spiritual greatness is still little known. Perhaps this was in keeping with her strong desire to imitate the hidden life of Jesus.

Taking the above words as a sign of Vincent's blessing, I continued to pursue my study of Louise's Spiritual Writings and Letters, several of her biographies and various articles. Through these I found a woman of faith, hope and love — a woman who was a prophetic model for Christians of the seventeenth century as well as for today. She was a woman of the gospel, a woman of the church, and a woman rooted in providence who, empowered by the Holy Spirit, was a tremendous agent for change in her society and whose legacy both spiritual and corporal has through her Daughters spread to the ends of the earth.

As the spirit and mission of Vincent and Louise could not be separated in temporal life, so they cannot be separated in eternal life. Hence it was with deep trust in their intercession and that of Catherine of Siena that I embraced this study and that I now share with you the reader, my journey into the spirituality of Louise de Marillac which in so many ways was intertwined with that of Vincent de Paul as they grew to become one heart and one hand in the providence of God. Through this humble effort may you come to know and love this valiant woman and may she be for you, as she has been for me, a source of comfort, light and hope in your journey with God. Through Louise de Marillac, may this work redound to the greater glory of God: the Father, the Son and the Holy Spirit.

General Situation

Louise de Marillac (1591-1660) was one of the most dynamic, prophetic and social reform women of seventeenth-century France. She was "une fille naturelle," an orphan, a wife, a mother, a widow, a consecrated woman, a foundress and a social reformer. Louise was a holy woman, the effects of whose works and spirituality have spread throughout the world. Yet, until this century she has been little known, especially in the English-speaking world, even by the many Congregations who claimed her as their spiritual foundress and mother. How could one so great be so forgotten? Perhaps this was in the providence of God, because this century and the next need the light of her vision and her witness as a sign of hope in the oft-times darkness of our societies which are so similar to hers. Perhaps too, she was seen mainly as the helpmate and collaborator of that giant of Charity and spiritual reform, her spiritual guide and beloved friend, Vincent de Paul. Whatever the reason, Louise de Marillac seems to be emerging from the shadows and coming into clearer focus in this our day. In her "Notes on The Meetings of the Ladies of Charity," Louise wrote:

It is very evident in this century that divine providence willed to make use of women to show that it was his goodness alone which desired to aid afflicted peoples and to bring them powerful helps for their salvation.[3]

Could not the echo of these words be heard from Christian women of today? Louise does, I contend, have a mighty message and a wise witness for all contemporary Christians. She was a woman of great prayer — a mystic — from which flowed her varied and extensive works of mercy. From her union with Christ and her imitation of his spirit and works came her sanctity. Her Cause for sainthood was introduced in 1895 during the pontificate of Leo XIII. In 1911 Pius X solemnly proclaimed her virtues; in 1920 Benedict XV beatified her; in 1934 Pius XI canonized her; and in 1960 Pope John XXIII proclaimed Louise de Marillac the Patroness of All Those Devoted to Christian Social Works, a fact that is also generally little known.[4]

With the recent publication of the *Spiritual Writings of Louise de Marillac:Correspondence and Thoughts* (1991), the English-speaking world now has greater access to the richness, the beauty and the depth of the woman Louise: her personality, her character, her talents, her struggles, her loves, all of which contribute to her spirituality. Through her letters and spiritual writings we come to know an oft "forgotten woman" as the Lord's "beloved one" whom he called to manifest his preferential love for the poor and the marginalized and whom he schooled in compassion through her personal experience of suffering and her journey from darkness to light. Through the power of the Holy Spirit and trust in providence she became a light in the darkness of the France of her day. Yet, for most Christians this light has been "hidden under a bushel" for nearly three hundred years. It seems that the time has come for more writers to catch the fire of Louise de Marillac and to let it glow so that in the darkness of hearts and societies it may bring the warmth and the hope of the love of Christ.

Description of Terms

1. Christian Spirituality

Spirituality is understood to include not merely the techniques of prayer but, more broadly, a conscious relationship with God, in Jesus Christ, through the indwelling of the Spirit and in the context of the community of believers. Spirituality is, therefore, concerned with the conjunction of theology, prayer and practical Christianity. A central feature is that spirituality derives its identity from the Christian belief that as human beings we are capable of entering into a relationship with God who is both transcendent and, at the same time, indwelling in the heart of all created things. This relationship is lived out, not in isolation, but in a community of believers that is brought into being by commitment to Christ and sustained by the active presence of the Spirit of God in each and in the community as a whole.[5]

2. The Confraternities of Charity

The "Confraternities of Charity" refer to the groups of women established in the parishes to assist the sick and the poor, both "corporally and spiritually." The first Confraternity was established by Vincent de Paul in the parish of Châtillon-Les-Dombes in August of 1617 and thereafter he established one in every parish to which he was in any way connected. The eighty-four-page manuscript containing the provisional rules, the definitive rules, the approbation of the Archbishop of Lyons and the official report of the erection of the Association of the "Confraternity of Charity" is on view in the Chapel of the Daughters of Charity in Châtillon.[6]

3. The Company of the Daughters of Charity

The Company of the Daughters of Charity initially began by helping the Ladies of the Confraternities of Charity; however, it was soon realized that a more united form of life under one

Superior was needed if the girls were to be totally dedicated to the service of the poor. Hence, on November 29, 1633, Vincent, after diligently seeking the guidance of providence, placed three or four girls under the care of Louise de Marillac and thus began their formation. Every precaution was taken to ensure that they would not be considered "religious" which would have meant the death of their charism. The Company of the Daughters of Charity was born with Vincent de Paul as their founder and Louise de Marillac as their foundress.[7]

4. The Company of Ladies of Charity

The "Ladies of Charity" were formed by Vincent de Paul in early 1634, through the requests of Mme Goussault and Archbishop de Gondi of Paris. The objective of the Company was primarily to be of spiritual assistance to the patients in the Hotel Dieu Hospital of Paris. Vincent de Paul was named the perpetual director and Mme Goussault the President. By July 25, 1634 from 100 - 125 Ladies of rank were members.[8]

5. The Congregation of the Mission

The Congregation of the Mission was formed on April 17, 1625 by Monsieur and Madame Gondi and it was to be under the direction of Vincent de Paul. The priests of the Congregation were "to devote themselves . . . unreservedly to the salvation of poor country folk by preaching, catechetical instruction and the hearing of general confessions."[9] By 1626 the Company consisted of Vincent de Paul and three other priests. Vincent obtained episcopal approbation for the Congregation from the Archbishop of Paris, John Francis de Gondi on April 24, 1626 and Letters of Patent from the King granting it legal status in May, 1627. Papal approbation was granted by Pope Urban VIII on January 12, 1633.[10] The "Priests of the Mission" were the one half of the future "Double Vincentian Family" and their Superior General would be so for the future Daughters of Charity as well.

Sources

The primary sources utilized in this study consist of the Correspondence and Spiritual Thoughts of Louise de Marillac, Documents directly related to her, Conferences of Vincent de Paul to the Daughters of Charity and Correspondence between Vincent and Louise. These original documents are preserved in the Archives of the Daughters of Charity at rue du Bac in Paris. Other primary sources related to Vincent de Paul are taken from works based on materials preserved in the Archives of the Motherhouse of the Congregation of the Mission, rue du Sèvres, Paris. The secondary sources consist of Biographies, Major Studies, Articles and Related Studies. These sources will be noted within the Selected Bibliography.

Notes

1 . Pierre Coste, C.M., *The Conferences of St. Vincent De Paul to the Sisters of Charity*, translated by Joseph Leonard, C.M. (Maryland: Christian Classics, Inc., 1968). IV, 315. Hereinafter cited as Leonard, *Conferences*. These are the words of Vincent de Paul to the Daughters of Charity during the first Conference "On The Virtues Of Louise de Marillac," July 3, 1660.

2 . J.P. Sheedy, C.M., *Untrodden Paths: The Social Apostolate of St. Louise de Marillac* (London: Salesian Press, 1958), p. 1.

3 . Louise Sullivan, D.C., ed. and trans., *Spiritual Writings of Louise de Marillac: Correspondence and Thoughts* (New York: New City Press, 1991), p. 789, A.56.

4. Sheedy, p. 1.

5 . Philip Sheldrake, S.J., *Spirituality & History* (London: SPCK, 1991), p. 52.

6 . Pierre Coste, C.M., *The Life & Works of St. Vincent de Paul*, 3 vols., trans. Joseph Leonard, C.M. (New York: New City Press, 1987), I, 83.

7. See Coste, *Life & Works*, I, 226-231.

8. Coste, *Life & Works*, I, 237-242.

9. Coste, *Life & Works*, I, 148.

10. Coste, *Life & Works*, I. See Chapter IX, pp. 144-159.

The Life and Times of Louise de Marillac: A Woman of Yesteryear

Historical Framework (1591-1660)

How often does one's lifespan of sixty-nine years witness the drama of three kings, two Queen-Regents, two powerful political cardinals and forty years of unrelenting war with its resultant destruction of the social, economic, political and religious fabric of the country? Such was the historical setting for the life of Louise de Marillac who was born August 12, 1591 and died March 15, 1660. Her birth occurred during Henri IV's struggle to claim the throne of France and her death occurred just prior to the fullness of the splendorous reign of Louis XIV. In the intervening years her life was strongly marked by the history of her day. Louise was no mere observer of the events but one whose life was dramatically affected by the occurrences of the times. Every aspect of her country's history impinged upon her personal life and to a great extent determined the focus of the activities of the second half of her life. From the shadows of political intrigue and the darkness of war and destruction Louise was to emerge with Vincent de Paul as a central figure of light and hope to the suffering masses of many parts of France. The direct influences of history on her personal life we shall see shortly but first let us view the historical panorama which constituted the background of her life.[1]

Born in August of 1591, Louise entered the scene of France almost concurrently with Henri IV who had become its rightful king in 1589 upon the assassination of Henri III. But, because of his Protestant religion the staunch Catholics of France would not accept him. Thus, in an effort to claim his throne Henri had to battle with Catholic extremists who had joined forces with the Spanish king, Philip II. During this time of war, Paris suffered terrible economic conditions which forced people to eat horses, dogs and rats to survive. One author records that some even disinterred children's bones to be ground for flour.[2] In the midst of this chaos Henri tended to be a merciful enemy allowing the old and weak to leave the city. "Paris must not become a graveyard," he said, "I do not wish to reign over the dead."[3] After nearly four years of fighting Henri was successful and finally was accepted as King of France in 1593 when he renounced the Calvinist religion and publicly accepted Catholicism. Henri IV's years of leadership tended to be positive as he somewhat alleviated the tax burden of the poor, granted religious freedom to the Huguenots[4] and with his able minister Sully began repairing the damages of war. Together they succeeded in developing agriculture and new prosperity ensued. For these blessings Henri was dubbed "the good king".[5] This is not surprising when epidemics and famine ravaged the provinces killing thirty to forty per cent of the population, when the infant mortality rate was fifty per cent, and when the average life span of the peasant was between twenty and twenty-five years.[6] With Henri's assassination by a madman on May 14, 1610, darkness fell over France. Despite his lax personal life Henri had contributed positively to France's history and is remembered even today as one of the most popular rulers of France.[7]

Since Henri's son, Louis XIII, was only nine years old at this time, his mother, Marie de Medici, became Queen-Regent. Inefficient as a ruler she aligned herself with her Italian friends, particularly the Concinis who became powerful figures at Court. In time, both the feudal lords (seigneurs) and Protestants began to stir up trouble in opposition to the Court abuses which had depleted the treasury built up by Henri IV and Sully. Eventually, Louis XIII on the advice of his friend the Duc du Luyne, requested that Concini be eliminated and subsequently he was shot in front of the Louvre on April 24, 1617. Later his wife, because of her influence over the Queen Mother, was convicted of witchcraft and was beheaded. Then the Queen Mother herself was banished to Blois on May 3, where she remained for several years.[8]

With the deposition of the Queen Mother, Louis XIII began to reign but disorder continued until he appointed Cardinal Richelieu as his Prime Minister. With Richelieu order ensued. His first move was to demand obedience to the King from the seigneurs and the Huguenots. In spite of wars, Richelieu, a genius of organization, restored order and abolished the privileges of the nobility thus giving royalty the ascendancy.[9] In his own right, Louis XIII was an active prince who became an excellent soldier and collaborated with Richelieu in the tasks at hand. However, his mother, Marie de Medici and his wife, Anne of Austria would gladly have seen him gone but even more so they would have rejoiced over the exit of his Prime Minister, Richelieu. This was evident in their major plot to overthrow Richelieu in 1630 when during the King's illness both wife and mother endeavored to turn him against his Prime Minister. The Queen Mother had already persuaded Michel de Marillac, Louise's uncle who was Keeper of the Seals, that he could overthrow and replace Richelieu. Should Louis not recover from his illness, Anne would marry his brother Gaston d'Orleons and be secure in her position. The plot failed; the Queen Mother was banished; Marillac was imprisoned and Richelieu was the victor. In history this day is known as "The Day of Dupes". Yet, even in exile the Queen Mother continued to try to overthrow Richelieu. As a lesson to her, Jean-Louis de Marillac, Maréchal of France and an ally of the Queen Mother, was arrested on the charge of profiting from his military posts and was beheaded in May of 1632. In August of the same year, Michel de Marillac died in prison at Châteaudun ending the almost two-hundred-year political life of the Marillac family. It was Louise, "la fille naturelle", who was destined to continue to carry the noble name into the pages of history.

Louis XIII continued to reign and with the astuteness of Richelieu they persevered in their attempts to secure France in the midst of the threat of foreign hostilities. In 1633, the King's troops occupied Lorraine and in 1634 Colmar. They declared war on Spain in May of 1635.[10] In August of 1636, Richelieu's campaign to crush the power of the Spanish and Austrian Hapsburgs and their German allies came home to Paris and its suburbs when these troops, led by the Bavarian General Johann von Werth and the young Cardinal Infant Ferdinand of Spain, crossed the northern border of France and overran Picardy, driving the French back toward Paris. On August 5, they swept into the town of Corbie and by August 14 controlled the fortress which protected Paris on the Amiens road. The French defeat was intensified by fleeing peasants, monks and nuns who were intermingled with the exhausted troops, all seeking refuge in Paris which became chaotic.[11] Vincent de Paul described the situation thus:

> . . .Paris is expecting a siege by the Spaniards. They have entered Picardy and are pillaging it with a powerful army whose vanguard extends to within ten or twelve leagues from here. As a result, the people from the plains are fleeing to Paris and Paris is so terrified that many are running away to other cities. Nonetheless, the King is trying to assemble an army to fight that of the Spaniards because his own troops are either outside the kingdom or at its borders; and the place where the companies are being trained and armed is here in our house. The stables, woodshed, halls, and cloisters are full of weapons, and the courtyards filled with soldiers.
>
> The feast of the Assumption is not exempt from the noisy commotion. The drum is beginning to roll already although it is only seven o'clock in the morning. That is why they have been able to drill seventy-two companies here in the past week.[12]

This war ensued until November of 1636 when the King, leading his troops in person, recaptured Corbie and on November 21 reentered Paris in triumph.[13] The major threat seemed to be overcome but internal battles still surfaced for the remaining few years of Louis XIII's life and the state of the country villages, especially Lorraine, was desperate as they were ravaged by the effects of war, famine and the plague. Pierre Coste describes the situation as follows:

> The greater part of the population died of starvation; men and women might have been seen wandering about from place to place with haggard eyes looking for anything to eat, fighting with domestic animals for acorns and grass and with carnivorous beasts for the flesh of horses, dogs and rats. . . . The corpses of men either killed or dead from want of nourishment were not spared, and children were seen digging up the corpse of a father or mother to devour it. Even the living were attacked and men were hunted like hares. . . . One mother made a bargain with another to eat her own child on condition that the other would afterwards do likewise.[14]

May 1638 which saw the birth of the dauphin, Louis XIV, at Saint-Germain-en-Laye brought great rejoicing to the French. It was another hint of sun through the pervading clouds.

The final five years of Louis XIII's reign saw a revolt in Normandy (1639), the limitation of the power of Parliament (1641), the death of Sully (1641), Mazarin receive the Cardinal's hat (1641), the death of Richelieu (1642) and his own final illness. Louis XIII died at Saint-Germain on May 14, 1643 assisted by the humble curé, Vincent de Paul, who the following day in a letter to Bernard Codoing in Rome described the King's death thus:

> It pleased God to dispose of our good King yesterday, which is the same day he began to reign thirty-three years ago. His Majesty wanted me to assist him at the hour of death, together with the bishops of Lisieux and Meaux, his

principal chaplain and his confessor, M.Dinet. As long as
I have been on this earth, I have never seen anyone die in
a more Christian manner. . . . Never have I seen greater
elevation of the soul toward God, greater tranquillity,
greater apprehension of the smallest atom that seemed to
be sin, greater kindness, or better judgment in a person in
this state.[15]

In 1643, when his father died, Louis XIV was five years old;
hence his mother, Anne of Austria became Queen-Regent. She
chose as her Prime Minister the Italian, Cardinal Mazarin[16] and
gave him full power to govern which he did, defending the
interests of royalty while at the same time amassing his own
fortune. He lived extravagantly and he entertained lavishly while
the people paid. As usual, increasing taxes fell most heavily on
the poor, sowing the seeds of discontent and revolt everywhere.
By 1648 Mazarin had brought the war with Germany to an end
and by the Treaty of Westphalia, Alsace belonged to France; but,
in a few short months he faced civil war within Paris. In reaction
to continual taxation, the nobles and citizens closed ranks against
the Court and Parliament. Fighting and turmoil once again
reigned in the streets of Paris. Queen Anne and her son Louis
fled Paris on January 6, 1649; the gates of the city were closed
and another siege of Paris was imminent. Inside was an army of
nobles and common soldiery while outside was the recently
disbanded army loyal to the King. The *War of the Fronde* had
begun.[17]

In 1650, Spain entered the war in league with the Queen and
Mazarin. Again the Provinces became the battlefield and Picardy
and Champagne were once more ravaged by war, famine and
pestilence. Vincent de Paul sent his missionaries and their accounts paint a horrible scene:

No tongue can utter, no pen express, no ear listen to, what
we have seen in the early days of our visits. . .Churches
profaned, priests slain, houses demolished, harvests carried

off, almost universal famine and death, corpses without burial and for the most part exposed as a prey of wolves. The poor . . .lie hidden in roofless cabins or holes into which they can scarcely squeeze. Their faces are black and disfigured, and they resemble ghosts rather than men.[18]

In June of 1652, the relics of St. Geneviève, the patroness of Paris, were carried in procession to Notre-Dame to beg God for an end to the suffering. Louise mentions this in a letter of June 11, 1652 to Sister Barbe Angiboust at Brienne:

The messenger will tell you about the beautiful ceremony which was held today for the procession of the reliquary of Saint Geneviève. Oh, how good it is to be faithful to God, who bestows so much honor upon his good servants as a sign of his eternal love.[19]

Before long conditions in Paris became nearly as crucial as in the Provinces. A letter of Vincent de Paul of June 21, 1652 describes the distribution of soup every day at the house of Mlle. Le Gras (Louise de Marillac) to 13,000 poor and in the faubourg of Saint-Denis to 800 refugees and in the parish of St. Paul alone, to 5,000 poor and to another sixty or eighty ill. . .[20]

Thus was the plight of the "ordinary folk" of Paris at this time and it was to worsen before it improved.

On July 1, 1652 the popular troop, led by Condé and pursued by the King's army under Turenne, passed near Saint-Lazare. Louise described the situation in a letter to M. Vincent:

This alarm truly frightened all of us. . . . I do not think that we can go to buy any wheat since there is none in the surrounding villages, and there is the danger of losing the money if we go further. I informed her (Mademoiselle de Lamoignon) that the city administrators judge it safe to have it delivered by several archers whom we would pay for their trouble. I do not think there is any other way to prevent these poor little children from dying of hunger.

The majority of the people are moving out of this quarter. Shall we not follow their example?. . .It seems that Paris is abandoning this district. However, I hope that God will not abandon it and that his goodness will have mercy on us.[21]

Condé managed to escape Turenne's troops and to enter Paris. However, during the ensuing months conflict between him and the Parliament resulted in anguish for the people of Paris. Anarchy reigned in the streets; murder and massacre were common and reports came from the country of growing distress.[22] Failing in a personal attempt to have Mazarin return the King and Queen to Paris, Vincent de Paul appealed to Pope Innocent X on August 16, 1652. He wrote:

Most Holy Father, may I dare, full of confidence in that fatherly kindness which welcomes and gives ear to the least of your children, to set before you the lamentable state of our country, France, which is certainly most deserving of pity? The Royal Family, torn by dissension; the people, split into factions; the cities and provinces, afflicted by civil war; the villages, hamlets and towns, overthrown, ruined and burned; tillers of the soil placed in such a position that they cannot reap what they have sown and no longer sow for the following year. Soldiers deliver themselves up with impunity to all manner of excesses. The people are exposed not only to acts of rapine and brigandage, but also to murder and all forms of torture. Such of the inhabitants of the country districts as have not perished by the sword are dying of hunger; the priests, who are not spared any more than others, are inhumanly and cruelly treated, tortured and put to death. Virgins are dishonored and even nuns themselves exposed to their licentiousness and rage; the temples of God are profaned, plundered or destroyed;. . .

I am well aware that your Holiness may rightly accuse me, who am but a private nameless individual, of great temerity for venturing to expose such evils to the head and common Father of Christians, who is so well and so fully instructed on the affairs of all nations and especially of all Christian nations. But I implore you, Holy Father, not to be angry with me if I do speak. I will speak to my Lord, even though I be but dust and ashes. In truth, Most Holy Father, no other remedy remains for our evils than that which can proceed from the paternal solicitude, the affection and the authority of your Holiness. . . .[23]

With no answer forthcoming, Vincent de Paul again contacted Mazarin, this time in writing, asking him to have the King and Queen return to Paris:

I venture to write to your Eminence; I beg you to allow me to do so and to say that I now see the city of Paris again returned to its former condition, asking for the King and Queen with its whole heart and soul;. . .Accordingly, My Lord, I think your Eminence will perform an act worthy of your goodness if you advise the King and the Queen to take possession of their city and of the hearts of Paris.[24]

Vincent received no response; but in October, Louis XIV, who was now fourteen years old, returned to Paris accompanied by Turenne. Coste recounts the welcome thus:

. . .the Parisians loudly manifested their joy at the sight of the young King who had thus returned to them; they pursued him with their cheers up to the Louvre, his new residence, and one more easily defended than the Palais Royal."[25]

The Cardinal's return was inevitable but he had the prudence to wait until February of 1653 when the exuberance of the King's homecoming had subsided. The War of the Fronde appeared to be over but the devastating results lingered on. Peace had returned to Paris but fighting still persisted in the country where Condé in alliance with Spain desired to rule France. The winter of 1653 found crowds of abandoned soldiers and refugees descending upon Paris who along with the regular beggars created a horde of starving, desperate people. The authorities did nothing to alleviate the situation.[26] In April of 1656 the French State responded to the situation of beggars in Paris and elsewhere, not in light of their human dignity, but rather to rid the streets of the "menace". This they did by the royal decree forbidding all begging. According to one author, it was in fact a declaration of war against the poor:

> We expressly prohibit and forbid all persons of either sex, of any locality and of any age, of whatever breeding and birth, and in whatever conditions they may be, able-bodied or invalid, sick or convalescent, curable or incurable, to beg in the city and suburbs of Paris, neither in the churches, nor at the doors of such, nor at the doors of houses nor in the streets, nor anywhere else in public, nor in secret, by day or night. . .under pain of being whipped for the first offense, and for the second condemned to the galleys if men and boys, banished if women or girls.[27]

Obviously the authorities saw beggars as an evil to be eradicated from public and thus pursued their policy of forcibly institutionalizing such poor.[28]

The respite from fighting was brief and in 1656 war broke out with renewed intensity. By 1658 the end seemed in sight. Two French armies were facing each other near Dunkirk. Condé had been joined by the Spanish army and Turenne had been joined by the English under the command of Cromwell. A decisive battle was expected and should the King's forces succeed, England would gain Dunkirk. Members of the Court including the King and Queen Mother went to Calais to be near the action. Fighting was fierce and the plague raged. A hospital was established to care for the wounded. Appeal was made to the Queen in Paris to send assistance.[29]

In 1659 peace came at last with the defeat of Condé and Spain becoming France's ally through the marriage of the Spanish Infanta Maria Thérésa with the young king, Louis XIV. This marked the beginning of a new era for France. Mazarin died in 1660 and Louis XIV, aged twenty-two, grasped the reins of power to commence one the most illustrious and longest reigns in history - seventy-two years. In that same year of 1660, Louise de Marillac died on March 15 in her 69th year and a few months later on September 27, Vincent de Paul died at the age of 79. In spite of chronic illness and the rigors of intense work both had lived unusually long lives in a time when even the bourgeoisie did not expect to live past fifty. Furthermore, Vincent and Louise had left their indelible mark on the history of France. The greater part of their lives had been dominated by the effects of war; they were bounded by Henri IV's battle for his throne (1589-93) and the Civil Wars of the Fronde (1649-1659). In the middle were the Wars of Religion (1618-1648). Into this pervasive darkness of human agony and despondency Vincent de Paul and Louise de Marillac had brought the light and warmth of the unconditional love of God. In 1660, as one "sun" of France was rising another was setting; there is little doubt as to which left the enduring rays of light and hope in the hearts and lives of the common people of France.

The Life of Louise de Marillac: A Short Survey

Louise's Early Years (1591-1613)

Louise de Marillac was born on August 12, 1591 in or near Paris. Her biographers differ on the exact location suggesting Paris (Gobillon),[30] the Parish of St. Paul (Baunard),[31] and Far-rières-en-Brie (Dirvin).[32] Each supports his hypothesis with circumstantial evidence but since no record of Louise's baptism has been found there is no certainty as to the place of her birth or baptism.[33] As well there is no record of her mother's identity. What is known then is that Louise was the illegitimate daughter[34] of a proud nobleman, Louis de Marillac, "sieur de Ferrières et

Farinvilliers" who at the time of her birth was an officer in the service of King Henri III.[35]

Louise was born between her father's two marriages. His first wife, Marie de la Rozière, died childless in 1588 or 1589; Louise was born in August of 1591 and Louis remarried in January of 1595 a widow, Antoinette Le Camus who had four children.[36] Louise was not to be part of this family and perhaps in one way providence was kind to her because the marriage was fraught with turmoil, conflict and eventual public notoriety.[37]

Louis de Marillac although unable to provide a stable family situation for his daughter certainly recognized her as his child and attempted to provide for her well-being financially[38] and educationally by placing her with other children of noble birth in the Royal Abbey of Poissy in the care of her great aunt, the Dominican nun Mère Catherine Louise de Marillac.[39] Whether Louise was placed there in infancy or at the age of three when her father remarried is not certain. Dirvin suggests that she was likely placed in Poissy in infancy because it would have provided a safe, honorable and discreet home for her and such care was not at all an uncommon practice for well-born little girls of the time. It also would have prevented the probable talk and speculation had her father kept her at home with a nurse or governess. Dirvin also posits that her birth may not have been generally known.[40]

At any rate Louise's formative years were spent at the Convent in Poissy where she received a liberal education in the arts beyond that of most girls of her day and where she was grounded in solid spirituality.[41] In spite of the rather luxurious living of religious at the time, the Convent at Poissy had a reputation for great learning and piety and Louise's great aunt, Catherine Louise de Marillac was, according to Hilarian de Coste, one of the leading pious and literary figures of the early seventeenth century.[42] In this environment young Louise studied literature, art and Latin. She also learned the lessons of charity to the poor exemplified by their patron St. Louis IX whom Louise adopted as her patron saint.[43] As well, Louise would have been steeped in the teachings of Catherine of Siena and the importance of love of God, love of neighbor and prayer. Her association with Catherine is evident in her writings wherein we find her invoking her protection.[44] In the magnificent Royal Monastery at Poissy, Louise would have been surrounded with treasures such as: hangings, rugs, furniture, and sacred vessels of gold and silver studded with jewels.[45] These years saw a development of her appreciation for beauty, art and culture plus an understanding of her station in life. Guy states that Louise was marked for life by the "scholarship, intellectual elegance and true culture of the Dominican nuns."[46] Elisabeth Charpy suggests that Louise remained at Poissy until she was about twelve years old when she was sent to a *pension* in Paris operated by a poor lady.[47] Of this residence, Louise herself was to have told her Sisters that "when she was young, she had been a boarder with a good,devout, spinster, along with other young girls."[48] Gobillon asserts that this change of residence was made by her father.[49] Gobillon, Baunard and Broglie all remark on the contrast between the convent, the culture and the simplicity, almost poverty of this new residence, "pension bourgeoise."[50]

While here, Louise, in order to help the poor mistress of the house, performed daily housekeeping chores and organized the other girls to obtain orders from merchants for handwork in order to earn money to assist in the upkeep of the *pension*. Even at this early age Louise was willing to help those in need and also was utilizing her gentle persuasion and organizational skills to recruit the assistance of others. How long Louise remained at this *pension* is not known but it is known that at the time of her marriage in 1613 she was living with her aunt, Valance de Marillac, Marquise d'Attichy.[51]

The only two references that Louise makes to her early life is the preceding one regarding the mistress at the *pension* and a reference in her writings to personal suffering:

> God who has granted me so many graces, led me to understand that it was his holy will that I go to him by way of the cross. His goodness chose to mark me with it from my birth and he has hardly ever left me, at any age, without some occasion of suffering.[52]

That suffering was a hallmark of Louise's early life is indisputable. She was an illegitimate child and as such was deprived of the legal rights of her family station. She spent her early years in a convent setting removed from ordinary family life, then lived in a *pension* or boarding house following which she resided with an aunt and uncle where she helped to care for their children. In addition to the pain of not really belonging or having any place to set down roots, she naturally suffered the lack of the love and tenderness of a mother and the longing for more of her *part-time* father. This suffering was intensified by his death on July 25, 1604 just prior to her thirteenth birthday. Furthermore, at the age of nineteen she was involved in a legal action with her uncle Michel in order to claim her rightful inheritance from her father.[53] As time will show family involvements tended to be complicated and often painful for Louise.

The Marillac family was closely connected with the religious life in Paris at this time and Louise became part of this circle. It is known that she enjoyed privileges at the Convent of the Capuchin nuns[54] which was located close to the d'Attichy home, that their Provincial, Père Honoré was her spiritual director and that so great was her desire to live their life that she made a promise to God to join them. To her utter sorrow, the Provincial refused her request on the grounds of "delicate health" which would prevent her from living such an austere life. Either in consolation or in prophecy he left her with these words: "Dieu a d'autres vues sur vous."[55]

Although the picture of Louise's youth appears to be very dark there certainly were rays of light in her young life. Her father loved her dearly and expressed this in his will two days before his death. He stated: "She has been my greatest consolation in this world. She was given to me by God to calm my spirit in the afflictions of life."[56] In the convent at Poissy, Louise undoubtedly experienced the warmth and caring of her aunt Catherine Louise, the security and beauty of her surroundings and the companionship of other children, although the sting of *aloneness* likely came when families visited and on other special occasions as her awareness developed. Perhaps too, Louise contented herself in her reading, her studies and her art, all of which she loved and at which she was proficient. There is no indication that her days at the *pension* were unhappy and in all likelihood her visits to the Franciscan Convent were joyous times for her. It is not the intent of this brief survey to speculate upon the movements of Louise's heart but it is evident that she experienced major losses in her early life. It is also clear that through the power of grace, the love of a husband and friends she became a very generous and compassionate woman who could identify with and reach out to others in their sufferings.

Louise's Married Life (1613-1625)

Since Louise seemed not to be called to cloistered life, marriage would be her future. Although she had no parents, Louise de Marillac was a member of an illustrious family with close Court connections.[57] It was likely through her uncle by marriage, Marquis d'Attichy that Louise was introduced to Antoine Le Gras, secretary to the Queen Mother, Marie de Medici.[58]

Antoine Le Gras would not have been a stranger to the Marillacs since they were from the same part of Auvergne. The Le Gras family were long-time residents of Paris with notable connections with the parish of Saint-Gervais, and were of substantial fortune, noted for their charity to the poor.[59] Thus there would be some common ground for the couple. No courtship is mentioned but on February 5, 1613 Antoine and Louise were married in the stylish church of Saint-Gervais. On February 4, the marriage contract had been signed at the home of Count and Madame d'Attichy. All the renowned Marillac relatives were present as noted on the contract but were identified as "friends" of Louise. No parents were present and Louise is noted as the "natural daughter" of the late Louis de Marillac. The d'Attichy's spoke for her and Antoine's mother spoke for him. No other Le Gras relatives are listed as present. Since Antoine Le Gras was a member of the *bourgeoisie* and not a nobleman, Louise would be known as Mademoiselle Le Gras rather than Madame Le Gras.[60] Although this was to be an occasion of joy, a tinge of sadness must have darkened Louise's spirit as again her family did not legally recognize her and the situation of her birth was announced publicly. In spite of this, the marriage was to usher in a period of relative peace and happiness wherein Louise would know the initial joy of human love and motherhood.

The twelve years of Louise and Antoine's marriage knew their share of joys and sorrows. At the age of 22, Louise, now married, officially entered the social circles of the Court and shared in the royal favors lavished upon the Marillacs whose fortunes and futures were connected with the Queen Mother and Concini.[61] The newlyweds lived well. They lived in a hotel in the fashionable Marais section in the parish of Saint-Merri on the right bank and then later moved to Saint-Sauveur. In the Marillac circle they would have been frequent visitors to the Hôtel d'Attichy, the Hôtel de Marillac, Uncle Michel's home on the rue Saint-Avoye and the Petit Luxembourg where Uncle Jean-Louis and Catherine Medici had their suite. Calvet mentions that she was frequently seen about the Court to which her duty bound her.[62] These new social endeavors did not preoccupy Louise's time or mind. Gobillon, her first biographer states that during the first years of her marriage she visited the sick poor of the parish tending to both their physical and spiritual needs and even preparing their bodies after death.[63] A servant woman of her household also testified that Louise brought them sweets, washed their sores and cleaned them of their vermin.[64] She communicated her enthusiasm for the poor to other ladies of noble birth and as at the *pension* she gently persuaded them to help.

On October 18, 1613, Louise and Antoine were blessed with the birth of their son Michel Antoine, who was baptized the following day in the church of Saint-Merri with René de Marillac and Valance d'Attichy as godparents. The couple thus began their family life and little is noted until the shadows of difficulties began to fall. In 1614, Marquis d'Attichy, Louise's uncle, died suddenly leaving his wife with seven children. Three years later she died. Michel de Marillac, another uncle of Louise, was named the legal guardian but apparently asked Antoine Le Gras to oversee the situation so in reality this family responsibility fell to Louise and Antoine who began to devote themselves to caring for the d'Attichy family and their precarious financial situation. That the children fared well is attested to by their successes in life.[65] That it imposed a grave burden, especially financial, upon the Le Gras' is attested to by Louise in a letter to Vincent de Paul in 1643:

> What I did was to write two days later to Father d'Attichy to tell him that the only motherly duty in which I seemed to have failed my son was in not letting him know that my late husband had devoted all his time and his life to looking after the affairs of the d'Attichy family while completely neglecting those of his own family.[66]

Undoubtedly this would be one reason why Louise was left so financially insecure at the time of her husband's death. However, this also indicates that Antoine, in the spirit of his family, was very charitable, perhaps even to a fault. In addition to the responsibility of the d'Attichy children, apprehension concerning Antoine's employment emerged with the assassination of Concini and the Queen Mother's subsequent exile to Blois in May of 1617. As well, it was becoming evident that little Michel who had been premature at birth was both delicate in health and somewhat slow in learning. Hence after four years of marriage the young couple was faced with grave family responsibilities, financial uncertainty plus anxiety about their child. In the midst of these ongoing trials, Antoine, in 1621-2, became ill with a disease that was to last for nearly four years. Dirvin suggests that the ailment was a form of tuberculosis.[67] This was a tragic blow for them and Louise found herself coping with a husband whose personality was changing for the worse. Gobillon who knew Louise personally stated the following regarding the onset of Antoine's illness: "Three or four years before his death, he fell into frequent illnesses which put him in a tiresome and fretful humour."[68] As the years progressed Antoine required constant nursing and Louise unsparingly devoted herself to him. Antoine died on December 21, 1625.[69] Louise in writing to Père Hilarion Rebours described his final hours as an agony in which he "suffered in the whole of his body, and lost all of his blood, while his mind was almost always occupied in meditation on the Passion. Seven times he lost blood from the mouth, the seventh time ending his life upon the instant."[70] Louise was alone with him to assist him on this important journey and she recounts his final words to her which would be engraved forever upon her heart: "Pray to God for me, I can do no more."[71]

That a strong love had grown between Louise and Antoine is evidenced by the fact that every year on the anniversary of their marriage she assisted at Mass and Communion for him and thirty years later in her last will and testament she "entreated her son to remember to pray often for the repose of his father's soul, to remember his good life, his strong faith in God and especially his patience in suffering the great illnesses that came upon him in his final years in which he practised great virtue."[72]

This enduring quality of their relationship was no doubt rooted in their mutual life of prayer, their devotion to the poor, their struggles through family difficulties, and their bondedness in the ongoing agony of a terminal illness. That Louise suffered her own agony during these years is unquestionably attested to.

As has been seen, the bliss and security of family life and social life were short-lived for Louise. The crosses she bore gradually took their toll on her and probably under the strain of physical, emotional and mental fatigue she struggled with recurring depression. Louise endeavored to cope with this in the manner that she knew by prayer, sacrifices and seeking the advice of wise directors. That she had renowned directors and spiritual assistance available to her during these years is apparent. Her regular director was Bishop Camus[73] who understood her and was compassionate with her. In a letter to her around 1622, he stated:

I sympathize with you in the inertia of mind in which you find yourself on account of the illness of your dear hus-

band. Come, then, here is your cross, and why should I be
sorry to see it on the shoulder of a daughter of the cross?
To carry it well, you do not lack skill, nor counsel, nor
books, nor mind. God desires also that you should not lack
the courage.[74]

In 1619 Louise met Francis de Sales whose books had become
the staple of her spiritual reading and who visited with her a
number of times on his visits to Paris. Perhaps her meeting may
have been through Camus who was a close friend of Francis.
Undoubtedly Francis de Sales would have given Louise counsel
and support.

Mère Catherine de Beaumont, superioress of the Paris Visitation was Louise's friend and advisor. She too tried to comfort
Louise in her struggles. She wrote thus:

I sympathize greatly with your sorrow, my very dear
daughter, but all the same, I have no fear, but rather the
hope that the hand which has inflicted the wound will
work the cure. O God! Be therefore very gentle and
courageous, to support with patience what is given you
with so great a love. . . .pay less attention to what you
yourself are feeling and suffering; but unite your will to
that of our heavenly Father, that you may do and suffer
whatever pleases him; then after that, do everything you
can for the health of your dear husband, leaving the
outcome to the good pleasure of God.[75]

At times Louise sought the advice of her Uncle Michel who was
noted for his piety but he tended to be rather detached with her
advising her in terms of general self-abnegation. His letters are
thorough pieces of spiritual advice but not really what Louise
needed at that time. Calvet comments on Michel's advice as follows:

Marillac is probably dealing here with scruples and anxieties with which Louise was beset and haunted; he probes

the recesses of her conscience, and excites in her a sense of sin to which she was in any case only too liable. She stood more in need of encouragement than of humbling.[76]

Louise possessed a sensitive conscience and a keen spirit. She hungered for holiness especially through doing the will of God in her life. Camus cautions her against her "certain spiritual avidity which needs to be controlled."[77] It was this avidity that intensified the spiritual anguish in Louise. In the midst of trials it is a very natural initial impulse to ask, "Why me? What have I done wrong?" With Louise this became a trial in itself. She wondered whether or not her family was being tried because of her. Was God displeased because she had not kept her promise to enter the cloister? As time went on the darkness settled in and her spiritual assistants seemed unable to guide her. Bishop Camus says: " I am always waiting for serenity to return to you after the clouds which prevent you from seeing the beautiful brightness of the joy which belongs to the service of God."[78] Was it an attempt to regain serenity by "making up to God" that prompted Louise to pronounce a vow of widowhood on May 4, 1623, the feast of St. Monica or was it a direct inspiration from God?[79] Of this vow Louise was to write: "In the year 1623, on the Feast of St. Monica, God gave me the grace to make a vow of widowhood should he call my husband to himself."[80] Hence Louise saw this action as a grace from God. In all likelihood it was made with the permission of Bishop Camus who was in Paris at the time and on May 8,1623 gave written permission for Louise and Antoine to read the sacred scriptures in French.[81] Peace ensued for a few weeks but then on Ascension Day, May 25, Louise entered into a dark night which lasted until Pentecost, June 4. We have her own testimony of this ordeal which caused her "incredible anguish". The spiritual trial consisted of three grave doubts: whether or not she should leave her husband to make good her first vow and to have greater liberty to serve God and her neighbor; whether or not she had the capacity to break the attachment she had for her director which might prevent her from accepting another and her doubt concerning the immortality of the soul.[82] On the Feast of

Pentecost June 4, during Mass or while praying in the church, Louise's mind was instantly freed of all doubt and she received what she termed her "*Lumière*". In this enlightenment she was advised to remain with her husband and was given the insight that the time would come when she would make vows of poverty, chastity and obedience; she would be in a small community where others would do the same, where she could help her neighbor and where there was to be much coming and going. This she could not understand. She was also assured that she should remain at peace about her director and that God would give her one whom he seemed to show her. Although it was repugnant to her to accept him, nevertheless she acquiesced.[83] Her third doubt was removed by the inner assurance she felt that it was God who was teaching her these things and that believing there is a God she should not doubt the rest.[84]

Louise always believed that she received this grace from the Blessed Bishop of Geneva, Francis de Sales, because she had greatly desired to communicate her trials to him before his death in December of 1622 and since then had great devotion to him and had received many graces through him.[85]

Reassured and strengthened by this gift of "Light", Louise continued to nurse her husband, care for her son, attend to family responsibilities and reach out to the poor. Gradually the illuminations of the Holy Spirit began to unfold. In October of 1623 Bishop Camus wrote to inform Louise that he could no longer frequent his beloved Paris but must remain in his see at Belley. Gobillon suggests that it was through the high opinion that Francis de Sales had of Vincent de Paul that Camus knew he could find no wiser guide with whom to entrust Louise.[86] Dirvin proposes that it was the influence of Bishop Camus and their mutual friendship with Francis de Sales that convinced Vincent de Paul to accept the direction of Louise because both he and Louise had reservations but for different reasons.[87] The cross was not to leave Louise and her sensitive, anxious spirit would be with her for life. However, God had now sent her that special spiritual guide and friend who would share the journey with her. Thus in late 1623 or early 1624, Vincent de Paul assumed his lifelong care of Louise's soul.[88] Through her personal losses and her anxieties he would guide her with gentle firmness; he would recognize and channel her talents for the service of the poor. For her part, she would support, graciously challenge and be concerned for his well-being and his work. God had brought together two souls who had experienced a "dark night"[89] and who would burn with the light and fire of the Holy Spirit - the love of God. Vincent no doubt assisted her during the final months of Antoine's illness but it was during her widowhood that he would become, in an unique way, God's instrument of grace for her.

Louise's Widowhood (1626-1633)

The years 1626-1633 were a period of transition for Louise. They were years in which she experienced the effects of significant changes in her life. She journeyed from the grief of widowhood, through turbulent family struggles, to the dynamic servant of the poor who finally saw the promise of her "*Lumière*" of Pentecost 1623 become a reality with the foundation of the Daughters of Charity in November of 1633. During this period while Louise ardently sought God's will for her life, she was schooled in the lessons of contemplation and action which prepared her for her future work. The cross had been her companion in the past and so too it would accompany her during this stage of her life, but through its lessons of dying and sur rendering she would be given new life and freedom to become the instrument of the Holy Spirit in addressing the social ills of her time, the results of which would resound throughout the world and through the ages.[90]

Following the death of her husband Antoine in December of 1625, Louise devoted herself even more diligently to her spiritual life, to discovering God's will for her and to the service of her neighbor. She had already drawn up her detailed "Rule of Life in the World" which outlined her daily horarium, her daily prayer life, her commitments to charitable works, her spiritual devotions, her penances, her yearly retreats and her desire to be attentive to the Word of God.[91] Now she made her "Act of Consecration" in which she renewed her baptismal profession, irrevocably resolved to love and serve God with greater fidelity and to give herself entirely to him by renewing her vow of widowhood and her resolution to practice the virtues of humility, obedience, poverty, suffering and charity in order to honor those virtues in Jesus Christ who had often called her to imitate him. Promising to abandon herself to the designs of divine providence and to the accomplishment of his will in her life, Louise sacrificed and dedicated herself to God and to the fulfillment of his holy will which she chose as her supreme consolation. Recognizing her own weakness, she implored the Holy Spirit to grant her the grace of immediate conversion should she fail to keep her holy resolutions because she desired never to remain for an instant in a state displeasing to God. Louise completed her Consecration in the following words:

> O my God, deign to confirm my consecration and my holy resolutions and to accept them as a fragrant offering! Since you inspired me to present these gifts to you, grant me the grace of perfecting them. You are my God and my All. I recognize you as such and adore you, the one true God in three Persons, now and forever.

> May your Love and that of Jesus crucified be eternally exalted!
> (signed: Louise de Marillac)[92]

In her "Oblation to the Blessed Virgin", Louise asked Mary to be the protectress of her son and herself in these words: "Most Holy Virgin, deign to take my son and me into your care. Welcome the choice I make of you as our protectress."[93]

In the midst of her grieving, Louise professed her total consecration to God, her dependence on the power of the Holy Spirit, her commitment to the crucified Jesus and her devotion to the Blessed Virgin. She was beginning a new phase in her life and she desired it to be totally in harmony with the will of God. One's spiritual life is not lived in isolation from everyday reality and

Louise found herself coping with the changes ensuing from Antoine's death particularly the void in her and Michel's hearts and home. Following a letter of condolence of February 22, 1626 from Bishop Camus a second attests to her grief when he says:

> I do not understand why your spirit is troubled and believes itself to be in darkness and abandoned. To what purpose? You are no longer divided. You determined long since to want only him, and now that he has broken your bonds and you ought to offer him a sacrifice of praise, you are astonished![94]

Louise did desire to be totally God's but her human heart felt the anguish of the loss of one "greatly loved"[95] and she needed time for the gentle healing power of the Spirit to soothe the wound and bring new vitality to her being. But, life must go on and in the process, Louise had to face the demands of daily life in her family and household. Besides the realization that she and Michel were now alone, she had to confront the situation of depleted financial resources. Thus in 1626 she changed residences and moved from the stylish area of rue Corteau-Vilain to rue Saint-Victor in the parish of Saint-Nicolas-du-Chardonnet. Here she was near the motherhouse of the newly-formed Congregation of the Mission, the Collège des Bons Enfants and near schools for Michel. Biographers suggest various reasons for the move such as the desire to be closer to her director, Vincent de Paul, the desire to be removed from the proximity of court life, as she desired to live a more simple lifestyle, and the reality of financial burdens.[96]

Whatever Louise's motivations, she settled in the area, registered Michel in *the petit seminaire* near the Church of Saint-Nicolas-du-Chardonnet and consumed with the desire to know God's will for her life, devoted herself to prayer and works of mercy among the poor. In her struggles with doubt and depression, Vincent's counsel was forthcoming even though he might be away on business. Michel, who was now thirteen years old needed male influence, and both he and his mother would benefit from a healthy space from each other. In a letter to Vincent on June 5, 1627 Louise wrote:

At last, my Most Honored Father, after some worry, my son is placed in school. Thanks be to God, he is happy and is doing well there. If that continues, I shall be very relieved concerning him.[97]

With Michel provided for, Louise had more time to devote to charitable works. That she was becoming involved in assisting Vincent is evidenced in this same letter when she stated: "The work which your Charity gave me is finished. If the members of Jesus need it and you want me to send it to you, Father, I shall not fail to do so."[98] This letter also suggests the deepening relationship between Vincent and Louise and the openness of their communication. It read:

I hope that you will excuse the liberty I am taking in telling you how impatient I have become because of your long absence, troubled as I am about the future and not knowing where you are or where you are going.[99]

As well, we see the beginnings of the unfolding of the promise of her "*Lumière*" about serving her neighbor with others. Louise wrote:

Allow me, Father, to bother you again about the 28-year-old girl that they wish to send from Burgundy and confide to my care. From what I hear, she has a good background and is virtuous. Prior to this, the good blind girl from Vertus had told me that her 22-year-old companion might also come here. She has been under the direction of the Oratorians for the past four years and is a true country girl. . . .I humbly implore you to tell me what I should do in this matter.[100]

The next two years of Louise's life (1628-29) appear to be characterized by her desire to do God's will, her son's education, and her association with Vincent both as director and as co-worker. The frequent correspondence between Louise and Vincent attest to this as do Louise's personal Spiritual Writings.[101]

The reference to Louise's desire to do God's will in her life is a recurring refrain in the correspondence between herself and Vincent and in her "Spiritual Thoughts". A few examples from their Letters illustrate this point: "These past days I have greatly desired you to remember to offer me to God and to ask of him the grace of accomplishing his holy will in me despite the opposition of my misery."[102] ; "O my very dear Father, offer my will to the divine mercy for I want, with the help of his holy grace, to be converted . . ."[103]; "Be then his dear daughter—quite humble, submissive, and full of confidence—and always wait patiently for the manifestation of his holy and adorable will."[104]; "Mademoiselle, be quite cheerful in the disposition of willing everything that God wills."[105] In her "Spiritual Thoughts" of this period we find similar references to the will of God: "I am entirely yours, most Holy Virgin, that I may more perfectly belong to God. Teach me, therefore, to imitate your holy life by fulfilling the designs of God in my life."[106]

Regarding Michel's education and happiness we read of his waning desire to remain in the seminary and Louise's concern: "Either God does not want him to become a priest at this time, or the world has raised obstacles to his doing so because his fervor has greatly diminished. . . . I will explain to you if God grants me the grace, which I greatly need, of seeing your return."[107] We read of Vincent's counsel to leave Michel alone and to surrender him to the Lord's will: "Leave him alone then, and surrender him completely to what Our Lord wills or does not will."[108] The struggle of Louise's letting go and of Vincent's joy at her freedom from the excessive attachment to Michel is also expressed in their letters: "However, I am telling your heart in advance that I praise God because it has freed itself from the excessive attachment it had to the little one (Michel), and because you have made it correspond to reason."[109]

That Louise and Vincent's relationship was developing during this period both from the standpoint of spiritual sharing and charitable works is evident from their correspondence. Attestations to this are seen in the following excerpts from their letters, especially from those of Vincent. With respect to the ease and openness of their relationship one reads: "I am writing to you about midnight and am a little tired. Forgive my heart if it is not a little more expansive in this letter." [110] Vincent's letters continue:

And because it is his good pleasure that we remain always in the holy joy of his love, let us remain in it and attach ourselves to it inseparably in this world, so that we may be one day but one in him, in Whose love I am, . . .[111];

I could not tell you how ardently my heart desires to see yours in order to know how this has come about in it, . . .Oh! what a tree you have appeared to be today in God's sight, since you have borne such a fruit! May you be forever a beautiful tree of life bringing forth fruits of love, and I, in that same love, your servant. . .[112];

What shall I tell you about the one whom your heart loves so dearly in Our Lord? . . .My heart could not hide it from yours, . . .I must conclude by telling her that my heart will have a very fond remembrance of hers in that of Our Lord and solely for that of Our Lord. . .[113];

. . .Therefore, patience until then, my dear daughter, I beg you. I assure you that I thought about you again this morning for a rather long time, and that I am and shall be all my life, in the love of Jesus and his holy Mother, your servant.[114]

Surely such expressions bespeak a deep human affection rooted in the love of Christ. It is the essence of true love to manifest itself in deeds of love. Such was the spirit animating the works of charity which Vincent and Louise shared. Her continuing involvement in Vincent's undertakings is illustrated in the following excerpts from his letters:

> Since your good lady wishes that . . .we distribute what she gave you right now . . .I beg you to send us by M.du Coudray, . . .the sum of fifty livres. . . . .Please send us also four shirts, and convey our most humble respects to your good lady.[115];

> . . .Get ready to do an act of charity for two poor girls whom we have decided should leave here. We shall send them to you. . .and ask you to direct them to some good woman who can find them work as servants. . .[116];

> Father de Gondi sent me word to come by coach to see him in Montmirail. That will perhaps prevent me from having the honor of seeing you , because I am leaving tomorrow morning. Do you feel like coming, Mademoiselle? If so you would have to leave next Wednesday on the coach to Châlons. . .[117]

The positive response to this invitation to visit the Charity on the De Gondi estates at Montmirail formally initiated Louise's co-operative efforts with Vincent in the ongoing organization and evaluation of the Charities. Herein her active apostolate officially commenced.

Gobillon described these years of Louise's life as a kind of novitiate which served to augment and to affirm her resolution to embrace every occasion for charity which presented itself. As well, he contended that her faithfulness and perseverance finally obliged Vincent to associate her with his mission for the poor.[118]

From May 1629 until November 1633, Louise labored tirelessly in assisting the Charities.[119] Vincent recognized her astuteness, her organizational abilities, her unflagging zeal and most of all her solid spirituality. With the gentle strength of the soul friend he had become, he both encouraged and cautioned her in her efforts to serve the poor. He continuously counseled her to wait for providence and to act only when she was certain of God's will. During this time Louise was beset with major crises in the Marillac family. Again the cross would weigh upon her as she shared the family grief. Most characteristic of these years was Louise's apostolate with the Charities and her earnest desire to know and to do God's will concerning the promise of her *"Lumière"*. A brief survey of these three and half years attests to this.

In May of 1629 with her visit to Montmirail, Louise launched her apostolic activity. Vincent missioned her with the following words: "Go, therefore, Mademoiselle, go in the name of Our Lord. . . .May he be pleased to bless your journey, giving you his spirit and the grace to act in this same spirit, and to bear your troubles in the way he bore his."[120] Gobillon described the beginning of Louise's first missions thus: "St. Vincent commença de l'employer dans ces fonctions saintes en l'année 1629, et il l'envoya visiter dans les villages les confréries de charité qu'il y avait établies."[121] During the ensuing two and half years, not only did Louise visit several Confraternities in the villages, she also assisted with St. Sauveur in Paris and even established one herself in the parish of St. Nicolas-du-Chardonnet. In all, her goal was to assist the Ladies in the Charities by: encouraging those who were working well, rekindling the spirit of those who were growing cold, instructing girls who would teach, caring for the spiritual and physical needs of the people, and evaluating the overall operation of the Charity.[122] During her first year of 1630 Louise made several significant visitations. In February she visited the Charity of St. Cloud. She set out for this trip on the anniversary of her wedding day, February 5, and during the morning Mass she experienced a special grace which seemed to her like a spiritual marriage with Christ.[123] Undoubtedly, this encouraged her for the upcoming journey and work. While in St. Cloud, Vincent wrote to her inquiring about her health and admonishing her about her excessive concern for her son Michel:

. . .I beg you to let me know right away whether your lung
is being irritated by your talking so much, or your head by
so much confusion and noise. . . . As for your son, . . .what
shall we say about this excessive affection? I certainly
think, Mademoiselle, that you have to try before God to
rid yourself of it.[124]

In this letter Vincent also inquired about Marguerite Naseau:
"Let me know whether that good young woman from Suresnes
who visited you before and spends her time teaching girls, has
come to see you as she promised me last Sunday. . ."[125] It appears
that Louise may have directed Marguerite to Vincent. The
pentecost promise continued to unfold.

In April of 1630, Louise visited the Charity of Villepreux, east
of Paris. Here she encountered difficulties with the pastor because she had begun her visitation without first consulting him
and he was determined not to let "that missionary woman" speak
in his parish.[126] When Louise shared her difficulties with Vincent,
he counselled her to apologize to the pastor and to leave if need
be. Her humility in apologizing won her the ensuing staunch
support of this pastor.[127]

In May of 1630, Louise's zeal was so strong that Vincent had to
remind her that: "Our Lord wants us to serve him with common
sense, and the opposite is called indiscreet zeal."[128] During this time
her desire for community continued to grow but Vincent encouraged patience and satisfaction with her present lifestyle.[129]

In November of 1630, Louise again experienced the cross in
her family life. Both her uncles were arrested. Michel de Marillac
who had been directly involved with the Queen Mother's plan
to overthrow Richelieu was arrested and imprisoned. Subsequently, his brother Jean-Louis who was Maréchal of France in
Italy was arrested and imprisoned on charges of profiting from
his position in the army.[130] Thus began a two-year period of
anguish for the entire family.

In December of 1630, Louise left to visit the Charities in
Beauvais. When she began her meetings, the ladies came in great

numbers and were charmed by the spiritual conferences which she gave them in which she encouraged and exhorted them in their Christian lives. Although men were not part of the Confraternities of Charity and thus not invited to attend, Louise was such an engaging speaker that the men came and hid in order to hear her talks.[131] At this time such conferences might last for three hours and Louise did not spare herself with the result that she often lost her voice. Her vigor in her work also caused her to have migraine headaches and Vincent frequently cautioned her to prudence. At one point he wrote: "It seems to me that you are killing yourself from the little care you take of yourself."[132]

In the ensuing months Louise continued to work with the Charities in Paris. In March 1631 she was back on the road, this time to Montreuil where she made suggestions and checked the rules for the Confraternity.[133] Here Vincent informed her of her son's unrest and suggested that she send him to study with the Jesuits while she was away. A few weeks later Vincent assured her that he had the word of Father Lallement, head of the Jesuit College to take Michel as a boarder.[134] The uncertainty of Michel's vocation and future weighed heavily upon Louise for years.

Vincent's appreciation and value of Louise's expertise was illustrated in his request for her to return to Paris in April of 1631 because the Charity of Saint-Sulpice needed her.[135] In the correspondence of these months there appeared to be hints of the ongoing topic of Louise's pentecost promise of women coming together and going forth among the poor. In Letter 67, Vincent said: "On my return we shall discuss this whole plan and your trip to the country." Then, in Letter 71 we read: "As for the rest, I beg you, once and for all, not to give it a thought until Our Lord makes it evident that he wishes it, and at the present he is giving indications to the contrary."[136] It was at this time that Louise founded the Charity at St. Nicolas-du-Chardonnet, showed her administrative ability in adapting the general rule for the Charities, and received Vincent's affirmation of her efforts.[137]

With the coming of fall, Louise again began to visit the outlying Charities. On September 2, 1631 she left for Montmirail, then visited surrounding parishes. In mid-September she received word from Vincent that Madame de Marillac was very ill.[138] A following letter brought Louise news of her aunt's death on September 15, probably the result of a broken heart and of the physical and mental exhaustion from her efforts to procure her husband's freedom from prison. Vincent, endeavoring to console Louise, advised her to adore God's providence and also encouraged her to express her natural sorrow.[139] To somewhat lessen the pain of this news the letter also informed Louise that her son Michel was fine and that his mind was developing more and more.

October found Louise in Le Mesnil where she worked with the Confraternities. In November she returned to Paris experiencing the failure of not succeeding with the Bishop of Châlons and suffering from the pain of gossip that was circulating regarding her and a gentleman who maintained she had promised to marry him. Vincent told her to have courage and to strengthen herself within because this false accusation and the resultant suffering would bring good to her both in this world and the next.[140] In these situations Louise felt the cross that may often befall one in active ministry.

For Louise, the year 1632 was marked by suffering in the Marillac family, her continuing desire to do God's will regarding a community and her ongoing work in the Charities.

The major family crosses centered on the public execution of Jean-Louis de Marillac on May 10 on the Place de Grève in Paris and Michel de Marillac's death on August 7 at the prison in Châteaudun. Their deaths ended nearly two years of imprisonment and the family's struggle to have them freed. After Jean-Louis' execution, Vincent wrote to Louise:

> The way our relatives go to God is of no importance to us, provided they go to him. Now, the good use of this kind of death is one of the most certain paths to eternal life. Let us not feel sorry for him then, but let us accept the adorable will of God.[141]

Undoubtedly, the deep faith of the Marillacs sustained them in these long trials and gave Louise the strength to accept the permissive will of God in these events.

The recurring allusion to the formation of a group of women to dedicate themselves totally to the care of the poor was evident in the letters of Vincent to Louise and in Louise's "Spiritual Thoughts" during this year.[142] Particularly in Letter 122, Vincent made reference to Marie Joly joining Louise and he directed her to draw up the rule.[143] In her retreat notes of 1632, Louise wrote:

> I must have great trust in God and believe that his grace will be sufficient to enable me to fulfill his holy will, however difficult it may appear to be, provided the Holy Spirit is truly calling me. I shall know this by listening to the advice which he will permit me to receive.

And further in the same notes she wrote:

> Thus, closely united to God, I shall await the time when he shall be pleased to reveal what he is asking of me. . . .I must perseveringly await the coming of the Holy Spirit although I do not know when that will be. I must accept this uncertainty as well as my inability clearly to perceive at this time the path which God wishes me to follow in his service. I must abandon myself entirely to his providence so as to be completely his. In order to prepare my soul for this, I must willingly renounce all things to follow him.[144]

During 1632 Louise continued to work with the Charities within Paris as well as visiting those in the country. July found her trying to reestablish the Charity in Villeneuve and visiting the village of Crosnes.[145] It appears that 1632 also saw Louise enter into ministry with the prisoners in Paris. Vincent in L.115 encouraged her in this work and even suggested that perhaps her Charity of Saint-Nicolas assume responsibility for it for a time.[146] It was evident that Louise was now fully involved in the charitable works of Vincent, not only as an assistant but as a collaborator whom he deeply respected and appreciated.

As 1633 progressed the reality of the birth of the community became more dominant as Louise continued her work among the poor and sought the confirmation of God's will. Vincent, seeking it as well, remained cautious but began to speak more openly about the foundation. References to the establishment of the community are found both in Louise's "Spiritual Thoughts" and in Vincent's letters to her from April of 1633 to January of 1634.

In L.138 of May 1633, Vincent wrote to Louise: "With regard to your employment, my mind is not yet enlightened enough before God concerning a difficulty which prevents me from seeing whether it is the will of his Divine Majesty."[147] In L.147 of September, 1633 Vincent mentioned a girl named Marie whom he thought the Lord had given to Louise to make use of through her.[148] Then in L.151 written in August or September, 1633 Vincent made two statements which could allude to the foundation. The first referred to Louise's health which was always a concern. Vincent exhorted her:

> I beg you, Mademoiselle, in the name of Our Lord, to do all in your power to take care of yourself, no longer as a private individual but as a person upon whose health a number of others are dependent.

The second concerned an inspiration:

> I think your good angel did what you told me in the letter you wrote to me. Four or five days ago, he communicated with mine concerning the Charity of your young women. It is true; he prompted me to recall it often and I gave that good work serious thought. We shall talk about it, God willing. . .[149]

In Letter 152 Vincent made a more direct reference to the foundation when he wrote:

We must surely meet before making a firm decision about the girls, and it can only be towards the end of the week. In the meantime, please send them away for the next twelve to fifteen days, at which time you can notify them through the student.[150]

Vincent encouraged Louise to have the girls remain in a spirit of indifference and he insisted that they must be trained in the knowledge of solid virtue before they could serve the poor.[151] This letter was written shortly before the foundation which is dated November 29, 1633.[152] The next letter which specifically mentioned the community is that of January, 1634 in which Vincent stated: "I received your letter yesterday and your outline of the rules for your Daughters. . ." He continued:

I have no doubt that they are as you describe them to me, but we have to hope that they will mature and that prayer will allow them to see their faults and encourage them to correct them. It would be well for you to tell them what constitutes solid virtue especially that of interior and exterior mortification, . . .[153]

Obviously Vincent became convinced of God's will in establishing the girls into a community and of Louise's leadership in their formation.[154]

In Louise's "Spiritual Thoughts" of this year we find continued references to the desire to do God's will and to serve her neighbor. Several of these references are: "No desires no resolutions. The grace of my God will accomplish whatever he pleases in me."; "I must even give myself to God to serve my neighbor in situations where I will be subject to blame in the eyes of the world."[155] Later we read the "Order Of The Day" observed by the First Daughters of Charity and the "Draft Of The Rule" which she submitted to Vincent.[156] The "Draft Of The Rule" stated the objective of the confraternity, its organizational principles, its spiritual foundations, its apostolate, and its community ideals. In these two documents of approximately three pages, Louise succinctly presented the embodiment of what we today would term our constitutions, our directives, our charism statement and our mission statement. The first paragraph of the "Draft Of The Rule" is worth noting:

> The Confraternity of widows and village girls has been instituted to honor Our Lord, its patron, and the Blessed Virgin, and to imitate, in some way, the women and young girls of the gospel who followed and ministered to Our Lord and his Apostles. While doing this, they shall work at their own perfection, for the salvation of their families, and for the corporal and spiritual assistance of the sick poor of this city and of the country, whom they shall serve themselves in their parishes and for whom they shall procure the able assistance of the Ladies of Charity in the villages. They shall provide funds from their common purse for the village Charities which would otherwise be unable to care for the poor and they shall see to it that all involved do their best to enable the poor who recover to lead a good life for the rest of their days and those who die to leave this world in a good state.[157]

This aspect of Louise's pentecost promise was now becoming a reality. She would be going and coming with other women who would be totally dedicated to God for the service of the sick poor. She had kept the promise in her heart, had nurtured it, had waited upon the Lord, had trusted in providence, and had finally received confirmation in Vincent's approval and support. Now a new phase of her life had begun -the journey that would imprint her and her Daughters upon the pages of history, that would ultimately lead to her canonization and to her designation as the "Patroness of Christian Social Workers." Perhaps it was in keeping with her desire to imitate the hidden life of Jesus that it took the Church nearly three hundred years to formally recognize her sanctity and her unprecedented contributions to apostolic women religious and to the welfare of the poor throughout the world.[158]

Louise and Her Daughters of Charity
(1633-1660)

In July of 1628 when Louise confided to Vincent her desire to devote herself to the service of the poor, Vincent responded with: "Oh! what a tree you have appeared to be today in God's sight, since you have borne such a fruit! May you be forever a beautiful tree of life bringing forth fruits of love . . ."[159]

This tree, deeply rooted in the love of God, began to blossom during Louise's "novitiate" in the service of the poor, particularly between 1629 and 1633 when she became deeply involved in the works of Vincent de Paul. The more involved she became, the deeper became her desire to serve the poor, the more evident became her virtue and her giftedness and the more apparent became the need for others who were totally dedicated to God to join her in this work.

Thus Vincent's prayer that she be a "beautiful tree of life bringing forth fruits of love" was being fulfilled and the years 1633-1660 would see this tree bear fruit a hundredfold in the consecrated women she would form and in their dedicated works for the glory of God and the service of the poor.

These final twenty-seven years of Louise's life were totally dedicated to the formation of her Daughters in preparation for their service of the sick poor. The words of Paul, "Caritas Christi Urget Nos" (2 Cor. 5:14) became the underpinning which she adapted to include, the Crucified Christ. Thus the motto and insignia for her life and that of her Daughters became, "The Charity of Christ crucified Impels Us," emblazoned on a background of the crucified Christ surrounded by fire.[160] As Vincent saw Christ in the poor, so too did Louise and together they inculcated in their Daughters the maxim that the poor were their lords and masters.[161]

Margaret Flinton in her book, *Louise de Marillac: Social Aspects of Her Work*, states:

From 1633, Louise de Marillac would exist only for the
Daughters of Charity, her spiritual children. Her thoughts,
her undertakings, her share in the organization of the
works, all centred on "her Daughters" and their Service of
the Poor.[162]

This brief survey of Louise's life with her Daughters will focus
mainly on illustrating her practical wisdom and foresight in
educating her Daughters in the consecrated life for ministry and
in firmly establishing the Confraternity so that its spirit and
uniqueness would be preserved. Her Daughters were to be the
most abundant fruit of love from her tree of life. They would
become new trees bearing fruits of love wherever they went and
as with her own tree of life so too with theirs, the love of Christ
would be the life-giving sap that would sustain and nourish them.

Let us now consider how Louise de Marillac, with Vincent de
Paul, nurtured the saplings of their Company: how through the
providence of God they incarnated in their Daughters - this
innovative group of women of seventeenth century France—the
charism, spirit and mission that was to motivate their spiritual
descendants for more than three hundred years and disperse
them to every nation of the world.

In 1633, the Daughters were formed to assist the Ladies of
Charity in their works for the poor. It had become evident
through the years that many of the tasks required in this service
could not be performed by the noble ladies and that the substi-
tution of their servant girls in the work was not suitable. The
Ladies needed the assistance of dedicated women who would care
for the poor with the respect and dignity that they justly deserved. It was to meet this need that Louise began to train country
girls who wished to dedicate their lives to the service of the poor.
For nearly twelve years they remained a community associated
with and dependent upon the Ladies of Charity. It was not until
1645 that Vincent de Paul petitioned the Archbishop of Paris
"to erect as a Confraternity this company of girls and widows."[163]
By this Ecclesiastical Approbation of 1646 the Company was

placed under the jurisdiction of the Bishop of Paris. Louise was very concerned about this and expressed her misgivings to Vincent over the next several years. She firmly believed that divine providence desired them to remain continuously under the guidance of Vincent and his successors both in spiritual as well as in temporal matters.[164] In 1647, Queen Anne even petitioned the Pope for this favor. When Vincent and Louise requested parliamentary registration of the Company in 1650, it was discovered that the original documents had somehow been lost and that the process had to be re-initiated. In writing the new text for the Bishop, Louise and Vincent included the *perpetuity clause* of the authority of the Superior General of the Congregation of the Mission. Approved in January of 1655 by the Bishop of Paris and signed in Rome by Cardinal de Retz, Ecclesial Approbation was secured. The Letters Patent of the King were obtained in November of 1657 and the *Confraternity* was registered in the French *Parlement* in 1658.[165] Louise was finally satisfied that the charism, spirit and mission of the Daughters would be preserved.[166] From 1633 to 1660 the little Company grew in number, in works and indeed in wisdom under the combined tutelage of Louise and Vincent, two persons whose hearts and souls were dedicated to the imitation of Christ in the service of the poor. They both identified the poor with Christ, seeing in them the reality of his Mystical Body. Totally imbued with this spirit themselves, they inculcated it in their Daughters and endeavored to have it permeate every aspect of their lives. This is evidenced in the many Conferences which Vincent delivered to the Daughters[167] and in the letters and exhortations of Louise.[168]

Thus the charism of this little band of consecrated women was to serve the poor both spiritually and temporally in imitation of Christ for the glory of God. Initially the poor for them were the sick poor in their homes and the poor girls who needed to be educated. Gradually their ministry to the poor extended to include the sick in hospitals, the galley slaves, the foundlings, the soldiers on the battlefields, the poor in war-torn villages, the insane and even the poor in Poland.[169] Baunard stated that the service of the poor was their first and final obligation and that they were to be "the voice of the voiceless."[170] Gobillon described their enterprise as "arduous but prepared by providence."[171]

That the Company was founded and prepared by providence was a constant theme in Vincent's Conferences. In his Conference of July 31, 1634 Vincent stated:

> Providence has brought the twelve of you together here with the intention, as it would seem, that you should honor his human life on earth. . . . You have been chosen to be at the disposition of divine providence and, if you do not fully submit to It, you will lose much.[172]

The Daughters were to honor the human life of Jesus through their service to the poor. So important was this that Vincent counselled the Daughters to "Leave God for God."[173] Again, in the Conference of July 19, 1640 Vincent reiterated the action of providence and the charism of the Daughters. He stated:

> By the permission of providence, the very first words of your rule run as follows: "The Company of the Daughters of Charity is established to love God, to serve and honor Our Lord, their Patron, and the Blessed Virgin.". . .God's design in establishing your Company is "to serve the sick poor corporally, by supplying them with all they need, and spiritually, by taking care that they live and die holily."[174]

Vincent often reminded the Daughters that providence was their founder, that neither Mademoiselle Le Gras nor he thought of founding them: "I have told you many and many a time, my daughters, that you should be perfectly certain that God is your founder. . ."[175] In addition to this Vincent impressed upon the Daughters the uniqueness of their Company: "Up to the present, nobody has ever seen the sick poor nursed in their own homes. . .this work was reserved for you. You were destined by God from eternity to be numbered amongst the first." Continuing, Vincent emphasized the power of God in their vocation:

If it was not God, my daughters, who brought about that which is visible in your vocation, would it have been possible for a girl to leave her native place, her relatives, the pleasures of marriage. . .to come to a place she has never seen, to live with girls from places far distant from her own, to devote herself, in voluntary poverty, to the service of convicts, to poor children abandoned by their parents, to the sick poor who are rotting in filth, and even to those in dungeons? Oh! no, my daughters, God alone could effect that![176]

Herein Vincent expressed the reality of the mystery of such a vocation and the resultant necessity of depending totally on the providence of God for the living out of such a calling "to serve Jesus Christ in the person of the poor."[177] Louise too reinforced the necessity of trust in providence which was a recurring theme throughout her Letters and Thoughts. In a treatise on providence she wrote: ". . .total dependence on divine providence . . .is one of the virtues which God clearly requires of us in order to insure the preservation of the Company."[178] Certainly these women had taken, to use a modern expression, a "preferential option for the poor and youth."[179] They endeavored to protect the dignity of the poor and to liberate them from the injustices in which they lived. Truly they were prophetic leaders in what would come to be known as the social doctrine of the Church in the modern age. Through Vincent and Louise they were educated to serve the poor with compassionate hearts while trusting totally in providence. They were to be aware always of the dignity of the person of the poor and their identification with Jesus Christ. In a letter of concern to the Sisters in Angers in 1644, Louise wrote:

Where are the gentleness and charity that you must pre-serve so carefully when dealing with our dear masters, the sick poor? If we deviate the slightest from the conviction that they are the members of Jesus Christ, it will infallibly lead to the weakening of these beautiful virtues in us.[180]

The spirit in which they were to serve the poor was that of simplicity, humility and charity. This lesson was continuously reinforced in the Conferences of Vincent de Paul to the Daughters. In Conference 52 of February 24, 1653 we read:

> May this spirit then always be apparent, when you go out and return; let the spirit of charity, humility and great simplicity be ever visible and never make use of artifice or cunning. If you live in this spirit, my dear Sisters, ah! how happy the Institute of Charity will be, how you will honor it, how it will be multiplied![181]

With respect to Charity, Vincent emphasized affective and effective love. In the words of one of the first Daughters, this meant: "Affective love causes one to love God tenderly and joyously; effective love causes one to proceed to practise good works when an opportunity arises of doing so."[182] Vincent continued the discussion with: "Now my dear Sisters, these two loves are necessary. The spirit of the Company of the poor Daughters of Charity consists of these two sorts of love for God and also our neighbor, beginning with one's Sisters;. . ."[183] Love and unity among the Sisters was essential. Both Vincent and Louise repeatedly called the Daughters to this. In a letter to her Sisters at Richelieu, Louise wrote: "Gentleness, cordiality and forbearance must be the practices of the Daughters of Charity just as humility, simplicity and the love of the holy humanity of Jesus Christ, who is perfect charity, is their spirit."[184] For Louise, the spirit of the Company was also a source of unity. She wrote the following to a Sister in 1657: "If humility, simplicity and charity, which produce support, are well established among you, your little company will be made up of as many saints as there are persons."[185] Louise often used the image of the Trinity as the basis and source of unity among them. This theme was frequently found in her Letters and Spiritual Thoughts. In Letter 111- An Account of Her Pilgrimage to Chartres in 1644, we read: "I prayed that he (God) might be the strong and loving bond that unites the hearts of all the Sisters in imitation of the union of the three Divine Persons."[186] Louise's correspondence to her Daughters is replete with references to the need for unity within the community because she realized that a solid community life based on prayer and mutual support was essential for the well-being of the apostolate. This is shown in a letter which Louise wrote to Barbe Angiboust in 1657:

> I was certain that all of you would have much to endure, but, by the mercy of God, you are generous enough to bear this burden and to help our Sisters to look upon it as the yoke of Our Lord. You also possess sufficient gentleness and forbearance to treat those with whom you deal without passion. This is one of the best ways to win them over. . . . We have great reason to praise God for the harmony that exists among you and for your fidelity in observing your Rules, insofar as the service of the poor permits.[187]

Not only was the charism and mission of the Daughters of Charity unique in the Church of the seventeenth century but also the lifestyle was totally distinctive. In 1633, the only type of communal life for consecrated women was that of the cloister. Both Louise and Vincent did not want to face the same fate of enclosure that Francis de Sales and Jane de Chantal had with their Sisters so they stressed that the Daughters of Charity were not religious nor were they lay with private vows. They took simple annual vows and lived in community but they were of a secular nature because they were not cloistered nor under perpetual solemn vows and thus not canonically religious.[188] Although the Daughters lived and worked "in the world" both Vincent and Louise stressed that they must be as dedicated and as spiritual as consecrated religious. Their commitment and their lifestyle marked the Daughters as an innovation in consecrated life by becoming a prophetic witness in forming a Society of Apostolic Life.[189] Presenting the Rule of the Parish Sisters, Vincent stated:

They shall bear in mind that they are not in a Religious Order, as this state is unsuitable to the duties of their vocation. Nevertheless, as they are more exposed to the occasions of sin than religious bound to enclosure, having only for a Convent the houses of the sick and that in which the Superioress resides, for a cell a hired room, for a chapel their parish church, for a cloister the streets of the city, for enclosure obedience, . . .for a grille, the fear of God, for a veil, holy modesty, making use of no other form of profession to assure their vocation than the continual confidence they have in divine providence and the offering they make to God of all that they are and of their service in the person of the poor, for all these considerations they should have as much or more virtue than if they had made their profession in a Religious Order.[190]

It was precisely the "duties of their vocation" in the service of the poor, that Louise wished to preserve when she insisted that the Daughters be under the jurisdiction of the Superior General of the Mission. She realized that the Priests would ensure the continuance of their charism, spirit and mission whereas the local Bishop could easily change their focus and even force them into enclosure thus robbing them of the essence of their foundation. Experience had shown that her vision and foresight were not unfounded.[191]

On August 8, 1655 at a Conference with Vincent de Paul, the final approbation of the establishment by his Grace the Archbishop of Paris and its confirmation by his Eminence Cardinal de Retz was read to the Sisters. The title of Society or Confraternity would remain and they would be subject to the Superior General of the Congregation of the Mission. The forty Sisters present signed the Act of Establishment.[192]

For the next five years Louise continued to support, guide and encourage her Daughters. Even when her health continued to decline, her thoughts, her prayers and her sufferings were with them. Although she had dedicated herself totally to the Company she had not forgotten her family. She had known Michel's struggles as a young man, had intervened with the Marillacs for his financial assistance, had seen him finally marry in 1650 and had rejoiced in the birth of her granddaughter Louise-Renée in 1651. The young family kept in close contact with Louise and her granddaughter was a joy not only to her but to the other Sisters as well. However, these last five years of Louise's life were marked by increased physical suffering and concern for the future of the Company.

From 1633-1660 she had witnessed through the grace of God and the assistance of Vincent de Paul the vision of her "*Lumière*" of 1623 become a reality beyond her furthest imaginings. From a small house with four women in 1633 to 65 houses in 1660 with "much coming and going to help the neighbor"[193] Louise knew the grace of her interior vision and its realization was the work of providence. Throughout these years she had endeavored to trust totally in providence and to school her Daughters in the ways of God. There had been many graces and successes but there had also been many sorrows and difficulties. Louise had known the sorrow of her Sisters in war and famine, as well as the sorrow of some departing from their ranks. Even within her lifetime, she and Vincent besought the Sisters to rediscover the initial spirit of the Company and to persevere in it.[194] Thus in her last years her thoughts turned to the future of the Company and the means which she saw as the hallmarks for the preservation of their charism and spirit. In her correspondence and writings Louise cited poverty and confidence in providence as the two "pillars" of the Company of the Daughters of Charity.[195] In a letter to Brother Ducourneau in January of 1658, Louise clearly expressed the lifestyle that aspirants would have to face in joining the Company. Her letter read thus:

> Rather they must continuously go to seek out the sick poor, in various places, in any kind of weather and at predetermined times. They will be very poorly clothed and nourished and will never wear anything on their heads except a linen

cornette in cases of great necessity. They must have no other intention, when entering the Company, than the pure desire to serve God and their neighbor.[196]

Louise's concern for the simple, poor lifestyle of the Sisters was expressed in a letter to Vincent in January of 1660. After presenting the difficulties the Sisters were experiencing Louise wrote:

All this, my Most Honored Father, leads me to realize how necessary it is for the Rules to continue to oblige the Sisters to live poorly, simply and humbly because I fear that if they settle into a way of life that requires great expenditures, is ostentatious and partially enclosed, they would thereby be obliged to find ways to maintain it . . .which is so dangerous for the continuation of the work of God which. . .your Charity has so firmly sustained against all opposition.[197]

Again we find the same theme expressed in Louise's Spiritual Writings of 1660 on "Problems for the Company." She wrote:

Oh, what a happiness, if, without offending God, the Company could be employed only in the service of those who are destitute in all things! To this end, this Company must never depart from nor change its poor manner of life. Thus, should divine providence provide them with more than is necessary, let them go to serve the corporally and spiritually poor at their own expense. If this passes unnoticed, what does it matter, so long as souls honor eternally the Redemption of Our Lord?[198]

In the last moments of her life, March 15, 1660 Louise's thoughts were for the poor and her Daughters. Although the light of her earthly body was being extinguished, the light of her spirit and the legacy of her charism were being passed on in her final Spiritual Testament:[199]

My dear Sisters, I continue to ask God for his blessings for you and pray that he will grant you the grace to persevere in your vocation in order to serve him in the manner he asks of you.

Take good care of the service of the poor. Above all, live together in great union and cordiality, loving one another in imitation of the union and life of Our Lord.

Pray earnestly to the Blessed Virgin, that she may be your only Mother.[200]

For twenty-seven years Louise, as Superioress, had been "the soul of the Company which animated the body and enabled it to carry out the plan of God for it."[201] Through her imitation of Jesus in his service to the poor she had formed her Daughters in the charism and spirit with which God had gifted her. She had learned to walk in the light of Christ in the midst of the darkness and suffering in her life and in his light that darkness had been turned into new light. With the cooperation of Vincent de Paul, she had engraved upon the hearts of her Daughters the charism of compassionate service to the poor in imitation of Jesus, given in a spirit of humility, simplicity and charity. Rooted in a spirit of poverty, trust in providence and devotion to the Blessed Virgin, Louise bequeathed to her Daughters the service of the poor. Truly she had been "a beautiful tree of life bringing forth fruits of love"[202] and imbued with her spirit so too would her Daughters be trees of life bringing forth fruits of love for God throughout the world. Louise's "*Lumière*" of 1623 would continue to shine. Empowered with the light and love of Christ, her Daughters would bring light and love to the poor of the world.

The spirit of Louise de Marillac has lived on for over three hundred years and has inspired thousands of women to devote their lives to the service of the poor. Through them, her "*Lumière*" continues to shine in the darkness of human suffering.

Notes

1. The general historical information for this section has been gleaned from four principal sources: Pierre Coste, C.M., *The Life & Works of St. Vincent de Paul, 3 Vols.*, trans. Joseph Leonard, C.M. (New York: New City Press, 1987); Lily Devèze, *A History of France* (Carcassone: Castel Printing Co., 1989); Joseph I. Dirvin, C.M., *Louise de Marillac* (New York: Farrar, Straus & Giroux, 1970); M.V. Woodgate, *St. Louise de Marillac: Foundress of the Sisters of Charity* (London: Herder Book Co., 1946).

2. Woodgate, *St. Louise de Marillac*, p. 4.

3. Woodgate, *St. Louise de Marillac*, p. 4.

4. Edict of Nantes, 1598.

5. Devèze, *A History of France*, p. 40.

6. André Dodin, *ST. VINCENT DE PAUL et la charité* (Bourges: Tardy Quercy, 1989), p. 6. Hereinafter cited as *St. Vincent de Paul*.

7. Devèze, p. 40.

8. This was the first of three "wars" between the Queen Mother, Marie de Medici and her son, Louis XIII.

9. 1627- The Huguenots at La Rochelle; Conflict with the German Emperor, the King of Spain and the English.

To the French Provinces (New France-Canada), Richelieu sent the powerful Intendents who represented the King and had full power to rule the colony. At home he created a Marine Corps and the French Academy of writers (L'Académie Française, 1635).

10. Dodin, *St. Vincent de Paul*, p. 164.

11. Dirvin, *Louise de Marillac*, p. 145.

12. Pierre Coste, C.M., ed., *SAINT VINCENT DE PAUL: CORRE-SPONDENCE, CONFERENCES, DOCUMENTS*, Vol. I (Paris: 1920) ed. Jacqueline Kilar, D.C.; trans. Helen Marie Law, D.C., John Marie Poole, D.C., James R. King, C.M.; ann. John Carven, C.M. (New York: New City Press, 1985), p. 331. Hereinafter cited as *V. de P.*, I.

13. Dirvin, p. 147.

14. Coste, *The Life & Works of St. Vincent de Paul*, II, 366-367. Hereinafter cited as *Life & Works*, II.

15. Pierre Coste, C.M., ed., *SAINT VINCENT DE PAUL:CORRE-SPONDENCE, CONFERENCES, DOCUMENTS*, Vol.II (Paris,1921), ed. Jacqueline Kilar, D.C. and Marie Poole, D.C.; trans. Marie Poole,D.C., Esther Cavanagh, D.C., James R. King, C.M., Francis Germovnik, C.M.; ann. John W. Carmen, C.M. (New York: New City Press, 1990), 435. Hereinafter cited as *V. de P.*, II.

During the reign of Louis XIII, Louise de Marillac experienced the joys and sufferings, the light and shadows of married life, of court life and of the family's fall from prominence which culminated in her uncle's execution in 1632. However, with Vincent de Paul, she also experienced the generosity of Louis XIII and Anne of Austria as they endeavored to assist the poor and suffering with money and with care as the Queen organized the women of "Blood" to work with the Ladies of Charity and the Daughters.

16. Cardinal Mazarin was not a priest. He was made a Cardinal in 1641, sent to France as the Papal Legate but later removed from this post by the Vatican. In 1642 he was appointed by the Queen to succeed Richelieu as First Minister on the Council of Conscience.

17. On January 14, Vincent de Paul secretly left Paris at night to plead with the Queen for the common good in preference to Mazarin but to no avail. For his efforts he had to remain outside Paris for several months, because his action, once known, would lead people to think he had gone to the other side.

18. Dirvin, pp. 317-318.

Vincent with the approval of Louise de Marillac sent their Daughters to work among the war-torn populace. Coste wrote:

They nursed the sick and wounded and fed the hungry. In this way, Vincent mobilized all his forces in the fight against human misery: to the destructive energy of those who were instruments of famine and death, he opposed the beneficent energy of those who had consecrated themselves to God to combat evil and bring life to others (*Life & Works, II*, 367).

19. Louise Sullivan, D.C., ed. and trans. *Spiritual Writings of Louise de Marillac:Correspondence and Thoughts* (New York: New City Press, 1991), p. 397. Hereinafter cited as SWLM.

20. Pierre Coste, C.M., ed., *St. Vincent de Paul*, 14 vols. (Paris: Gabalda, 1920-1925), IV, 407. (Hereinafter cited as *St.Vincent de Paul*).

21. *St.Vincent de Paul*, IV, 398-399.

22. Pierre Coste, *Life & Works*, II, 443ff. Chapter XLII, "The Relief of L'Ile-De-France" presents an excellent account of this situation.

23. Coste, *The Life & Works*, II, 466-467.

24. Coste, *The Life & Works*, II, 469.

25. Coste, *The Life & Works*, II, 472.

26. Elisabeth Charpy, *Petite vie de LOUISE DE MARILLAC* (Paris: Desclée de Brouwer, 1991), p. 125. In March of 1653, Vincent and Louise opened a house "The Name of Jesus" [Le Nom du Jésus] for the old and destitute. The objective of this house was to prevent the spread of mendicancy and to Louise's creative genius goes the success of the plan. The residents worked at their trades, made a little money and maintained their dignity as persons. Louise was careful to combine charity and justice in such enterprises.

The organization of the work incorporated concepts which foreshadowed present-day occupational therapy. Vincent Regnault, D.C., *Saint Louise de Marillac-Servant of the Poor,* trans. Louise Sullivan, D.C. (Rockford, Illinois: Tan Books and Publishers, Inc., 1983), p. 58.

27. Edward R. Udovic, C.M., "Caritas Christi Urget Nos: The Urgent Challenges of Charity in Seventeenth-Century France", *Vincentian Heritage, Vol.12, n.2* (Cape Girardeau, MO: Concord Publishing House, 1991), p. 86.

28. Udovic, "Caritas Christi Urget Nos. . ." p. 86. By 1657 the militia in Paris began to hunt down the remaining beggars and within a few years more than five thousand poor—men, women and children were detained in the various institutions of the General Hospital of Paris. The question of the beggars was a complicated issue. Initially Vincent obeyed the law to refuse them food but later contravened it.

29. The Queen sought Louise to send her Sisters to Calais. Vincent referred to this in an August conference:

> The Queen has called for you to go to Calais to nurse the poor wounded soldiers. What a motive for humbling yourselves is the thought that God wishes to make use of you for such great things! Ah! My Savior! Men go to war to slay their fellowmen, and you, you go to war to repair the harm they are doing (Dirvin, p. 368).

Cf. Conference 100 of St. Vincent To Four Sisters Who Were Sent To Calais, August 4, 1658. Pierre Coste, *The Conferences of St. Vincent De Paul to the Sisters of Charity,* trans. Joseph Leonard, C.M. (Maryland: Christian Classics, Inc., 1968), IV, 164. Hereinafter cited as *Conferences.*

30. M. Gobillon, *La Vie De La Vénérable Louise de Marillac, Veuve de M. Le Gras.* Revue par M. Collet (Paris: Librairie de Mme De Poussielgue-Rusand, 1862), p. 15.

31. Mgr. Louis Baunard, *La Vénérable Louise de Marillac (Paris: Poussielgue, 1898),* p. 3.

32. Dirvin, p. 4.

33. An historical family document published in 1908, supports Paris as the place of Louise's birth. It reads: "Louise de Marillac, née à Paris, le 12 août 1591, était fille de Louis de Marillac, seigneur de Ferrières, conseiller au parlement de Paris, . . ." De Marillac, *Documents Historiques Sur La Famille DE MARILLAC,* Receuillis Par Les Descendants De Jacques-Victor Hippolyte DE MARILLAC (Paris: Lahure, 1908), p. 220.

34. Louis de Marillac called Louise "ma fille, ma naturelle" in a legal document in which he set aside money for her upkeep. Dirvin, p. 5.

35. Regnault, p. 1.

36. Dirvin, p. 4.

37. Dirvin outlines the various difficulties in the marriage which culminated in court actions against Antoinette and her arrest and confinement

in the Hospital St. Gervais in May of 1601 (pp. 14-15). Regnault also makes reference to Louis' suit against his wife (p. 2).

38. August 15, 1591, Louis bequeathed to Louise an annual pension of 100 pounds in addition to land at Ferrières-en-Brie; January 2, 1595 he bequeathed a pension of 38 ecus to her; November 23, 1602-he added 1,200 pounds to his bequests to Louise and July 25, 1604 in his will he added another ten ecus of pension to be drawn from the profits of the land at Farinvilliers. Regnault, pp. 1-2; cf. Dirvin, p. 16.

39. Gobillon, p. 16: "Il la mit en pension dans le monastère des religieuses de Poissy, on il avait quelques parentes, pour lui donner dans cette maison les principes de la piéte chretienne."

40. Dirvin, p. 9. Coste suggests that Louise was older when she went to Poissy. *Life & Works,* I, 179.

41. Jean Guy, *Sainte Louise de Marillac: Femme au grand coeur, âme de feu* (Paris: Société Saint-Paul, 1960), p. 15: ". . .une large partie de la journée se trouvait consacrée à l'enseignement de la religion, du français, du calcul. Le latin n'était pas négligé, et les élèves les plus douées étudiaient le grec. Des classes étaient réservées aux arts d'agrément, à la bonne tenue et aux belles manières."

42. Pierre Coste states that one of the nuns, Louise de Marillac, was a woman of remarkable virtue for Hilarion de la Coste has given her a place in his *Lives of ladies illustrious for their piety and learning*; and, she was also of exceptional literary tastes since she composed hymns and a number of books of verse, as well as a translation of the *Office of the Virgin,* the *Penitential Psalms*, and a *Commentary of the Canticle of Canticles.* Coste, *Life & Works,* I, 179.

43. The Royal Abbey of St. Denis at Poissy was established by the grandson of St. Louis IX to honor his canonization in 1297. The chapel is on the site of St. Louis' birthplace. The Dominican nuns who took possession of it in 1304 were from the convent of Prouille, established by St. Dominic himself. Dirvin, p. 10.

44. SWLM, p. 117. L.105-To My Very Dear Sister Turgis, August 24 (1644):. . ."wishing for them the perfection of Saint Joan and of Saint Catherine of Siena, as I do also for you, my dear Sister. . ."

p. 266. L.225-To Monsieur Vincent, Friday [October 1648]:. . ."If Saint Catherine were alive, she would fear for me because of this, for my soul would appear to her to be without this love that I should certainly possess . . ."

45. Dirvin, p. 10.

46. Guy, p. 25: "Elle sera marquée, également, et pour toute son existence, par l'érudition, l'élégance intellectuelle, la vraie culture des Dames Dominicaines."

47. Charpy, p. 8: *"Vers douze ans, Louise est retirée de Poissy et envoyée dans une pension de famille tenue par <une demoiselle pauvre>."*

48. Dirvin, p. 17.

49. Gobillon, p. 16: "Lorsqu'elle fut suffisamment instruite, il (son père) la mit à Paris entre les mains d'une maîtresse habile et vertueuse pour lui apprendre à faire des ouvrages convenables à sa condition. . . . Il n'oublia rien de tout ce que la pouvait perfectionner dans les exercices du corps et de l'esprit."

50. Guy, p. 31.

51. Dirvin, p. 21. This information is recorded on Louise's marriage records. Dirvin posits that perhaps the family took her in after the death of her father in 1604.

52. SWLM, p. 711. A.29-ON CHARITY.

53. Regnault, p. 5.

54. These Franciscan nuns had been installed in Paris on August 2, 1606 and were known as the Daughters of the Passion. Louise dearly desired to join them and share in their life of penance and prayer. Calvet, p. 26; cf. Regnault, p. 5 and Dirvin, p. 19.

55. Gobillon, p. 18.

56. Regnault, p. 2. Cf. Gobillon, p. 17.

57. At this time, Louise's uncle Michel was a councillor of the King, her uncle Octavien Dony d'Attichy was superintendent of finances, and her uncle Jean-Louis was the husband of Catherine de Medici, aunt of the Queen Mother. Dirvin, p. 22.

58. Louise alluded to this fact in a letter to the Count de Maure in December, 1649 in which she said: "However, to whom could I pour out these troubles,. . .except to you Monsieur,. . .who hold in my regard the place of those whose conduct has led me to embrace this life which has placed me in the situation in which I now find myself."

The Count de Maure was the husband of Anne d'Attichy, Louise's cousin with whom she lived prior to her marriage. "Those" clearly refers to Monsieur and Madame d'Attichy and "the situation" refers to her financially-fraught widowhood. SWLM, p. 308. L.274.

59. Dirvin, p. 22.

60. Dirvin, p. 23.

61. Dirvin, p. 26.

62. Calvet, p. 33.

63. Gobillon, p. 19:
    She applied herself from the first years to visiting the sick poor of the parish where she lived. She herself gave them broths and remedies, made their beds, instructed them and consoled them by her exhortations, disposed them to receive the sacraments, and buried them after their death.

64. Gobillon, p. 18.

65. For example: Henriette became Mère Angelique de Jesus of the Parisian Carmel; Louis became Père d'Attichy of French spiritual literature and Bishop of Riez; Antoine became Marquis d'Attichy; Anne became Lady in Waiting to Marie de Medici and married the Comte de Maure. Dirvin, p. 33.

66. SWLM, p. 97. L.96-To Monsieur Vincent. Calvet says: "He neglected his own business, pledged his property, and parted with a great deal of his capital" (p. 34). Even so the d'Attichy children took offence at his assiduous efforts.

67. Dirvin, p. 40.

68. Gobillon, p. 17.

69. Baunard states: "M. Le Gras allait mourit. Il venait d'être pris d'une crise cérébrale qui fut près de l'emporter" p. 34.

70. Calvet, p. 44.

71. Baunard, p. 35.

72. Baunard, p. 37.

73. Bishop Camus was Louise's director, who upon his assignment to Belley, was instrumental in having Vincent de Paul accept Louise for direction.

74. Calvet, p. 38.

75. Calvet, p. 40.

76. Calvet, p. 36.

77. Dirvin, p. 39.

78. Dirvin, p. 42.

79. It is interesting to note in passing that Louise too would spend her life praying for the well-being of her son, Michel.

80. SWLM, p. 1. A.2-LIGHT.

81. Dirvin, p. 42.

82. Dirvin, p. 42.

83. The reference is to Vincent de Paul.

84. This experience of Louise seems to meet the criteria of "an intellectual locution" described as one of the principal extraordinary phenomena observed in the lives of the saints and mystics. Jordan Aumann, O.P., Spiritual Theology (London: Sheed & Ward, 1980,1993), pp. 427-428.

85. SWLM, p. 1. A.2-LIGHT.

86. Francis de Sales had asked Vincent de Paul to be the Superior of the Visitation Convent in Paris, an office which he carried out until his death in 1660. Coste, Life & Works, I, 191. He was also directing Madame de Chantal. Dirvin, p. 52.

87. As a result of Vincent's experience in directing Mme de Gondi, he was reluctant to undertake the direction of another lady of noble birth, lest

she also be too demanding. Louise, on her part, was disinclined to change directors and also was not initially attracted to Vincent, perhaps because of the difference in their social station.

88. Dirvin, p. 51. Louise soon realized the wisdom and holiness of Vincent de Paul and completely entrusted her soul to him.

89. Vincent de Paul had anguished through three to four years of spiritual darkness when he assumed the doubts of a priest who was a famous doctor of theology. Only when Vincent promised to dedicate the remainder of his life to the poor did the dreadful doubts leave him. Coste, *Life & Works*, I, 49.

90. Three hundred and sixty years later (1993) the Daughters of Charity had 27,000 members with 72 provinces throughout the world.

91. SWLM, p. 689. A.1. No specific date is given for this document but it is placed prior to 1621. During this time it was not unusual for devout persons to establish such a rule of life.

92. SWLM, p. 693. A.3-ACT OF CONSECRATION. This Consecration was probably written shortly after Antoine's death because of the renewal of her vow of widowhood and the use of her maiden name. It is also situated before her "Act of Consecration to the Blessed Virgin" in which she dedicates herself and her son to Mary's protection.

93. SWLM, p. 695. A.4-OBLATION TO THE BLESSED VIRGIN (c.1626). This oblation was probably made shortly after Antoine's death in December of 1625.

94. Dirvin, p. 55.

95. Dirvin, p. 55. The phrase used by Bishop Camus in his letter of condolence to Louise, February 22, 1626: "He has deprived you of him whom you greatly loved."

96. Gobillon, p. 36.

97. SWLM, p. 5. L.1-To Monsieur Vincent, June 5, 1627.

Michel was a source of anxiety for Louise for many years. He found studies difficult; he had distress in deciding his vocation during which he experienced periods of unrest, unhappiness and irresponsible behavior. Vincent often admonished Louise about her excessive concern for her son. Finally she was able to surrender him and his future to God and gain peace of soul for herself.

98. SWLM, p. 6. L.1-To Monsieur Vincent, June 5, 1627.

99. From the context of the letter it appears that Vincent might have been away for a lengthy time: "For the past month our good God has permitted . . ."

100. This seems to suggest the beginning of Louise's queries with Vincent regarding God's will in the calling of other women to serve with her. Such discussion and discernment would continue until 1633.

101. Louise's Spiritual Writings are divided into her "Letters" and "Thoughts" and will be classified as such in this study.

102. SWLM, p. 6. L.1-To Monsieur Vincent, June 5, 1627.

103. SWLM, p. 7. L.2-To Monsieur Vincent, January 13, 1628.

104. Coste, *V. de P.*, I, 24. L.12-To Saint Louise de Marillac, October 30, 1626.

105. Coste, *V. de P.*, I, 36. L.23-To Saint Louise, February 9, 1628.

106. SWLM, p. 695. A.4-OBLATION TO THE BLESSED VIRGIN-c.1626.

107. SWLM, p. 7. L.2-To Monsieur Vincent, January 13, 1628.

108. Coste, *V. de P.*, I, 34. L.22-To Saint Louise, January 17, 1628.

109. Coste, *V. de P.*, I, 37. L.24-To Saint Louise, February 1628.

110. Coste, *V. de P.*, I, 27. L.15-To Saint Louise, 1627.

111. Coste, *V. de P.*, I, 35. L.23-To Saint Louise, February 9, 1628.

112. Coste, *V.de P.*, I, 46. L.27-To Saint Louise, c. July 30, 1628.

113. Coste, *V.de P.*, I, 54. L.29-To Saint Louise (Between 1626 and May 1629).

114. Coste, *V. de P.*, I, 60. L.33-To Saint Louise (Around 1629).

115. Coste, *V. de P.*, I, 28. L.16-To Saint Louise, October 8, 1627.

116. Coste, *V. de P.*, I, 34. L.22-To Saint Louise, January 17, 1628.

117. Coste, *V. de P.*, I, 63. L.38-To Saint Louise (April or May 1629).

118. Gobillon, p. 37.

119. The Charities were the organizations of women in the various parishes who devoted themselves to aiding the poor. They were also called Confraternities of Charity. Each operated under a general structure and rule.

120. Coste, *V. de P.*, I, 64. L.39-To Saint Louise, Montmirail, May 6, 1629.

121. Gobillon, p. 39.

122. Gobillon, p. 43.

123. SWLM, p. 704. A.50-(VISITS TO THE CONFRATERNITIES OF ASNIÈRES AND SAINT-CLOUD): "I left on the Feast of Saint Agatha, February 5, to go to Saint-Cloud. At the moment of Holy Communion, it seemed to me that Our Lord inspired me to receive him as the Spouse of my soul and that this Communion was a manner of espousal."

124. Coste, *V. de P.*, I, 67. L.40-To Saint Louise in Saint-Cloud, Paris, February 19, 1630. Vincent's reasoning is full of practical wisdom: "All it does is weigh upon your spirit and deprive you of the peace Our Lord wishes in your heart and the detachment from love of everything that is not himself."

125. Coste, *V. de P.*, I, 68. Marguerite Naseau was considered by Vincent to be the first Daughter of Charity.

126. Elisabeth Charpy, "Come, Wind or High Water", *Echoes of the Company,* 4, April 1987. p. 147.

127. Coste, *V. de P.,* I, 75. L.46-To Saint Louise, in Villepreux.

128. Coste, *V. de P.,* I, 79. L.48-To Saint Louise in Villepreux.

129. Coste, *V. de P.,* I, 71. L.43: "You belong to Our Lord and his holy Mother. Cling to them and to the state in which they have placed you until they make it clear that they wish something else for you. . ."

130. The irony of the charges was that the law had been introduced and passed only recently by Michel de Marillac when he was Keeper of the Seals.

131. Gobillon, p. 48.

132. Coste, *V. de P.,* I, 145. L.95-To Saint Louise.

133. Coste, *V. de P.,* I, 102. L.64-To Saint Louise in Montreuil.

134. Coste, *V. de P.,* I, 104. L.65. It is of interest that Father Lallement was martyred in Quebec in 1665.

135. Coste, *V. de P.,* I, 105. L.66.

136. Coste, *V. de P.,* I, 107, 111.

137. SWLM, p. 707. A.46-(RULE OF THE CHARITY.) Coste, *V. de P.,*I, 114. L.74: "You are a skillful woman to have adapted the rule of the Charity in this way; I think it is fine."

138. Madame de Marillac was the wife of Jean-Louis de Marillac.

139. Coste, *V. de P.,* I, 126. L.84:
Come now! This will grieve you; but then, since Our Lord has willed it this way, we must adore his providence and strive to conform ourselves in all things to his holy will. . . . The Son of God wept over Lazarus; why should you not weep for that good lady? There is no harm in it so long as, like the Son of God, you conform yourself in this matter to his Father's will. I am confident that you will.

140. Coste, *V. de P.,* I, 138. L.92-To Saint Louise.

141. Coste, *V. de P.,* I, 157. L.105-To Saint Louise.

142. Coste, *V. de P.,* I.

The following references may appear somewhat vague but in the context of preceding correspondence and the seeking of God's will for the future, they are accepted as alluding to the foundation of the Company:

Vincent states the following in L.95: "It will indeed be fitting for you to make some sort of pilgrimage for what you told me; but for the love of God, Mademoiselle, do not get sick on the way" (p. 145). L.97 reads: "As for the other matter we talked about yesterday, do not be concerned about it. He who has time at his command will take care of that affair in the time he has foreseen as appropriate from all eternity" (p. 146).

In L.119 Vincent exhorted Louise: "Take care of your health. It is no longer yours since you destine it for God" (p. 172).

143. Coste, *V. de P., I,* 174. L.122: "Draw up the rule; then I shall go over it and do what you asked me. Tell me the obstacles that you fear."

144. SWLM, p. 716. A.5-RETREAT

145. Coste, *V. de P.,* I, 162. L.110, July 7, 1632: "I certainly had no doubt at all that you would find it very difficut to reestablish the Charity and more so than you tell me. But blessed be God that there is some reason to hope you will set it up again!"

p. 164. L.111, July 10, 1632: "Please find out how the Charity at Crosnes is doing. . . .If you had a horse to go there, you would not lose any time."

146. Coste, *V. de P.,* I, 168. L. 115: "Charity towards those poor convicts is of incomparable merit before God. You have done well to continue in any way you can until I have the pleasure of seeing you . . .Give a little thought to whether your Charity at Saint-Nicolas would be willing to take on the responsibility for them, at least for a time."

147. Coste, *V. de P.,* I, 200. Footnote 3. Coste states that Abelly relates this to the institution of the Daughters of Charity.

148. Coste, *V. de P.,* I, 211.

149. Coste, *V. de P.,* I, 216.

150. Coste, *V. de P.,* I, 217. A certain number of young women had been living with Louise and she had been educating them in virtue to work with the poor.

151. Coste, *V. de P.,* I, 217.

152. Gobillon, p. 56: ". . .she began this little community on the 29th November, 1633 on the eve of the feast of Saint Andrew."

153. Coste, *V. de P.,* I, 223. L.156a-To Saint Louise.

154. Gobillon, p. 56.

155. SWLM, pp. 717-719. A.8-RETREAT.

156. SWLM, p. 726. A.55-ORDER OF THE DAY; p. 727. A.54-DRAFT OF THE RULE.

157. SWLM, p. 727.

158. Louise's cause was introduced in 1895 during the pontificate of Leo XIII. In 1911 she was proclaimed Venerable by Pius X. In 1920, Benedict XV beatified her and in 1934 Pius XI canonized her. In 1954 Louise's statue was erected in St. Peter's in Rome to occupy the fortieth and last niche reserved for founder-saints. Cited by J.P. Sheedy, C.M., UNTRODDEN PATHS, The Social Apostolate of St. Louise de Marillac (London: Salesian Press, 1958), p. 1.

159. Coste, *V. de P.,* I, 46.

160. Regnault, p. 134.

161. SWLM, pp. 36, 113, 320.

162. Margaret Flinton, D.C., *Louise de Marillac: Social Aspects of Her Work*

(New York: New City Press, 1992), p. 14. In this book Margaret Flinton gives an excellent exposition of the various works of Louise de Marillac and shows her to be a prophetic pioneer in the area of social work.

163. Coste, *V. de P.*, II, 603. L.773.

164. SWLM, p. 234. L.199-To Monsieur Vincent, November 1647.

Vincent de Paul seemed satisfied to allow the Daughters to be under the jurisdiction of the local bishop, whereas Louise consistently maintained that in order to preserve their identity and uniqueness, they must be under the jurisdiction of the Superior General of the Missions.

165. Coste, *Life & Works,* I, 355, 361, 362.

166. Dirvin, p. 338. The disposition of 1655 served for nearly 255 years until Pope Leo XIII gave it the virtue of his pontifical authority on June 25, 1882.

167. During the period of 1634-1660 Vincent delivered 120 Conferences to the Daughters which are extant. Many were preserved in Louise's own handwriting. Not only did she frequently request the Conferences but often suggested and outlined the topics to be discussed.

168. SWLM, p. 12. L.43-To Sister Barbe, c. 1636; p. 113. L.104B- To The Sisters at Angers, July 26, 1644; p.835- SPIRITUAL TESTAMENT OF LOUISE DE MARILLAC.

169. 1634- Work in the Hotel-Dieu in Paris; 1638- Commencement of work with the foundlings; 1639-First institutional mission outside Paris begins with the hospital in Angers; 1640- The Daughters go to the galley slaves; 1652- The Daughters go to Poland; 1653- The Daughters go to the battlefields at Châlons to nurse the soldiers. They also begin work with the insane in Paris.

170. Baunard, p. 430: "Elles sont la voix des sans voix."

171. Gobillon, p. 20.

172. Leonard, *Conferences*, I, 9.

173. Leonard, *Conferences*, I, 4: "My daughters, remember that when you leave prayer and Holy Mass to serve the poor, you are losing nothing, because serving the poor is going to God and you should see God in them."; I, 284: "To leave God only for God, that is to say, to leave one work of God to perform another, either of greater obligation or greater merit, is not to leave God." ; III, 83: "That is called leaving God for God." This explicit statement and lived reality of the correspondence between finding "God in the poor" and "God in prayer" may very well have been Vincent de Paul's original contribution to the history of spirituality.

174. Leonard, *Conferences*, I, 17. Cf. SWLM, p. 727, A.54-Draft of the Rule which Louise submitted to Vincent de Paul in January 1634 as the first draft prior to the Rule of 1645.

175. Leonard, *Conferences*, I, 216. Cf. p. 102

176. Leonard, *Conferences*, I, 219.

177. Leonard, *Conferences*, I, 223.

178. SWLM, p. 769. A.75-ON THE CONDUCT OF DIVINE PROVIDENCE.

179. Document de Puebla, IV, 2 as cited in *Libertatis Nuntius* (Boston: Daughters of St. Paul, 1984), #6, p. 16.

180. SWLM, p. 113. L. 104B. July 26(1644); cf. p.320. L.284B, May 4, 1650: "...be very gentle and courteous toward your poor. You know that they are our masters and that we must love them tenderly and respect them deeply. It is not enough for these maxims to be in our minds; we must bear witness to them by our gentle and charitable care."

181. Leonard, *Conferences*, II, 217.

182. Leonard, *Conferences*, II, 210. Cf. p. 206: "And there, you have in general the essence of affective and effective love; to serve Our Lord in his members both corporally and spiritually and to do so in their own homes, or indeed in whatever place to which providence may send you."

183. Leonard, *Conferences*, II, 211.

184. SWLM, p. 406. L.377, c. October, 1652.

185. SWLM, p. 532. L.505-To Sister Cécile Agnès, 1657.

186. SWLM, p. 122. Cf. p. 768, A.75: "It seemed to me that in order to be faithful to God we must live in great union with one another. Since the Holy Spirit is the union of the Father and the Son, the life which we have freely undertaken must be lived in this great union of hearts."

187. SWLM, p. 574. L.549, October 13, 1657.

188. SWLM, p. 293. L. 481-To Monsieur L'Abbé de Vaux, June 29 (1649): "I met with the Vicar General two or three times to explain to him that we were just a secular family and that because we were bound together by the Confraternity of Charity, we had M. Vincent, as General of the Confraternities, for our Director." Regarding the vows and those professed by the laity: "Let me say that they are not the same, for the laity usually pronounce them before their confessor."

At the beginning some Sisters pronounced perpetual vows but the custom of annual vows was soon adopted perhaps as another means of ensuring that the Sisters not be subject to enclosure as religious.

189. Sharon L. Holland, I.H.M., "Societies of Apostolic Life", *The Code of Canon Law: A Text and Commentary*. Edited by James A. Coriden, Thomas J. Green and Donald E. Heintschel (New York: Paulist Press, 1985), p. 535, Canon 731, #'s 1 and 2:

> The circumstances surrounding a society's foundation may well have shaped the form used for incorporation or for the undertaking of the evangelical counsels. The classic example of this is the Daughters of Charity of Vincent de Paul, whose apostolic labors

dictated using forms carefully distinct from those of religious life in an era when all women religious professed solemn vows and were strictly cloistered.

190. Leonard, *Conferences,* IV, 264. It is to be noted that Louise and Vincent collaborated in the formulation of the Rule even though the Conferences indicate that Vincent presented them to the Daughters. In general the responsibility for the formation of the Daughters was left to Louise but she consistently asked for Vincent's advice and input. She sometimes reminded Vincent that the girls were his Daughters as well as hers.

It is interesting that in the beginning the girls were known as "Filles de Charités, or "Servantes des Pauvres" and even "Filles de Mlle Le Gras". It was not until the 18th and more so the 19th century that they were called "Soeurs de Saint Vincent de Paul". L'Église leur a donné comme nom officiel celui de "Filles de la Charité de Saint Vincent de Paul" (Charpy, *Petite vie de Louise de Marillac,* p. 26).

191. Louise was prophetic in emphasizing with Vincent the need to ensure the preservation of the apostolic nature of the works of the Daughters of Charity. Their "Company" indeed prefigured and became a paradigm for future institutes dedicated to apostolic works. Through the teaching and formation of Louise and Vincent, the Daughters of Charity lived the reality and the spirit of apostolic institutes as expressed in CIC #675:

1. Apostolic action is of the very nature of institutes dedicated to apostolic works. The whole life of the members is, therefore, to be imbued with an apostolic spirit, and the whole of their apostolic action is to be animated by a religious spirit.

Is there an echo of Vincent here? "Now, my dear Sisters, you are not religious in name but you should be religious in deed, and you are more obliged to become perfect than they are" (Leonard, *Conferences,*IV, 261).

2. Apostolic action is always to proceed from intimate union with God, and is to confirm and foster this union.

Vincent said: "My daughters, remember that when you leave prayer and Holy Mass to serve the poor, you are losing nothing, because serving the poor is going to God and you should see God in them" (*Conferences,*I, 4). Yet, Vincent encouraged the Sisters to give prayer its place :

My dear Sisters, always do what you can so that, prayer being your first occupation, your mind may be filled with God for the rest of the day. It is true that, in case of necessity, you should prefer the service of the poor to making your prayer, but, if you take care, you will find plenty of time for both. . . .Hence, my daughters, I urge you . . .to make your prayer before going out and to make it together. . .I beg you to be exact about this holy exercise (*Conferences,* I, 29).

Vincent knew well the relationship between the interior life and the apostolic life; hence, he cautioned the Sisters thus: "Now, my Daughters, the soul without prayer is almost like a body without a soul; in what concerns the service of God; it is without feeling, movement, and has only worldly and earthly desires" (Conferences, II, 49).

3. Apostolic action exercised in the name of the Church and by its command is to be performed in communion with the Church.

Louise and Vincent constantly spoke of the Daughters as imitating the mission of Jesus which indeed is sharing in the mission of the Church.

Louise expressed the honor of being "Daughters of the Church" and wrote: "As long as we are part of the Church Militant, we must continue to fight. . . .Let us then, my dear Sisters, apply ourselves diligently to the corporal and spiritual service of the sick poor for the love of Jesus crucified. . ."(SWLM, p. 515. L.531B, 1656).

With their Approbations of 1646 and 1655, the Daughters of Charity were mandated by the Church to continue their apostolic action in the name of the Church. They were breaking new ground. As Vincent said: "To be true Daughters of Charity you must do what the Son of God did when he was on earth. . . . Since the time of the women who ministered to the Son of God and the Apostles, there has been no community established in God's Church with this end in view" (*Conferences,* I,13).

192. With this Act of Establishment, the Daughters of Charity and the Church officially ushered in a new form of *consecrated life* which today is embodied within the principles of "Societies of Apostolic Life". In their vision, Louise and Vincent were prophetic leaders in the mission of the Church. The nature of the Daughters of Charity prefigured both aspects of the Canon describing "Societies of Apostolic Life" (CIC, 731): They did not take religious vows; they pursued their apostolic purpose, lived a fraternal life in common and strove for the perfection of charity through their observance of their constitution [rules] — (CIC, 731, #1). Secondly, through their private vows they undertook to live the evangelical counsels (CIC, 731, #2).

It is interesting to note that the Approbation of the Company described the Company as a "Society or Confraternity" (Coste, *V. de P.,* I, 351, 362, 363; cf. also SWLM, p. 476).

Louise suggested to Vincent that the term "Confraternity" was not sufficient because of the form of "consecrated life" that had evolved in the Company (SWLM, p. 476. L. 445, 1655.) and that the term "Society" or "Company" was needed to designate their "consecrated life" (SWLM, p. 629. L.609, 1659). The "secular" aspect of the Daughters was ensured by the term "Confraternity" and their "consecrated" nature by the term "Society" or "Company". Both Vincent and Louise claimed that their Daughters were not *religious* but secular and they dissuaded any language or lifestyle that might equate them with religious. The founders did stress the Sisters' *consecrated life for service to the poor.*

Hence, the Daughters *resemble* institutes of consecrated life (CIC, 731, #1) and are reflective of the consecrated lifestyle by embracing the evangelical counsels (CIC 731, #2) but are not religious. Yet, they were forerunners to apostolic congregations of women religious of the ensuing centuries.

193. SWLM, p. 1. A.2-LIGHT

194. Leonard, *Conferences*, I, 280. Cf. III, 90: "As well, Louise and Vincent encouraged the Sisters to reflect upon the spirit and zeal of the deceased Sisters, a number of whom had died in and through their care of the poor."

195. SWLM, p. 518. L.489, July 1656.

196. SWLM, p. 583. L.561.

197. SWLM, p. 677. L.655-To Monsieur Vincent. Cf. p. 796, A.62: "The final means (to preserve the Company) is to strive to acquire the spirit of the Company through the love which we must have for Our Lord and by the practice of humility, simplicity and true charity. . ."

198. SWLM, p. 833. A.100-(PROBLEMS FOR THE COMPANY), 1660.

199. SWLM, p. 835.

200. SWLM, p. 835-SPIRITUAL TESTAMENT. Louise had a strong devotion to the Blessed Virgin which she inculcated in her Sisters. In 1626 she dedicated herself and her son to Mary (SWLM, p. 695, A.4). In 1632 Louise made a pilgrimage to Chartres to seek Mary's intercession to know God's will (V. de P., I. 145). In 1633 she dedicated the Company to Mary in the First Rule (SWLM, p. 727). On October 17, 1644 on the Feast of the Dedication of the Church at Chartres, Louise offered to God the designs of his providence on the Company (SWLM, p. 121, L.111). Louise always taught the Sisters to see Mary as their Mother and Protectress.

201. SWLM, p. 728. A.54-DRAFT OF THE RULE-THE SUPE-RIORESS.

202. Coste, *V. de P.*, I, 46.

A Study of the Spirituality of Louise de Marillac

Spiritual Framework (1591—1660)

The spiritual framework in which Louise de Marillac lived was that which is known as the French School of Spirituality. As the seventeenth century is known historically as "Le grand siècle," so too it might be termed "Un grand siècle" of spirituality.[1] It was during this century that numerous saints made outstanding contributions to the field of spirituality and during it that the division of theology and spirituality which had occurred during the scholastic period was reunited into an integrated whole. Major figures of this period include Francis de Sales, Jane de Chantal, Cardinal de Bérulle, Charles de Condren, Jean-Jacques Olier, Vincent de Paul, St. John Eudes, Père Lallement, Blessed Marie of the Incarnation,[2] Blessed Madeleine of St. Joseph, Margaret Mary Alacoque, Louis Marie de Montfort, Jean-Baptist de La Salle and of course Louise de Marillac. As well, the seventeenth century was a period in which lay leadership in spirituality was prevalent with such persons as Mme Acarie[3] and Michel de Marillac, uncle of Louise. Fruits of the period would include renewal of laity and clergy, foundation of seminaries, parish missions, spiritual direction, and the emergence of congregations devoted to apostolic works both within and beyond France.[4]

In this Introduction we shall limit ourselves to a brief overview of the French School of Spirituality by considering the major characteristics of the school and its theological principles.

The French School of Spirituality

In describing a school of spirituality, Raymond Deville in his book, *L'école française de spiritualité* posits that a spirituality or spiritual tradition is a certain manner of hearing and living the gospel. This is conditioned by a time, a milieu, and some influential principles. This particular way of hearing and living the gospel is incarnated in a group of people and prolonged through history, enriching or impoverishing itself. Such a spiritual tradition may be termed a school of spirituality.[5] Deville suggests the following five characteristics which determine a school of spirituality: i. Each school has certain aspects of the faith and life in the Spirit which it emphasizes. ii. It is distinguished by a certain manner of prayer and a certain approach to mission. iii. It always has its own elements of pedagogy which consist in practices aimed at nourishing the spirituality. iv. The school has its own preferred biblical texts. v. The school is rooted in a very strong spiritual experience.[6] Using these five principles, we shall now present a brief sketch of the French School of Spirituality. i. The four basic aspects of faith and life in the Spirit which the French School of Spirituality empasized are: Trinitarianism, Christocentricism, Marian, Pastoral and Ecclesial.[7]

It is an accepted fact that the major initiator in the development of the French School of Spirituality during this time was Pierre Cardinal de Bérulle. His spirituality was inspired by great saints and traditions and he in turn inspired great saints and traditions. Bérulle was born in 1575 and died in 1629. Deeply involved in Church and State, he was a mystic who transformed French spirituality and left a spiritual legacy to the Christian world.

Through a study of Bérulle's writings and the tradition of his works, several key principles emerge as the touchstones of his spirituality, which with some nuances contributed by his followers became the main characteristics of the French School of Spirituality: theocentric and trinitarian, Christocentric, Marian, pastoral and ecclesial.

In his theocentric trinitarianism, Bérulle saw God as infinitely immanent and infinitely transcendent.[8] God must be reverenced and adored for his perfection and grandeur. God must be adored in the unity of his essence and in the trinity of his persons. Jesus could not be separated from the Father whom he had come to image. The Holy Spirit, produced by the Father with the Word, is their "unity of love."[9] It was necessary to adore the Trinity, disposing oneself to this action for eternity and in time.[10] Bérulle maintained that persons were most themselves when they reflected the true relationship of love of God. Jesus was the perfect adorer of the Father, the perfect witness to this love relationship, and it was upon him that Bérulle focused his spiritual doctrine.[11]

The most characteristic principle of Bérulle's spirituality is its Christocentricism which focused on the Incarnate Word, Jesus. Through Jesus' humanity, persons enter into a new order. Humanity is deified through Jesus, who became man to make us gods. Bérulle uses the unique term "état" or "state" to develop this thought.[12] For Bérulle the pre-eminent state of the human Jesus was that of his servitude because in emptying himself of his divinity to become human, he assumed the state of one who was to be God's servant. It is Jesus who has come to heal the rupture of the relationship between God and humans. He, as the perfect adorer and servant, incorporates humans into his life and love and empowers them to imitate him in adoration and servitude of God. Particularly through the eucharist, it is by him and with him that Christians must render praise to God on earth as it is rendered to him in heaven by the angels.[13]

The mariological aspect of Bérulle's spirituality is centered in the mystery of the Incarnation to which he attaches his comments on the Blessed Virgin.[14] Through the Incarnation, Mary was in a profound way directly united with the Trinity. At the moment of the Incarnation, God the Father took her for his spouse, the Word chose her for his mother and the Holy Spirit executed these divine counsels within her.[15] Never did Bérulle separate the Son from the Mother. He repeated that it was necessary to go to Jesus through Mary and counseled his followers: "never to separate in their devotion that which God had joined together in the order of grace."[16] Bérulle focused on the totality of the humanity of Jesus and Mary's participation in all of these mysteries from his conception to his death and resurrection transformed her in the depths of her being.

Bérulle's ecclesial and pastoral focus was expressed particularly in the spiritual renewal of the clergy which culminated in his founding of the Priests of the Oratory in 1611. At this time the renewal of the priesthood was a crucial issue for the renewal of the Church but, although Bérulle concentrated on the priestly state, he had a very high opinion of the lay state. In his own experiences and especially through Mme Acarie's salon, he had interacted closely with lay people who were seeking perfection and who were most interested in the things of God and Church.[17] Bérulle maintained that "all were called to perfection through their own unique manner of participating in the various states of Christ" and that every soul must be regarded "as a subject of God's holiness which should shine and operate in him or her."[18] The sacramental life of the Church was also central to Bérulle's ecclesiology. He particularly emphasized the eucharist and its relationship between the mysteries of the Trinity and the Incarnation. For Bèrulle, "the way the divine persons reside in one another is somehow reflected in God's residence in Jesus as incarnate and as eucharistically present."[19]

These foregoing four theological principles form the basis of Bérulle's spirituality and the framework of what has come to be considered characteristics of the French School of Spirituality.

ii. In prayer, the founders and foundresses of the French School were identified as mystics. Their followers also would be considered to be contemplatives with some moving into the contemplative in action tradition. Regarding mission, it could be said that they had a strong ecclesial and pastoral orientation to mission expressed by all in their concern for priestly reform and by some in their concentrated concern for the spiritual and corporal needs of the poor. Most notable in this genre would be Vincent de Paul and Louise de Marillac.

iii. In its pedagogy and practices to express and to nourish its spirituality, the French School could be said to emphasize the sacraments of baptism, eucharist and penance. In its living out of the gospel, it expressed a strong imitation of Jesus and Mary, both in their external conduct and in their internal states of soul. In imitation of the "self-emptying" of Jesus, one was called to enter into oneself, to die to one's false self and to share in the state of adoration of God with Jesus. Through Jesus one was called to enter into union with the Trinity. These processes were manifested in the prayers of surrender and dedication, the vows of servitude, and the prayers of elevation.[20] In speaking of the pedagogy of the French School, Deville mentions the five following principles: the prayer of the Church (Liturgy), initiation into methods of prayer, the Cult of the Word and the eucharist, spiritual direction and the vows of servitude. All had the aim of assisting one to answer the call of the Lord, of surrendering to the Spirit, of adhering to Jesus, of serving the neighbor and of desiring to die to one's false self.[21]

iv. The scriptural basis of this spirituality is found primarily in Paul and John with emphasis on baptism, death and resurrection, dying to the old self, the Mystical Body, the sacrificial priesthood of Jesus and the operation of the Holy Spirit. Deville posits that the words of Paul in Galatians 2:20, "It is no longer I who live but it is Christ who lives in me." is the leit-motif of the spiritual doctrine of the French School and that their primary prayer is that of the early Christians, "Come Lord Jesus; Come and live in us."[22]

v. The original spiritual experience that would typify the French School was the experience of Jesus Christ, the Incarnate Word of God. This was fundamental to the reunion of spirituality and theology which Bérulle stressed and was central to all the ensuing doctrine of the school and its lived-out experience.

Notes

1. "Le XVII siècle est l'âge d'or de la spiritualité en France." A. Rayez, "Française (école)," *Dictionnaire de Spiritualité* (Paris: Gabriel Beauchesne et ses fils, 1937), t. V, col. 783. Hereinafter DS, V, 783.

2. Blessed Marie of the Incarnation, Ursuline, brought the Ursuline nuns to Quebec, Canada in 1639 to set up schools for girls. *Oxford Illustrated History of Christianity*, ed. John McManners (Oxford: Oxford University Press, 1992), p. 320.

3. Mme Acarie was later to join the Carmelites and to be known as "Marie of the Incarnation." She also was to become "Blessed."

4. For a fuller treatment of this period the following texts may be consulted: P. Cochois, *Bérulle et l'École française* (Paris: Éditions du Seuil, 1963); L. Cognet, *La Spiritualité Moderne* (Paris: Editions Aubier-Montaigne, 1966); R. Deville, *L'école française de spiritualité*—Bibliothèque d'Histoire du Christianisme n. 11 (Paris: Desclée, 1987); R. Deville, trans. Agnes Cunningham, *The French School of Spirituality* (Pittsburgh: Duquesne University Press, 1994); Louis Dupré, and Don E. Saliers, *Christian Spirituality: Post Reformation and Modern-World Spirituality* (London: SCM Press, 1990); Cheslyn Jones, Geoffrey Wainwright, and Edward Yarnold, S.J., Eds. *The Study of Spirituality* (New York: Oxford Press, 1986); P. Pourrat, *Christian Spirituality*, vol. III (MD: Newman Press, 1953); William M. Thompson, ed., trans. Lowell M. Glendon, S.S., *Bérulle and the French School Selected Writings*-The Classics of Western Spirituality (New York: Paulist Press, 1989).

5. Raymond Deville, *L'école française de spiritualité*-Bibliothèque d'Histoire du Christianisme n. 11 (Paris: Desclée, 1987), p. 102.
It is essential to recall that the French School of Spirituality is the term applied to the doctrine of spirituality developed in France during the seventeenth century. In the strict sense it is limited to the disciples of Bérulle who had an awareness of his originality and who followed the themes characteristic of his doctrine.

6. Deville, p. 102.

7. Deville, p. 13; P. Cochois, p. 146. Cf. Thompson, William M. ed., trans. Lowell M.Glendon, S.S., *Bérulle and the French School Selected Writings*-The Classics of Western Spirituality (New York: Paulist Press, 1989), pp. 33-66. Hereinafter cited as *CWS:Bérulle*. As the framework for the French School of Spirituality, Thompson identifies and discusses these characteristics in depth.

8. Molien, DS, I, 1549.

9. Bérulle as cited by Thompson in *CWS:Bérulle*, pp. 33-34. Cf. DS, I, 1566 (Col. 1203, Piété); Cochois, p. 98.

10. Molien, *DS*, V, 1549.

11. Deville, p. 45, Grandeurs de Jésus, Migne, 183-184.

12. The Bérullian term *état* referred to "the habitual dispositions of a person which both define the depths or the quality of this person and lie at the source of every action. It was distinct from actions" Dupré and Saliers, *Christian Spirituality* p. 66. Cf. DS, IV, 1372.

13. Molien, DS, I, 1554 (col. 1059, *Piété, LXXX*).

14. Molien, DS, I, 1559. (col. 430, *Vie de Jésus*, ch.v).

Cf. *Catechism of the Catholic Church* (Città del Vaticano: Libereria Editrice Vaticana, 1994), #721; #963. Hereinafter cited as *CCC* or *Catechism.*

#721: Mary, the all-holy ever-virgin Mother of God, is the masterwork of the mission of the Son and the Spirit in the fullness of time. . . . the Father found the *dwelling place* where his Son and his Spirit could dwell among men. . . .In her, the "wonders of God" that the Spirit was to fulfill in Christ and the Church began to be manifested.

#963: "Mary's role in the Church is inseparable from her union with Christ and flows directly from it. This union of the mother with the Son in the work of salvation is made manifest from the time of Christ's virginal conception up to his death. . . ."

15. Molien, DS, I, 1559. (col. 1106, Piété, xcvi).

16. Molien, DS, I, 1561. (Col. 1285, Piété).

17. The Lay Aristocracy played an important role in the renewal of the French Church. Mme Acarie's circle was a center for theological discussion and prayer. Through her and such associates the Renewed Carmelites were brought to Paris in 1604. It was also through the laity that the Capucines, known as the Daughters of the Passion, were brought to Paris in 1606.

18. *CWS:Bérulle*, p. 58. Cf. Bérulle as cited by Cochois, p. 114.

19. CWS:Bérulle, p. 58. Cf. pp. 138-139. (Grandeurs: Sixth Discourse).

20. The "vows of servitude" and "prayers of elevation" were particularly identified with Bérulle and the Carmelite nuns. The vows of servitude to Jesus and Mary were, according to Bérulle, "a prolongation of the baptismal vows" in which the Christian is marked by the radical servitude of Christ which in some way 'Christiforms' one's own existence" (*CWS:Bérulle*, pp. 15, 41).

"Prayers of elevation" refer to lifting up or aspirations to the divine and the God-Man Jesus (*CWS:Bérulle*, p. 99).

An elevation is a kind of prayer whose inner form is adoration and whose native expression is praise, which develops from initial acts of the honor of God to a habitual state of absorption in the mystery of God (Dupré and Saliers, *Christian Spirituality*, p. 66).

21. For a fuller treatment of these aspects see: Deville, pp. 118-123.

22. Deville, p. 107.

General Characteristics of the Spirituality of Louise de Marillac

Of the four theological characteristics of the French School of Spirituality, three may be said to form the framework of Louise's spirituality of which one constitutes her primary focus. From this stance the general framework of the spirituality of Louise de Marillac is Trinitarian, Christocentric and Ecclesial; the primary focus is the Incarnate Word of God — the humanity of Jesus, which could be identified as "Incarnational." From this latter perspective flow several related foci.

General Framework of the Spirituality of Louise de Marillac

For our study, the general framework of the spirituality of Louise de Marillac is identified as Trinitarian, Christocentric and Ecclesial.

Trinitarian

Reading the writings of Louise, one discovers the trinitarian foundation of her spirituality. Throughout her spiritual writings and letters, there are frequent examples of her devotion to the Trinity as a unity as well as to the individual persons of the Father, the Son and the Spirit. She wrote: "I wish to honor the three Persons separately and also together in the unity of the divine essence."[1]

Louise makes references to the Father as the Father of Jesus and of Mary. Certainly the Father-Son relationship of Jesus is rooted in Louise's knowledge of scripture and of the Fathers of the Church. In indicating the fatherly relationship to Mary, Louise, although cognizant of Mary's unique dignity, places her with us as the children of the "heavenly father."[2]

Louise's writings are replete with references to the Son as redeemer and model for the Christian life. It is Jesus that Louise seeks to imitate so that she too may be the "beloved of the Father" and enjoy the unity of the Trinity.[3]

For Louise, the Holy Spirit is her strength in the journey to eternity. Her spiritual reflections on and notations of her life experiences indicate the importance of the Holy Spirit in her Christian life. Louise always invoked the aid of the Spirit for direction in her decisions, for comfort in her trials, for joy in her times of depression, for light in her spiritual darkness and for strength in overcoming her weaknesses.[4]

In a meditation on preparing for the coming of the Holy Spirit Louise prayed:

> Eternal Father, I beg this mercy of you in the name of the design which you had from all eternity in the Incarnation of your Son and through his merits. My Savior, grant me this grace for the love which you bear for the Holy Virgin. Holy Spirit, operate this marvel in your unworthy subject by the loving union which you have from all eternity with the Father and the Son.[5]

Louise's prayers to the Trinity embrace the three persons and her prayers to and reflections about each person individually relate to the united Trinity. For Louise the Trinity is the source and essence of spiritual power and strength.[6]

In a reflection on the Epiphany, Louise incorporated a Trinitarian orientation in respect to prayer, fasting and almsgiving when she wrote: "Likewise we may present them to the Blessed Trinity: prayer to the Father, fasting to the Son and almsgiving to the Holy Spirit."[7]

The Trinity was a general focus of Louise's personal spirituality, but also she exhorted her Daughters and the priests of the Mission to be devoted to the Trinity.

In 1644 during her pilgrimage to Chartres, Louise prayed that "Jesus might be the strong and loving bond that unites the hearts of all the Sisters in imitation of the union of the three divine Persons."[8]

Then in 1645, Louise wrote to her Sisters:

> All the Sisters shall strive for true union . . . They shall always remember to honor the union of the Blessed Trinity, through which all order in the world has been made and is conserved, and to which . . . they submit themselves.[9]

Over the years, Louise repeatedly echoed in her letters to her Daughters the theme of unity in the Trinity.[10]

Writing on the end of the Congregation of the Mission, Louise also incorporated her Trinitarian focus:

> They shall honor the Blessed Trinity by great union among themselves. . . . By a communication of the Holy Spirit, they shall enter into a holy relationship with the Son of God who, by personally detaching himself, as it were, from his Father, willed to take our flesh for the salvation of the human race. . . .[11]

Louise's devotion to Mary is also situated within the framework of the Trinity. In this she may very well have prefigured the theological principles of devotion to Mary enunciated in the Counsels of Vatican II and *Marialis Cultus.*[12]

Reflecting on Mary's Immaculate Conception, Louise wrote:

That is why, throughout my life, in time and in eternity, I desire to love and to honor her to the best of my ability by my gratitude to the Blessed Trinity for the choice made of the Holy Virgin to be so closely united to the Divinity.[13]

For Louise, Mary's eternal blessedness will come through the Trinity as well:

May this precious body, united to so worthy a soul, be forever glorified because of the testimony of love which the Blessed Trinity will show to it throughout eternity.[14]

The foregoing excerpts from Louise's writings illustrate that within her spirituality the Trinity is a grounding principle of her theology and mainstay of her lived experience.[15] This theological motif spans her writings from those first recorded until those in the latter years of her life. In 1655, when three new Sisters were sent to Poland, Louise continued to encourage unity under the patronage of the Trinity:

My dear Sisters . . .in the name of the most Holy Trinity that you have so honored and must continue to honor, I beg you to open wide this heart to allow our three Sisters to enter into this cordial union. . . .[16]

In her final words to her Daughters, Louise implicitly suggested the Trinity as she exhorted them once again "to live in great union and cordiality, loving one another in imitation of the union and life of Our Lord."[17]

Christocentric

Central to Louise's spirituality is the Christocentric orientation characteristic of the French School. However, for Louise, it is not only the contemplation of the inner sentiments, states, mysteries and grandeurs of Jesus in his two natures that are to be her inspiration but as well it is to be the example of the *active service* of the man-Jesus.[18] He is "the way and the truth" (Jn. 14:6) to be followed in living the commandment to love both God and neighbor.

For Louise, Jesus is the exemplar of self-giving love and fidelity to the will of the Father. This was not solely an intellectual concept for her but an experience of gospel living which she tried to emulate in her life.[19] In her retreat notes around 1632 Louise wrote:

> All the actions and the entire life of the Son of God are only for our example and instruction . . . This should give me great courage and confidence to undertake all that he will ask of me because, what I am unable to do on account of my powerlessness or other obstacles in me, God will do by his kindness and omnipotence.[20]

Truly, for Louise, the humanity of Jesus, the God-Man, became the focus of her devotion, the source of her hope and her strength. In him she found too the model for her trust in the providence of God. These principles of spirituality Louise also endeavored to inculcate in her Daughters. In 1633 in the Order of the Day for the first Daughters of Charity, Louise prescribed the following: ". . .they shall read a passage of the holy gospel so as to stimulate themselves to the practice of virtue and the service of their neighbor in imitation of the Son of God." [21]

Louise endeavored to impart to her Daughters her love and appreciation of the gospels as a primary source of prayer and revelation of Jesus as their model in holiness and mission.[22] Not only were the Daughters to imitate the actions of Jesus towards the poor but also they were to imitate his spirit as well. In a letter of 1644, Louise gave the following counsel to her Sisters: "Enter upon this charge in the spirit of him who said that he had come not to be served but to serve."[23] Continuing the theme of the imitation of Jesus, she wrote to her Sisters in 1648:

> It is not enough to visit the poor and to provide for their needs; one's heart must be totally purged of all self-interest,

. . . In order to do this, my dear Sisters, we must continually have before our eyes our model, the exemplary life of Jesus Christ. We are called to imitate this life, not only as Christians, but as persons chosen by God to serve him in the person of his poor.[24]

Louise knew that only by keeping their eyes on Jesus would the Sisters be capable of living out both their baptismal call and their call to serve Jesus in the poor.[25] Inherent in this call is the call to holiness of which Jesus is the model and witness:

It is only reasonable that those whom God has called to follow his Son should strive to become holy as he is holy and to make their lives a continuation of his. What a blessing that will be for all Eternity! The merits of Jesus crucified have earned this grace for us.[26]

Louise was always aware that growth in holiness was a grace from God and not dependent totally on one's own efforts. Holiness was the result of being open to God's will in one's life and corresponding to God's love for us. In keeping with Paul, Louise would say that "Holiness is rooted in love, not our love for God but God's love for us" (Eph.2:8,9).

In a reflection from the latter years of her life, Louise exhorted her Sisters to consider the love of God in sending his Son as man and to reflect on this great gift of love:

Let us love this love and we will thereby grasp its endlessness since it depends in no way on us. Let us often recall all the actions of the life of our Beloved so that we may imitate them. . .[27]

By imitating Jesus in his spirit and works Louise wished that her Daughters would come to a deeper awareness that "by becoming like them, Jesus could bear witness to the fact that God had loved them from all eternity.[28]

Louise's recorded letters and reflections are replete with references to the Incarnate God, Jesus as the model of holiness, love and service that all Christians especially the Daughters of Charity were called to follow and imitate. Louise's spirituality and that of her Daughters was focused upon him and thus was Christocentric.

Ecclesial

Louise was a daughter of the Church. She realized that within the Church lay the source of her Christian life and the vocation to which she had been called. Rooted in her baptismal commitment she endeavored to live out the mission which she came to believe God had entrusted to her. The many works of charity and services to the poor which she initiated and directed were seen in the context of the Church continuing the mission of Jesus Christ, the Lord of Charity. This is reflected in one of her paintings which still hangs in the Motherhouse.[29]

Louise was keenly aware that through her baptism, she was a daughter of God and a daughter of the Church. She referred to this fact in her personal writings and letters. In her *Act of Consecration* c. 1626, Louise wrote:

> I, the undersigned, in the presence of the eternal God, having considered that, on the day of my holy baptism, I was vowed and dedicated to my God to be his daughter. . .[30]

In a similar vein, Louise wrote the following to Father Portail in Rome: "Monsieur, . . .we have the double happiness of being Daughters of the holy Church . . .children of such a Mother . . ."[31]

As a child of the Church, Louise saw this Mother as the source of her sacramental life and liturgical prayer, both of which were of great importance to her. Louise possessed a profound sense of her baptism, had a strong devotion to the eucharist and prayed in harmony with the liturgical feasts of the Church. In fidelity to these principles she exhorted her Daughters likewise to be faithful to the Church and to the source of life it offered.

Louise's prayers and reflections abound with references to the importance of the sacraments, to their lifegiving power and to the appropriate preparation for receiving them.

The sacraments which she mentioned most frequently were baptism and eucharist. For Louise, baptism was the source of life with Christ and the Church. The eucharist was the sustenance of that life through the continued presence of Jesus with and in his people.

Not only did Louise refer to her own baptism but she often counselled her Sisters to renew their own baptismal commitment and "to correspond with this precious gift" and the graces inherent therein.[32]

In one of her personal reflections on the Holy Spirit, Louise made reference to baptism thus:

> One of the greatest losses that a soul can experience by not participating in the coming of the Holy Spirit is that the gifts infused at baptism do not have their effect. . .[33]

For Louise, it was the power of the Holy Spirit that continued to activate the graces of baptism.

In the formula of vows for the Congregation, Louise again connected the evangelical consecration with baptism and rooted their mission therein:

> I, the undersigned, in the presence of God, renew the promises of my baptism, and I vow poverty, chastity and obedience to the Venerable Superior General of the Priests of the Mission in the Company of the Daughters of Charity in order to give myself, for the whole of this year, to the corporal and spiritual service of the sick poor, our true Masters. . .[34]

For Louise de Marillac, baptism opened to her the treasures of the kingdom of God and from these treasures, as a daughter of God and of the Church, she drew daily to imitate more closely the Word Incarnate, the Son of God.

Central to Louise's sacramental life was the eucharist. It was in the eucharist that she was nourished, experienced her Lord and Spouse intimately and was so richly blessed. Louise's profound understanding of the eucharist, its power and its relationship with the Church is illustrated in this extract from one of her meditations c. 1632:

> Holy Communion with the Body of Jesus Christ causes us truly to participate in the joy of the Communion of Saints in Paradise. This joy was merited for us by the Incarnation and the death of the Son of God. So powerful was this merit, that the reconciliation of human nature by means of it is so great that we can never again be separated from the love of God. Just as God sees himself united to man in heaven by the hypostatic union of the word made Flesh, so he wanted such a union on earth so that the human race would never again be separated from him.[35]

Here Louise presents her eucharistic doctrine clearly and simply, speaking as a theologian and a teacher. When one reads the "Decree on the Sacred Liturgy" #8, echoes of the above resound.[36]

Louise encouraged her Daughters to appreciate the eucharist and, unusual as it was for the time, to receive Communion frequently such as on Feasts and Sundays.[37] She also instructed that the sick in their care receive Communion every Sunday.[38] Furthermore, she was attentive to appropriate preparation for the reception of this sacrament. To this end, she schooled her Daughters and encouraged them, in turn, to prepare the sick and the children in their care. In a reflection, "On Holy Communion," Louise discussed three moments that were of great importance if one wished to receive Holy Communion well. These were: the period before Communion, the moment of reception and the time following reception. In each, Louise suggested means whereby one might prepare oneself to receive such an august gift of God. In the midst of all she said humbly: "However, we must preserve our souls in peace and await, with joy, the coming of Our Lord whom we must desire as the beloved of our souls."[39] In these writings we again see Louise as theologian and catechist.

Louise's concern for the proper dispositions for the sacraments also included Penance and Extreme Unction, the names given to these sacraments at that time. She wrote a short reflection on the preparation for Confession which focussed on the recognition of one's sinfulness, the request of God's grace to avoid sin and the gift of the love of God.[40] In her Daughters, Louise encouraged the "simple and humble" confession of one's sins,[41] saying that "succinct confessions are always the best."[42] In like manner, she encouraged trust in the sacrament. When writing to a Sister she said:

What are we looking for in this sacrament? Grace alone, and we can be certain that the divine goodness will not withhold it from us if we approach the sacrament with the necessary dispositions of simplicity, heartfelt sorrow and submission. I beg Our Lord to grant us these dispositions. . .[43]

As Louise catechized the Daughters of Charity with respect to the sacraments, so too, the Daughters were instructed in their rules to catechize those under their care. Specific directions were given to the Directress of the Seminary, the School Mistress and the Sisters nursing the sick. The following excerpts from the Rules for the Motherhouse illustrate this:

The Directress of the Seminary . . .shall instruct the new Sisters on the excellence of the sacraments, teaching the Sisters that it is through the merit of the Blood of Jesus Christ that the benefits of the sacraments are bestowed upon us.

The Schoolmistress . . .shall instruct her pupils well in the sacraments and in the esteem due to them. She shall teach them all that is necessary for the proper reception of these sacraments.[44]

They shall provide for those sick in need of instruction concerning salvation, so that they can make a general confession of their entire life. This should dispose the sick to go to confession and to receive Communion every Sunday, as long as their illness persists. It should also prepare them to receive Extreme Unction at the proper time.[45]

Louise's concern for the reception of the sacraments extended even to the Ladies of the Charities as is evidenced in this letter to Vincent:

These Ladies, or at least most of them, also go months without receiving Holy Communion. They need to have their fervor rekindled by a sermon when a priest goes there for the election of the Procurator.[46]

In conjunction with a strong sacramental life, Louise de Marillac also prayed in harmony with the liturgical year of the Church. In her writings, she spoke of the seasons of Advent, Christmas, Lent, Easter, and Pentecost. For her, the times of Advent and Pentecost were of special importance. In addition, Louise specifically mentioned the Feasts of the Trinity, of Corpus Christi, of the Immaculate Conception, of Christmas, and of the Incarnation.[47] In a reflection on Devotion to the Blessed Virgin, she said:

Let us celebrate, in a special way, the Church feasts honoring Mary, and meditate, during the day, on the mystery proposed.[48]

Louise's private prayer was also in keeping with the official prayer of the Church. She prayed parts of the Office: Vespers and the Office of the Blessed Virgin; she meditated on the scriptures of the day and read from the lives of the Saints.[49] In the formation of her Daughters, Louise also inculcated the habit of praying with the Church. This is evidenced in their Rules and in the counsels which Louise gave to them.[50]

Unity with and fidelity to the Church was found not only in the prayer life of Louise and her Daughters but in their loyalty to the Church in their concern and respect for bishops and priests. Louise always endeavored to collaborate peacefully with them in the undertakings of the Sisters and she always encouraged her Sisters to be respectful to the clergy and to pray for them: ". . .prier pour l'Église et principalement pour les prêtres, afin qu'étant tous de bonne vie, Dieu en soit plus honoré. . ."[51]

Even with her great respect and desire to work amicably with the clergy, Louise, a woman of indomitable will, was known to respectfully "wait out" local Church authorities when she perceived God's will. This was evidenced in her desire to gain a favorable response regarding the ultimate authority within the Congregation of the Daughters. Louise was steadfast in her belief that to have the charism and mission of the Daughters preserved they must, in perpetuity, be under the authority of the General Superior of the Congregation of the Mission and not under that of the Bishop of Paris as their first Ecclesial Approbation of 1646 had stated.[52] Staunch in her convictions, Louise even had to convince Vincent de Paul that this was indeed the will of God.[53] For nine years she prayed and waited patiently for this to become a reality.[54]

When convinced of injustice towards her Sisters and interference on the local level with their life, Louise respectfully but forcefully made her position known to the pastor and in one case eventually withdrew the Sisters.[55] Yet, she inculcated great respect for the priesthood in her Daughters[56] and they were urged always to be reserved with the clergy and to be grateful for the help they afforded them.[57]

Louise's life was a testimony to the belief that every person had a mission in the Church. For her, the Church's mission was not limited to that of the clergy and religious but definitely included the laity.[58] Certainly she would be at one with recent Church emphasis on the acknowledged role of the laity.[59] Louise was especially cognizant of the mission of women in the Church. This was clearly stated in her "Notes on the Meetings with the Ladies of Charity":

It is very evident, in this century, that divine providence willed to make use of women to show that it was his goodness alone which desired to aid afflicted peoples and to bring them powerful helps for their salvation.[60]

This fact was certainly attested to by the works of the Ladies of Charity and the Daughters of Charity whose apostolate, in a short time, spread to many areas of the world. Louise's Daughters were not religious of the day but were privately vowed women who lived in community and were dedicated to the mission of the Church in the person of their neighbor.[61] They were one of the first officially recognized congregations of consecrated women to devote themselves to apostolic works and therein paved the way for the future development in the Church of numerous groups of apostolic women *religious.*[62]

Louise herself founded and directed the first Charity in her parish in Paris, was a consultant for the Charities in the country and initiated numerous social works for the suffering and poor.[63] So prolific were her works that in 1960, Pope John XXIII named her *Patroness of All Those Devoted to Christian Social Works.*

Continuing to be a prophetic leader in ministry in the Church, Louise, in response to Vincent's request, and in collaboration with him began giving spiritual direction and retreats to women. This she did asking no remuneration and having the ladies, many of whom were nobility, stay in the Sisters' residence.[64] One may ask: "How new is the idea of retreat centers now blossoming in religious houses?"

In a recent article Fr. Bernard Koch, C.M. discussing Louise's retreat ministry wrote:

That a lay person, and even a woman, should give advice on spiritual direction was not, indeed, new in the Church: we think of Saint Catherine of Siena whom Saint Vincent was aware of and mentioned. However, to arrange that people who came to make the spiritual exercises should be guided by a woman, was perhaps more daring! In any case,

Vincent de Paul assigned this role to Louise de Marillac throughout her life. . .[65]

Dirvin commenting on this ministry says:

This apostolate to the rich and comfortable, the nobility and the bourgeois, carried on concomitantly with the basic apostolate to the poor, is very important in understanding the vocation of Vincent and Louise, which was essentially, like Christ's, a vocation to men and their most urgent needs — a vocation which very much concerned the fathers of Vatican Council II. Their first call was to the poor because they were, at the moment, the neediest; but, while never abandoning this first call, they did not hesitate to respond to other needs as they appeared.[66]

In today's terms it is interesting to note the "inclusivity" of Louise and Vincent's ministry and their "reading of the signs of their times." Truly Louise's mission was rooted in the broader mission of the Church which she served valiantly, pouring out her life and love for the less fortunate members of the Mystical Body of Christ. Throughout the years, Louise's letters and counsels to her Sisters attested to her deep conviction that the poor were indeed the continued incarnation of Christ in the world and must be treated as he himself deserved:

Where are the gentleness and charity that you must preserve so carefully when dealing with our dear masters, the sick poor? If we deviate in the slightest from the conviction that they are the members of Jesus Christ, it will infallibly lead to the weakening of these beautiful virtues in us.[67]

Louise encouraged her Daughters to respect and honor everyone but always with a *priority towards the poor*. In a letter of 1655 she wrote:

We must respect and honor everyone: the poor because they are the members of Jesus Christ and our master; the rich so that they will provide us with the means to do good for the poor.[68]

From her personal life, Louise would have known the invaluable assistance that the rich could give to the poor but also she must have learned this lesson especially well from her collaboration with Vincent de Paul.

It was as members of the Church that the Sisters were to exercise their ministry to the poor of Christ, in him and through him. This Louise stressed:

As long as we are a part of the Church Militant, we must continue to fight. If God, in his goodness, shows us his mercy and admits us into the Church Triumphant, we shall then enjoy that intimate union with him which we can never completely attain here on earth. Let us then, my dear Sisters, apply ourselves diligently to the corporal and spiritual service of the sick poor for the love of Jesus crucified . . .[69]

Louise's love and concern for the Church was extended even to Vincent's Congregation of the Mission about which she wrote in 1628:

In the design of serving the Church, it shall have a knowledge of God, recognizing him as sovereignly worthy of being fittingly honored. To this end, each one in particular shall give himself entirely to work for the salvation of souls insofar as he can hope to do so by the love of God. This work will be greatly advanced by their example and their instructions on the duties of a Christian as well as by the grace of the sacraments worthily administered in the Church. This will happen and the glory of God will be greater when the only priests are good priests.[70]

In this reflection, Louise sounds like a prophet addressing the discrepancy between the call of the ordained minister and the reality of the situation at that time. In some ways she may seem presumptuous to challenge those over whom she had no authority but her concern for the Church and for Vincent's Congregation led her to speak clearly, profoundly and simply to Vincent and to his priests.[71]

In instructing her Sisters in the Orphanage at Cahors, in May of 1657, Louise counselled them and the girls "to offer their work for universal peace and union in the holy Church and for the grace that the Holy Sacrament be well administered particularly in that house."[72]

In this directive, Louise manifested a realization and a concern for the broader church and for the difficulties it was facing in France with respect to the unrest caused by the threats of Jansenism and the impoverished state of the clergy.[73]

Louise's love of the Church was such that she expressed in her Will of December, 1645, the desire to live and to die in the Roman, catholic, apostolic church.[74]

It was her desire as well that her son and her spiritual Daughters remain faithful to their baptismal calling. In her final blessing of Michel and his family, Louise, on her deathbed, prayed that they might be "attached to Christ and live as good Christians."[75] Her blessing to her Daughters was to love their vocation and to remain faithful to the service of the poor.[76] Thus in her final moments on this earth, Louise implored for those she loved most the grace of perseverance in their Christian commitment.

Louise de Marillac was truly a woman of the Church. She was convinced of her baptismal calling and endeavored to live it fully in the arms of Mother Church and in the service of her privileged members, the poor. As she lived, so she died.[77]

The Incarnation — Devotion to the Humanity of Jesus —
Primary Focus

The design of the Blessed Trinity from the creation of man was that the Word should become flesh so that human nature might attain the excellence of being that God willed to give to man by the eternal union that he willed between himself and his creature, the most admirable state of his exterior operations.[78]

The primary focus of the devotion of Louise may be said to be "incarnational" in that she was devoted to the humanity of Jesus in all its facets.[79] Her writings reveal that she meditated upon the childhood of Jesus, his hidden life, his public ministry, his passion and death and his resurrection. The hidden life, public ministry and sufferings of Jesus became particular focal points for Louise's inspiration and model for her Christian life.[80]

The Childhood of Jesus: Pre-natal and Infancy

Louise's devotion to the humanity of Jesus addressed his humanity in its earliest stages. Beginning with Jesus in the womb of Mary, Louise found cause to praise and thank God for the wonder of the greatest gift to humankind.

In her prayer life and in her counsels to her Daughters, Louise reflected her esteem for and devotion to the Child Jesus. This devotion was manifested throughout her life and was mentioned particularly at the Feast of the Incarnation, March 25, and the Christmas season.

In Louise's writings prior to the founding of the Daughters of Charity in 1633, several references to the Child Jesus are found.

In 1628, in her first Rule of Life, Louise noted the following:

Exactly at midday, I shall meditate for a quarter of an hour in order to honor the instant when the Incarnation of the Word took place in the womb of Mary.[81]

Again, in a December Retreat note of 1632, Louise wrote:

I shall honor the serenity of the crib by a disposition to replace desire by contentment in the possession of God who never denies himself to the soul that truly seeks him. I shall calmly adore the divinity in the Infant Jesus and imitate, to the best of my ability, his holy humanity, especially his simplicity and charity which led him to come to us as a child so as to be more accessible to his creatures.[82]

And in a following Retreat prior to 1633 is found:

To love abjection since God is to be found there. Jesus teaches us this by his birth. He wanted us to know that this abjection filled heaven with astonishment and gave glory to the Father.[83]

In the period between 1633-1647, this same devotional theme is evident in Louise's writings and actions. At some point during this time she sent to the Motherhouse a statue of Mary holding a chaplet of nine beads in honor of the nine months which Our Lord spent in her womb."[84] She also wrote to Vincent in 1646 concerning her devotional practice to the Humanity of Jesus, saying:

It honors the hidden life of Our Lord in his state of imprisonment in the womb of the Blessed Virgin and congratulates her on her happiness during those nine months.[85]

Through this devotion, Louise interceded for her Company:

By means of this little exercise I intend to ask God, through the Incarnation of his Son and the prayers of the Blessed Virgin, for the purity necessary for the Company of the Sisters of Charity and for the steadfastness of this Company in keeping with his good pleasure.[86]

On the eve of the Feast of the Incarnation of 1646, Louise sent the following to Vincent: ". . .I am unworthy of the grace which I desired in order to prepare myself for our very dear Feast of the Incarnation."[87]

In a reflection on the Feast of the Epiphany, Louise suggested adoration at the crib by means of fasting, prayer and almsgiving: "Thus we are able to adore our Incarnate God with the angels by prayer, with the Kings by almsgiving and with the shepherds by fasting; . . ."[88]

Within this Christmas theme, Louise focused on the birth and infancy of the Child Jesus, and the adoration that was due to him.

In a reflection on The Virgin Mary, Louise prayed:

> Most Holy Virgin, you know the emotions of my heart today at the thought of your divine Son in the crib and how great this mystery seemed to me when I considered that it was the introduction of the law of grace granted to all mankind. . .[89]

Louise's devotion to the Child Jesus also expressed itself in the closing of a Christmas letter: "I am in the love of the Infant Jesus who began to shed his precious blood in the crib. . ."[90]

From the foregoing, it is evident that Louise de Marillac had a deep devotion to the humanity of Jesus from the moment of his conception and that she saw the beginnings of his life in reference to the end of his life, when through the shedding of his Precious Blood on the cross, he won salvation for all human-kind.[91] It is interesting to note the frequency of the references to blood in Louise's writings on the Infant Jesus. Might this be the prelude to her devotion to the Passion of Christ?

In a Christmas letter of 1659, Louise wrote to the Sisters at Chantilly, exhorting them to imitate the virtues of the Child Jesus:

> Let me tell you that, this year, the crib is in a little grotto at the feet of Jesus crucified. . . .You will learn from Jesus, my dear Sisters, to practice solid virtue, as he did in his holy humanity, as soon as he came down upon earth. It is from the example of Jesus in his infancy that you will obtain all that you need to become true Christians and perfect Daughters of Charity.[92]

It is noteworthy that in this passage, Louise embraces the totality of the humanity of Jesus from the crib to the cross. As she modelled her life on the humility, simplicity and charity of Jesus, so too, she imbued this spirit within her Daughters.[93]

In an unique way, Louise's devotion to the Child Jesus was evidenced in her poem to the New-born Jesus in which she lauded "his kingship, his mercy and his poor and glorious throne before which her poor, little, timid company was called."[94]

The Hidden Life of Jesus

A strong emphasis in Louise's spirituality is that of her desire to remain hidden in God alone. She gradually grew to a sense of detachment from the limelight of society, from the aspiration to be in leadership and from the natural desire to be recognized for her achievements. The strength for this detachment she found in pondering the hidden life of Jesus. It was Jesus "meek and humble of heart" that she wished to emulate in her life; and, in his hidden life Louise discovered the basis for the journey into her inner self and the resultant gifts of her own self-knowledge, simplicity and humility. She knew that like her, Jesus shared in the ordinariness of daily life.[95]

In her adult life, Louise had been accustomed to Court circles but during the illness of her husband and after his death she found her social status changed. Even though she desired to live a less conspicuous and more humble lifestyle, she felt the pain of poverty and the sting of social descent. In these circumstances spiritual growth came for her through her imitation of the hidden and humble life of Jesus. This is seen in the following reference from her writings of 1632:

> To go to my new home with the motive of honoring divine providence which is leading me there. . . .By this change of residence, to honor the changes made by Jesus and the Blessed Virgin when they moved from Bethlehem to Egypt and then to other places, not wanting, any more than they, to have a permanent dwelling here on earth.[96]

Herein, there appears to be a sense of economic insecurity in Louise, which leads to a gathering of strength through trusting in divine providence and imitating the Holy Family.

Louise's detachment from worldly goods also extended to detachment from worldly prestige. In a retreat reflection around Christmas 1632 Louise wrote:

> Our Lord, born in poverty and obscurity, teaches me the purity of his love which he does not manifest to his creatures. . . . Thus, I must learn to remain hidden in God, desiring to serve him without seeking recognition from others or satisfaction in communicating with them, content that he sees what I am striving to become. To this end, he wants me to give myself to him so that he can form this disposition in me. I did so with the help of his grace.[97]

Even in her interior, Louise wished to become simpler and hidden from honor. As early as 1628, this desire was present in her:

> I must practice interior humility by a desire for abjection and exterior humility by willingly accepting all the occasions which occur for humbling myself. I shall do this in order to honor the true and real humility of God himself in whom I shall find the strength to overcome my pride, to combat my frequent outbursts of impatience and to acquire charity and gentleness toward my neighbor. Thus I shall honor the teaching of Jesus Christ who told us to learn of him to be gentle and humble of heart.[98]

Certainly, Louise's growth in the spirit of detachment and humility was founded on her imitation of the hidden life of Jesus and was rooted in his grace. In no way did she believe that it was the result of her own efforts. Only the grace of God could bring about this change in her.

Throughout her life as Louise aspired to imitate the virtues of the hidden life of Jesus, she endeavored to school herself in detachment from the natural desire to be recognized for her accomplishments and her abilities. This journey was evidenced in her spiritual writings and letters.

In 1632 in her notes, Louise recorded the following imitation of Jesus in his hidden life:

> Filled with consolation and happiness at the thought of being accepted by him to live my entire life as his follower, I resolved that in everything, particularly in uncertain or questionable circumstances, I would consider what Jesus would have done and honor his submission to his Mother during the years when he was dependent upon her as her Son.[99]

Not only did Louise endeavor to imitate the hidden life of Jesus, but she counselled her Sisters to do the same. This is manifested in her letters to them. In a letter of December, 1659, Louise encouraged a Sister who was experiencing discouragement in her work:

> Be thoroughly consoled, my dear Sister, by the thought that you are imitating the state in which the Son of God found himself when, after leaving the temple where he had been working for the glory of God, he went with the Blessed Virgin and Saint Joseph to obey. . . .

> We do not know, my dear Sister, why divine providence has put you aside, leaving you hidden in the service of the Son of God. Nevertheless, by working unostentatiously and quietly in the service of the poor, you are most certainly fulfilling the designs of divine providence.[100]

Commenting on the good works of the Sisters in 1660, Louise recalled the injunction to honor the hidden life of Jesus:

> All this was done under a veil of silence. Would to God that it had not been necessary to mention it, since this manner

of acting is in keeping with the first commandments of the Founder of the Company, Jesus Christ, speaking through his servant. We are told to honor his hidden life. This is essential for the strength of this Company . . .[101]

In contemplating the virtues of the hidden life of Jesus, especially his detachment and humility, Louise de Marillac discovered her refuge from the natural inclinations to seek honor, recognition and approval for herself, her work and her community. As she came to the end of her life, she had truly endeavored to live her resolve of 1632: "I must spend the rest of my days honoring the hidden life of Jesus on earth."[102]

The Public Ministry of Jesus

It was the study and meditation of the gospels that opened to Louise the riches of the public ministry of Jesus. In her prayer she plumbed the actions of his public life and discovered the spirit that permeated them. Herein she understood her Lord of Charity and what is now called his *preferential* love for the poor and suffering. His love drew her to himself and she desired to give her all to imitate him and to continue his loving service of the poor. In serving them she would serve him and through them she would be united to him.

In her "Rule of Life" c. 1628, Louise manifested her desire to follow Jesus in his life of poverty and service to her neighbor. Herein she wrote:

May the desire for holy poverty always live in my heart in such a manner, that freed from all bonds, I may follow Jesus Christ and serve my neighbor with great humility and gentleness, living under obedience and in chastity all my life and honoring the poverty that Jesus Christ practiced so perfectly.[103]

That Louise meditated on the gospels is evident from her retreat notes of 1632 in which she referred to "the contemplative and active life of Jesus, the evangelical counsels set forth in the Sermon on the Mount and the humility which Jesus taught."[104]

For Louise, meditating on the life of Jesus was essential in order to imitate him in her life so that she might truly be a Christian conformed to Jesus.[105]

For her Sisters too, the gospels were to be the source of knowing Jesus and thus were included in the directives of 1633 for their "Order of the Day":

> . . . they shall read a passage of the holy gospel so as to stimulate themselves to the practice of virtue and the service of their neighbor in imitation of the Son of God.[106]

It was upon the spirit and ministry of Jesus in the gospels that Louise modelled her own ministry and that of her Daughters. In her counsels, in her letters and in her reflections this is evident. In a letter to some of her Sisters she wrote:

> What can you do in this situation my dear Sisters? Nothing but practice patience and imitate, as far as you are able, the example of Our Lord who consumed his strength and his life in the service of his neighbor.[107]

In one of her own reflections, Louise expressed the dignity of those called to carry on the ministry of Jesus:

> Blessed are those persons who, under the guidance of divine providence, are called upon to continue the ordinary practices of the life of the Son of God through the exercise of charity.[108]

In Louise's contemplation of Jesus, she wished to imitate not only his ministry in the "ordinary practices of life" but also the spirit in which he lived it: the spirit of poverty, humility, simplicity, and charity. This spirit would transform the "ordinary" practices of life into the "extraordinary" practices of true Christian life. The ordinary would be done in an extraordinary manner.[109] In her own life and in her counsels to her Sisters, Louise emphasized the necessity of acting in this spirit of Jesus. In 1647, she wrote to her Sisters:

> That is why it would be well if every morning each Sister would individually pray . . .for the blessing of our good God in order that they might act in the manner of his Son while he was on earth as they carry out the works of charity to which they have been called. Better yet, they should pray that the same Spirit that acted in him should act through them.[110]

In one of her earliest recorded retreats, Louise reflected on the humility of Jesus in service to others and this spirit became a hallmark of her life. In 1633, she wrote:

> I must bear in mind the fact that the humility which Our Lord practiced at his baptism is not only a source of humiliation for me but it must also serve as an example which I must imitate. . .

Then she continued:

> . . . He did not shrink from humbling himself to the point of washing the feet of his Apostles immediately before his passion.[111]

In imitation of Jesus, Louise was similarly adamant in her call to the spirit of poverty for herself and her Sisters. In a Letter of 1639, she counseled her Sisters thus:

> Cultivate a love for poverty in imitation of the Son of God. By so doing you will obtain the graces necessary to be a true Daughter of Charity. Otherwise I doubt very strongly that you will persevere.[112]

Louise frequently reminded her Sisters that Jesus "had come to serve, not to be served"[113] and that this service was rendered in a spirit of simplicity, devoid of self-interest. For Louise, the external action of service to the poor was not sufficient to fully imitate Jesus; purity of intention must also be present:

> It is not enough to visit the poor and to provide for their needs; one's heart must be totally purged of all self-interest, and one must continually work at the general mortification of all the senses and passions. In order to do this, my dear Sisters, we must continually have before our eyes our model, the exemplary life of Jesus Christ. We are all called to imitate this life, not only as Christians, but as persons chosen by God to serve him in the person of his poor.[114]

Inherent in the imitation of Jesus in his ministry was the universal call to holiness and Louise reminded herself and her Daughters of this:

> It is only reasonable that those whom God has called to follow his Son should strive to become holy as he is holy and to make their lives a continuation of his. What a blessing that will be for all Eternity! The merits of Jesus crucified have earned this grace for us. . .[115]

Louise realized that the struggles of community life would require great virtue and in this she called upon her Sisters to imitate the spirit of Jesus:

> . . .this is a time when our souls must be moved, despite the weakness of our nature, to practice heroic virtue by spontaneous acts of humility and gentleness of heart and to prove that we desire to be truly Christian. Thus we will honor Jesus Christ by practicing the virtues which he, himself, in his holy humanity taught us.[116]

Through the contemplation of Jesus in the gospels, Louise discovered her call to ministry, its spirit and its source; and herein, she understood her call to holiness. As with all gifts of the Spirit, Louise's call and ministry was not for her alone but was to be shared with others as Jesus had shared his call and ministry. Louise was cognizant of this and thus was willing to share with many the fruitfulness found in her life of loving service to the poor in Jesus and to Jesus in the poor. In ministry her paradigm was Jesus' ministry: a holy life of contemplation and action characterized by simplicity, humility and charity. Hence, from the Public Ministry of Jesus, Louise drew the meaning and the model for her own public ministry and in turn became a model for others.

Passion and Death of Jesus, the Redeemer

In her devotion to the Passion and Death of Jesus, Louise exhibited her deepest identification with Jesus in the outpouring of his life in obedience to the will of the Father. As doing the will of the Father was the "food of Jesus," one might say that the desire to imitate him in doing the will of God was also the spiritual hunger and food of Louise de Marillac. This is an underlying theme found in many of her writings and was a resolution Louise made before she began her life of ministry with the poor. She formulated it thus:

> I hereby renounce self-love with all my heart and choose your holy will as the directing force in my life. I shall recognize your will by reflecting upon the life which your Son led upon earth, to which I shall strive to conform my own. O Holy will of my God! How reasonable it is that you should be completely fulfilled! You were the meat of the Son of God upon earth. Therefore, you are the nourishment which will sustain within my soul the life received from God. . . .May your will alone be the rule of my life![117]

As the cross became the ultimate sign of Jesus' acceptance of the Father's will, so too, for Louise the cross became the symbol of her life and of her union with Jesus crucified. She firmly believed that the cross was her route to sanctification and that it had been with her from the day of her birth. This she expressed in a spiritual reflection written prior to 1633:

> God, who has granted me so many graces, led me to understand that it was his holy will that I go to him by way of the cross. His goodness chose to mark me with it from my birth and he has hardly ever left me, at any age, without some occasion of suffering.[118]

In contemplating the cross of Jesus and finding in him the grace to surrender to God, Louise gained the strength to accept the crosses of her life, to surrender to God's will and thus to blossom in newness of life and understanding:

> Since grace had many times enabled me to esteem and desire this state, I trusted that his goodness would, again today, grant me a new grace to carry out his holy will. I begged him, with all my heart, to place me in this state no matter how painful I found it.[119]

In the death of Jesus, Louise understood the depths of his mercy and love. Herein she found hope and new life for herself and others in the merciful love of Jesus. Louise continually invoked the mercy of Jesus and requested her Daughters to do likewise for her and for themselves:

> I beg you all also, my dear Sisters, to ask Our Lord for mercy for me at the hour of my death, through the merits of his most precious death.[120]

> Let us pray to the divine goodness for one another that his mercy may pour out on us his blessings of grace and light so that we may glorify him eternally.[121]

In her imitation of Jesus, Louise tried to extend this mercy to those who had injured her. As well, she counselled her Sisters to be understanding and compassionate towards one another and towards those they served. This was particularly evident in her instructions to them regarding the galley slaves:

> The Sisters must never reproach them nor speak rudely to them. Moreover, the galley slaves should be treated with great compassion, as much for their spiritual state as for their most pitiful corporal state.[122]

For Louise, the mercy of Jesus as signified in the cross became her only hope—her "Spes Unica." In some form, this symbol spanned the adult years of her life, appearing as her personal seal and in the closing words of her letters.[123] This was the seal she adopted for the Congregation and the final symbol she chose to denote her life.[124] As scripture says, "Set me like a seal on your heart, like a seal on your arm." (SS 8:6). . . The cross indeed seemed to be the seal that God had set on Louise's heart and life and through her acceptance of it God schooled her to great compassion and love. Louise experienced in her own life the power of the passion, death and resurrection of Jesus and thus could encourage others to remain in their embrace:

> I trust, my dear Sister, that Our Lord has let you taste the sweetness reserved for souls filled with his love amidst the sufferings and anguish of this life. If such is not the case and you are still standing on Calvary, rest assured that Jesus crucified is pleased to see you retire there and to know that you have enough courage to want to remain there as he did for love of you. You may be certain that you will emerge from there gloriously.[125]

How wonderfully encouraging for one who has to suffer!

The Risen Jesus

Although the resurrection of Jesus is not explicitly emphasized in Louise's writings, it is mentioned on various occasions and its importance is present implicitly.[126] Louise was deeply aware that the suffering and death of Jesus — his cross — was not the end but the means to eternal life and resurrection. The cross of Jesus was the sign of hope for the future — the life of eternal happiness with the Trinity. This theme is relevant to Louise's writings and thus supports her cognizance of the importance of the resurrection. In the time in which Louise lived, the cross may very well have been more emphasized than the resurrection, but nonetheless, the resurrection being the touchstone of Christian life, was inherent to the Christian message and hence to the Christian life.

Allusions to the resurrection are found in Louise's writings when she speaks of sharing in the Paschal Mystery. One must die with Christ before one can rise with him and this dying consists in renunciation of one's "old self":

On Easter Sunday, my meditation was on my desire to rise with Our Lord. Since, without death, there can be no resurrection, I realized that it was my evil inclinations which must die. . .[127]

Specific reference to the resurrection is evident in Louise's reflection on the Easter season:

The Holy Communion of Eastertime is the only one commanded by the Church, which tells us thereby that its children will receive their inheritance from its Spouse today. . . . This obliges us to choose the life of Jesus crucified as the model for our lives so that his resurrection may be a means for glory for us in Eternity.[128]

On several occasions Louise referred to the Resurrected Christ in the closure of her letters.[129]

That the resurrection was a source of strength and peace to Louise is evidenced in the following excerpt from a letter to her Sisters:

> I beg all of them for the love of the death of our dear Master, to renew themselves in his resurrection, receiving the peace that he gave us so many times in the person of his apostles.[130]

Louise's great devotion to the humanity of Jesus included his glorified humanity. This she expressed both in her writings and in her paintings of the Lord Jesus which depicted the Resurrected Christ:[131]

> To keep my mind as fully occupied as possible in honoring the glory which the holy humanity of Our Lord receives in heaven, remembering the way in which he lived on earth, with the desire to imitate him.[132]

For Louise, imitation of Jesus in his service and sufferings in this life, gave the promise and hope of eternal union in glory in the next. In her devotion to the Incarnate God, Louise embraced all stages of the life of Jesus from his infancy to his glorified humanity. As she desired to be one with him on earth, so too, she hoped to be one with him in heaven: "The risen Christ lives in the hearts of his faithful while they await that fulfillment."[133]

Related Foci to the Incarnate Jesus

Related to the primary focus of Louise de Marillac's Incarnational Spirituality are devotions inherently connected with Jesus, the Second Person of the Blessed Trinity. These are the eucharist, the Holy Spirit, the Blessed Virgin and the Church, the Mystical Body of Christ.

The Eucharist in Relation to the Incarnate Jesus

For Louise de Marillac, the eucharist was the continuation of the Incarnate Jesus on earth. Under the appearance of the earthly food of bread and wine, Jesus, the risen God-man was truly present. Herein lay Louise's spiritual strength and her source of deepest union with Jesus. The eucharist called her to be united with Jesus and she experienced a deep awareness of the reality of this union. It was frequently in the context of eucharist that Louise received the special graces of her life: her Lumière and her mystical espousals.[134] Even when she felt unworthy to receive the eucharist, Jesus himself seemed to call her to it:

> On the Feast of All Saints, I was particularly overwhelmed
> by the thought of my lowliness, when my soul was made
> to understand that my God wanted to come to me.[135]

Louise received Communion as often as possible for that time and encouraged her Sisters to receive as well.[136] The Mass held a central place in the prayer life of Louise and in that of her Sisters. From the time of recorded references in her life it appears that Louise attended Mass daily. This is evidenced in the daily schedule of her "Rule of Life in the World" c. 1628 and later was incorporated into the horarium for her Daughters.[137]

Louise frequently mentioned her great desire to be worthily prepared for the reception of the eucharist. In the following prayer she implored the Holy Spirit to prepare her soul for Jesus:

> Most Holy Spirit, the Love of the Father and of the Son,
> come to purify and to embellish my soul so that it will be
> agreeable to my Savior and so that I may receive him for
> his greater glory and my salvation. I long for you with all
> my heart, O Bread of Angels.[138]

How penetrating are these final words, "I long for you with all my heart, O Bread of Angels"?

Within the eucharist, Louise also reverenced Mary as the Mother of the Redeemer and congratulated her on this title:

On August 15, 1659, during the Holy Sacrifice of the Mass at which I was to receive Holy Communion, I reflected on the greatness of the Blessed Virgin as Mother of the Son of God who desired to honor her to such a degree that we may say that she participated in some way in all the mysteries of his life and that she contributed to his human-ity by her virginal blood and milk. Considering her in this light, I congratulated Mary on her excellent dignity which unites her to her Son in the perpetual sacrifice of the cross, reenacted on our altars.[139]

United with the glorified Jesus in the eucharist, Louise saw herself as united with the Godhead and recreated through Jesus. Through the eucharist, Louise experienced the power to be transformed in Christ. This belief she expressed profoundly in the following reflection on Holy Communion:

We should rejoice in contemplating this admirable inven-tion and the loving union by which God, seeing himself in us, makes us, once again, like unto him. This he does by communicating not only his grace but himself. He thus effectively bestows upon us the merits of his life and death, thereby giving us the capacity to live in him as he lives in us.[140]

For Louise, the eucharist was the continued presence of the Incarnate God with humankind, bestowing the merits of his life and death, pledging the glory of union for eternity and giving the means for the realization of that reality.

The Holy Spirit: The Spirit of the Risen Jesus

That the Holy Spirit was a most important aspect of Louise's faith life and devotion cannot be disputed. Major experiences in her faith journey occurred at the time of Pentecost: notably her great spiritual "Light" at Pentecost of 1623 which she termed her "pro-found interior conversion" and a significant witness to God's providential care of her and the community at Pentecost of 1642.[141]

To mark these pentecostal experiences, Louise encouraged that her Sisters have a great devotion to this Feast. She wrote to M. Vincent: "I then thought that our entire family should have great devotion to the Feast of Pentecost and total dependence on divine providence."[142] Consequently, Louise instructed her Sisters to prepare for the Feast of Pentecost with great attention. They were to do this by means of novenas, fasting from Communion, and interior recollection.[143] If possible, those at the Motherhouse were to make their annual retreat at this time. The rule read thus:

> Each year, from the Ascension to Pentecost, all our Sisters shall practice interior recollection in honor of the plan of the Son of God when he commanded his Apostles to remain in a state of inactivity while awaiting the coming of the Holy Spirit. They shall strive to imitate the life of the Blessed Virgin and the Apostles in their deprivation of the visible presence of Jesus. Henceforth, if possible, the Sisters of the Motherhouse shall make their retreat at this time. . . . (before 1647).[144]

Early in her life, Louise herself had resolved to make an annual retreat in preparation for Pentecost:

> I would like to spend eight to ten days in retreat twice a year. One would be during the period between the Feast of the Ascension and Pentecost in order to honor the grace which God bestowed on his Church by giving it his Holy Spirit to guide it and by commissioning his Apostles to preach the gospel to all nations.[145]

This deep devotion to the season of Pentecost remained with Louise throughout her life and later she wrote to M. Vincent: "It is true that I have a special affection for the feast of Pentecost and this time of preparation for it is very dear to me. . ."[146]

Louise invoked the grace of the Holy Spirit in all circumstances and trusted in that power to enable her to live her Christian life fully and to grow in holiness and union with God. This is found in her earliest "Rule of Life":

> Upon awakening, may my first thought be of God. . . .Reflecting on my lowliness and powerlessness, I shall invoke the grace of the Holy Spirit in which I shall have great confidence for the accomplishment of his will in me, which shall be the sole desire of my heart.[147]

Several years later, Louise expressed her continued confidence in the call of the Spirit when she wrote:

> I must have great trust in God and believe that his grace will be sufficient to enable me to fulfill his holy will, however difficult it may appear to be, provided the Holy Spirit is truly calling me. I shall know this by listening to the advice which he will permit me to receive.[148]

Similarly, it was Louise's custom to encourage her Daughters to invoke the power of the Holy Spirit in their lives and to trust in the grace of the Spirit's gifts. An example of this is recorded in a letter of 1642 in which she spoke to a Sister about feelings of depression. She wrote:

> I share in the suffering that I know you are enduring because of your attacks of sadness and depression. . . .I advise you to do your best to overcome this dangerous temptation by asking the Holy Spirit for joy, which is one of his seven gifts.[149]

So important was Louise's trust in the Holy Spirit's guidance of the Congregation that she suggested to M. Vincent that the elections for officers be held during the season of Pentecost:

> Allow me to ask you if it should not be every year, during this period of the Feast of Pentecost, that we hold the

election of Officers, either to elect new ones or to prolong the terms of those holding office.[150]

Louise's writings are filled with references to the Holy Spirit and the Feast of Pentecost held such a special call for her that she wrote two profound meditations on the dispositions required to prepare for receiving the Holy Spirit and the signs by which one would know if one had received the Holy Spirit.[151] Among the dispositions Louise indicated as required for receiving the Holy Spirit, were: desire for the gift, detachment of heart, humility and love. The main sign she stated for having received the Holy Spirit was bearing witness to Christ through a life lived in charity.[152]

Louise's deep belief in the power of the Holy Spirit to empower one is seen in the following excerpt from one of her reflections on the preparation for Pentecost:

> The Holy Spirit, upon entering souls that are so disposed, will certainly remove any obstacle to his divine operations by the ardor of his love. He will establish the laws of holy charity by endowing them with the strength to accomplish tasks beyond their human powers so long as they remain in a state of total detachment.[153]

Louise frequently requested the Sisters to invoke the Holy Spirit for the Congregation but especially during the season of Pentecost. In these requests she identified the Holy Spirit with the Christ:

> Pray for us, my dear Sisters, that Our Lord Jesus Christ may bestow his Spirit upon us on this holy feast so that we may be so filled with his Spirit that we may do nothing or say nothing except for his glory and his holy love in which I am, my very dear Sister, your very humble Sister and very loving servant.[154]

For Louise, the Holy Spirit was related to the Incarnate Jesus through the Trinity, as the Spirit of the Risen Jesus come to empower Christians to carry on the mission of Jesus, the Redeemer, the Lord of Charity.[155]

Blessed Virgin Mary and the Incarnate Jesus

Louise de Marillac possessed a strong and focused devotion to Mary which was founded on Mary's motherhood of Jesus, the Incarnate Word. Louise wrote:

All truly Christian souls should have great devotion to the Blessed Virgin, especially in her role as Mother of God. . . . We should rejoice with her and congratulate her for the choice which God made of her by uniting his humanity and his divinity within her womb.[156]

Louise's two principal foci for devotion to Mary were her Immaculate Conception and her motherhood. For Louise, Mary's great dignity stemmed from this relationship with Jesus. Mary's Immaculate Conception was a necessary grace in preparation for the Conception of Jesus; Mary's maternity, in all its facets, was inseparable from Jesus Incarnate.[157]

Louise frequently congratulated Mary on her great honor as the Mother of Jesus. She prayed to her and united herself with her as she carried Jesus in her womb, nursed him as an infant, cared for him as a child, suffered with him in his agony and death and rejoiced with him in his resurrection. Jesus was redeemer and Louise saw Mary as "co-redemptrix"[158] and the "channel through which the graces of the Incarnation and exemplary life of Jesus came" to humankind.[159]

No earthly person was closer to Jesus than Mary and no one knew him as intimately; hence, Louise invoked Mary's intercession to assist her in her quest to know and to love Jesus.[160]

That devotion to Mary was integral to Louise's faith life was evidenced by her desire to place herself and her own son under Mary's protection, by her dedication of the Congregation to Mary and by her final exhortation to her Daughters to take Mary as their only mother.[161]

Perhaps Louise's strong devotion to Mary stemmed from the circumstances of her own birth and childhood wherein she did not know her natural mother or the loving care of such a mother throughout her life.[162] In such cases God frequently provides other sources of nurturing and love and often religiously inclined children will tend to choose Mary as their spiritual mother and develop a deep devotion to her. Louise herself believed that her devotion to Mary was a gift of God. She believed also that God granted her special insights into Mary's graces. Louise expressed this in her writings and also desired to share this gift of understanding with others. In a reflection on Mary, Louise wrote the following:

O my God, why am I unable to reveal to the world the beauty which you have shown me as well as the dignity of the Blessed Virgin? Everything is comprised in her title of Mother of the Son of God.

And addressing Mary, in the same reflection, Louise continued:

I shall manifest my gratitude to you by the praise I offer, by my zeal in helping others to recognize your greatness, and by renewed devotion and trust in your powerful intercession with God. Help me, I implore you, most Holy Virgin, to put such appropriate resolutions into practice.[163]

Louise's devotion to Mary also stemmed from the great mystery of the Incarnation and for this reason the Feast of the Annunciation or the Incarnation and of the Nativity were major sources of joy for her.[164] As a mother, Louise resonated with the joys of Mary as she carried the child Jesus in her womb, nourished him with her blood, brought him to birth, sustained him with her milk and nurtured him. On several occasions, Louise mentioned the use of Mary's blood to form the body of the Child Jesus. Louise honored Mary and praised God for this:

Blessed may you be forever, O my God, for the choice
which you made of the Holy Virgin! . . .You used the blood
of the Blessed Virgin to form the body of your dear Son.
O admirable goodness![165]

For Louise, Mary was the exemplar of discipleship and Louise
chose her as her model to show her how to follow Jesus and thus
lead her to union with him and the Trinity. [166] Louise desired to
model herself on the hidden life of Jesus and Mary which
nourished her spirit enabling her to reach out in compassion to
the poor and the suffering. As well, Louise encouraged her
Daughters to model their lives on that of Mary:

Let us take Our Lady as the model for our daily lives and
bear in mind that the best way to honor her is by imitating
her virtues. . . .her purity since we are spouses of Jesus
Christ,. . . her humility which led God to do great things
in her. Following the example she gave. . ., we must be
detached from all things.[167]

Louise's writings are permeated with references to Mary and
most relate to her maternity of Jesus Incarnate. Hence it is
evident that for Louise, devotion to Mary could not be separated
from devotion to her Son Jesus. It was from Jesus that Mary drew
her humble greatness. For the Incarnation, Louise praised God:
"Blessed may you be forever, O my God, for the choice which
you made of the Holy Virgin!"[168]

The Mystical Body of Christ: Continuation of the Incarnate Jesus, Especially in the Poor

Another related focus of Louise's *Incarnational* spirituality is
that of the Mystical Body of Christ — the Church. Louise referred
to the Church as the Mystical Body of Christ when she wrote:
"You bring to completion the work of founding the Holy
Church. . . .You infused into this Mystical Body the union of
your works . . ."[169]

For Louise, the Church was in reality the Mystical Body of Jesus Christ and in his members, Jesus was present to her to be ministered to and to be loved.[170] For her Christians were called to bear witness to Jesus through charity. In her reflections she stated:

Blessed are those persons who, under the guidance of divine providence, are called upon to continue the ordinary practices of the life of the Son of God through the exercise of charity.[171]

Louise found Jesus incarnated in her neighbor, particularly in the poor. In a letter to one of her Sisters she wrote: "Oh, how true it is that souls who seek God will find him everywhere but especially in the poor!" [172] Jesus led Louise to the poor, suffering members of his Body and in turn they led her to a deeper union with Jesus. All of her service to the poor was centered in Jesus: in the imitation of his ministry to the poor and in seeing him in her suffering neighbor. She exhorted her Sisters thus: ". . . Practice patience and imitate, as far as you are able, the example of Our Lord who consumed his strength and his life in the service of his neighbor."[173]

As Jesus had compassion on the suffering, so too, Louise in union with him, compassionately touched the bodies, hearts and minds of her poor whether they were her own Daughters, the beggars, the orphans, the Ladies of Charity or the galley slaves. In Paris, Louise became, with Vincent de Paul, the caring and compassionate hand of providence to those in need. This same spirit of *serving with compassion*, Louise and Vincent inculcated in their Daughters instructing them to *leave Jesus for Jesus*, to leave prayer for the poor when need be.[174] Indeed the suffering poor were the members of Jesus and in them the Sisters would find Jesus.[175] In and through the poor, they would carry on the mission of Jesus to the world bringing hope and new life, setting people free from the bonds of poverty and ignorance and renewing personal dignity through the spiritual and corporal ministry of the Company. This was not an easy task but Louise always encouraged the Sisters in their mission as is seen in this excerpt from one of her letters:

In order to do this, my dear Sisters, we must continually
have before our eyes our model, the exemplary life of Jesus
Christ. We are called to imitate this life, not only as
Christians, but as persons chosen by God to serve him in
the person of his poor.[176]

In so many ways, Louise herself spent her adult life enriching the
quality of life for others. She ministered to the poor, the sick, the
orphan and the elderly gifting them with dignity. She directed and
educated women. She taught her Sisters so that they might be
empowered to teach, to nurse, to lead and to serve others in the
Spirit of Christ. From Vincent de Paul, Louise learned well the
lesson that "affective love must pass on to effective love."[177] Together they instilled this truth in their Daughters.[178] Truly, Jesus
was to be found in his Mystical Body, particularly in the person of
the poor and this truth was to be the guiding principle of the mission
of Louise and Vincent and of their Daughters of Charity.

Concluding Remarks

Having reflected on the general framework of the spirituality of
Louise de Marillac, one might describe her overall spiritual landscape thus: The ground of her spirituality was her strong trinitarian
devotion and deep prayer life. From this rootedness emerged the
focal tree of her life — the Incarnate Jesus, through whom, with
whom and in whom, was the source of her ecclesial works of charity.
These deeds were the fruits of an integrated spirituality wherein
Louise drew deeply from the Holy Spirit of God and in imitation
of Jesus gave herself in loving service to her neighbor. As for Jesus,
so for Louise, love and service of God her Creator could not be
separated from the love and service of her neighbor.

Thomas McKenna, speaking of Vincent de Paul states: "His
integrated spirituality cannot be described neatly, but some traits
can be distinguished."[179] This statement might also describe the

spirituality of Louise de Marillac. Having looked at the general characteristics of her spirituality, a mosaic takes shape, the background hues of which are her strong trinitarian devotion and her contemplative prayer. The more predominant colors of the foreground are the imitation of the Incarnate Christ in the ministry to the poor and the suffering: the practical application of a life of union with Christ concretized in the ongoing mission of Jesus in the active life. The fine black lead delineating these two intensities of color is Louise's passionate devotion to the suffering Jesus based on his desire to do the will of God and his trust in God's providence. This mosaic presents a simple portrayal of the rootedness of the life of Louise in her faith in God: the Father, Son and Holy Spirit.

Notes

1. SWLM, p. 831. A.31B.

2. In 1974, Pope Paul VI also expressed this reality in the words: "Mary, in fact, is one of our race, a true daughter of Eve — though free of that mother's sin — and truly our Sister, who as a poor and humble woman fully shared our lot" Pope Paul VI, *Marialis Cultus* (Boston: Daughters of St. Paul, 1974), p. 47.

3. SWLM, p. 709. A.19; p. 715. A.5.

4. SWLM, p. 819. A.26; p. 339. L.118B; p. 74. L.102.

5. SWLM, p. 819. A.26.

6. SWLM, p. 820. A.26: "O Trinity perfect in power, wisdom, and love!"

7. SWLM, p. 735. A.45B.

8. SWLM, p. 121. L.111.

9. SWLM, p. 752. A.84. Is there a seed here of true "Creation Spirituality" in creation and in the ongoing creativity of God in its providential sustenance?

10. SWLM, p. 289. L.248,1649; p. 353. L.429,1651; p. 478. L.447,1655; p. 828. A.27.

11. SWLM, p. 696. A.38 (before 1628).

It is interesting to note Louise's poetic imagery in the use of the simile "detaching himself as it were from his Father." It is precisely this spirit of detachment that Louise felt called to emulate in her own life. As Jesus detached himself from the Father to be united with us in all but sin, led by the Spirit, she grew to detachment from herself and the things of earth to be united to the Father.

12. Devotion to the Blessed Virgin . . .is based on the singular dignity of Mary, Mother of the Son of God, and therefore beloved daughter of the Father and Temple of the Holy Spirit. . . *Lumen Gentium,* 53: AAS 57(1965), p.58; *Marialis Cultus,* 1974, p. 46.

13. SWLM, p. 831. A.31B.

14. SWLM, p. 815. A.32.

15. In her Trinitarian grounding, Louise was firmly rooted in the ongoing tradition of the Church's teaching. The *Catechism of the Catholic Church* #261 states: "The mystery of the Most Holy Trinity is the central mystery of the Christian faith and of Christian life. God alone can make it known to us by revealing himself as Father, Son and Holy Spirit."

16. SWLM, p. 478. L.447.

17. SWLM, p. 835. SPIRITUAL TESTAMENT.

18. Deville, p. 106.

19. To illustrate that this focus was ongoing, the selected references will span the years of Louise's life from 1632—1660.

20. SWLM, p. 715. A.5.

21. SWLM, p. 726. A.55-ORDER OF THE DAY, 1633. It is to be noted that the gospel and the imitation of Jesus were primary in the spirituality of Vincent de Paul and thus both he and Louise shared this focus with their Daughters.

22. It is noteworthy that in *Perfectae Caritatis,* 1965, the Second Vatican Council called all religious to make the gospel the prime source of their spirituality, saying: "Since the final norm of the religious life is the following of Christ as it is put before us in the gospel, this must be taken by all institutes as the supreme rule" (PC, 2a) Austin Flannery, O.P., *Vatican Council II, The Conciliar and Post Conciliar Documents,* I (Collegeville: Liturgical Press, 1992), p. 612. Canon 619 of the 1983 Code also states: "They (superiors) are frequently to nourish their members with the food of God's word and lead them to the celebration of the liturgy."

23. SWLM, p. 118. L.125B, September 9,1644.

24. SWLM, p. 260. L.217, August 29,1648.

25. It is interesting to note that Louise relates the consecrated call of the Sisters to serve the poor to the living out of their baptismal commitment. How timely she was as in the post-Vatican era this has been re-emphasized in reference to the consecrated life. *Perfectae Caritatis,* 5 states: "This (dedication to his service) constitutes a *special* consecration, which is deeply rooted in their baptismal consecration and is a fuller expression of it" (Flannery, I, 614).

26. SWLM, p. 371. L.328, September 22, 1651.

It is noteworthy that Bérulle spoke of the Incarnation of Jesus as the prolongation of the Trinity upon earth and Louise speaks of the life of a true Christian as the continuation of the life of Jesus on earth.

27. SWLM, p. 827. A.27.

28. SWLM, p. 827. A.27.

29. Louise often referred to Jesus as the Lord of Charity. The painting attributed to her in the Motherhouse at Rue du Bac presents the resurrected Jesus under this title.

30. SWLM, p. 693. A.3-ACT OF CONSECRATION. Cf. p. 786. A.23-THOUGHTS ON BAPTISM. This *Act of Consecration* was a private devotional act wherein Louise renewed her baptismal promises, her vow of widowhood, her resolution to imitate Jesus and her dedication to fulfilling God's will. This Consecration was received by her director, Vincent de Paul.

31. SWLM, p. 202. L.179, June 21, 1647.

32. SWLM, p. 666. L.647.

33. SWLM, p. 817. A.26-REASONS FOR GIVING ONESELF TO GOD IN ORDER TO RECEIVE THE HOLY SPIRIT.

34. SWLM, p. 782. A.44B-FORMULA OF THE VOWS.

It is very noteworthy that Louise states that the vows are taken for mission —the service of the poor. Herein is the foundation of "Societies of Apostolic Life" and the basis for the majority of modern institutes of apostolic women religious (CIC #731).

The vows of the Daughters were and still remain private vows. On March 25, 1642, Louise and four other Sisters bound themselves by perpetual vows. In the ensuing years several others did likewise but there is no further trace of perpetual vows after the death of Vincent de Paul and by 1718 the practice of taking annual vows had become universally established (Coste, *Life & Works*,I, 349).

35. SWLM, p. 713. A.15-CONFORMITY TO THE DIVINE WILL.

36. Flannery, O.P., *Vatican Council II, The Conciliar and Post Conciliar Documents*, I, "Sacrosanctum Concilium," 1963, p. 5:

> In the earthly liturgy we take part in a foretaste of that heavenly liturgy which is celebrated in the Holy City of Jerusalem. . .With all the warriors of the heavenly army we sing a hymn of glory to the Lord, venerating the memory of the saints. . .

37. SWLM, p. 727. A.55-ORDER OF THE DAY, 1633.

38. SWLM, p. 742. A.91.

39. SWLM, p. 822. M.72.

40. SWLM, p. 816. M.70.

41. SWLM, p. 816. M.70.

42. SWLM, p. 520. L.157B.

43. SWLM, p. 520. L.157B.

44. SWLM, p. 754. A.91B-RULE FOR THE MOTHERHOUSE. "Seminary" is the term used by Louise and Vincent to denote the first formation period or novitiate. The term is still used today.

45. SWLM, p. 746. A.88-HOSPITALS; p. 233. L.196B; p. 749. A.84; p. 742. A.91.

46. SWLM, p. 7. L.3B. The Ladies of the Charities were women of the parish who assisted the poor. They were usually of the aristocracy and wealthy.

47. SWLM, p. 734. A.22; p. 817. A.26; p. 734. M.35B; p. 701. A.21; p. 768. A.75; p. 718. A.8; p. 690. A.1; p. 142. L.137.

48. SWLM, p. 785. M.33. This principle is stated in the *Documents of Vatican II,* in the Decree on the Sacred Liturgy, # 13: ". . .devotions should . . .harmonize with the liturgical seasons, accord with the sacred liturgy, be derived from it, and lead the people to it. . ." Cf. *Marialis Cultus,* p. 28.

49. SWLM, p. 689. A.1; p. 734. M.35B.

50. SWLM, p. 726. A.55; p. 738. A.91; p. 746. A.88; p. 768. A.75.

Calvet, one of Louise's biographers, notes that the "framework and the texture of Louise's teaching was the liturgy and the liturgical year." Calvet, p. 117.

51. *Documents,* p. 968. A.48. Cf. SWLM, p. 372. L.285; p. 348. L.521; p. 292. L.481; p. 540. L.513; p. 361. L.313; p. 773. A.85.

52. Louise feared that if after Vincent's death, the Sisters came under the jurisdiction of the Bishop or his delegate, enclosure might be imposed upon them. Even Queen Anne petitioned the Pope in 1647, requesting that in perpetuity, the Sisters be under the authority of the Superior General of the Missions. The process of final approbation is described in Chapter I of this study.

53. SWLM, p. 140; L.130D, p. 187; p. 461.

54. Fr. Jose Maria Roman states: "The establishment of the Superior General of the Congregation of the Mission as Superior General of the Daughters of Charity is, consequently, one of the contributions of Louise de Marillac to the institutional configuration of the Company of the Daughters of Charity" ("Configuration of the Institute," *Echoes of the Company,* May, 1993, p. 229).

55. SWLM, p. 560. L.527B; p. 559. L.529B.

56. SWLM, p. 116. L.105; p. 560. L.529B. Even if the Sisters were unjustly treated and humiliated publicly, they were encouraged to remain silent and to trust in providence for their justification.

57. SWLM, p. 386. L.337; p. 151. L.141,

58. Corpus Juan Delgado, C.M., "Luisa de Marillac y la Iglesia," *Evangelizare: 30, 1991* (Salamanca: C.E.M.E), p. 307: ". . .en la iglesia, todo laico y, ciertemente, la mujer tiene una mision."

59. Decree on The Apostolate of Lay People, Vatican II, 1965, #3. "Inserted as they are in the Mystical Body of Christ by baptism and

strengthened by the power of the Holy Spirit in confirmation, it is by the Lord himself that they are assigned to the apostolate" (Flannery, I, 768). Cf. *Christifideles Laici*, 1990.
    60. SWLM, p. 789. A.56. This notation is so timely that it could easily be attributed to a present-day writer. Louise's prophetic gift of vision has much to say to women of today.
    61. *Documents*, p. 899. Doc.783, #2, #3: "Que les Filles de la Charité ne sont pas religieuses, mais des filles qui vont et viennent comme des séculiers. . ." #2.
    "Notre petite compagnie s'est donnée à Dieu pour servir le pauvre peuple corporellement et spirituellement, et cela dès son commencement, en sorte au'à même temps qu'elle a travaillé au salut des âmes pour les missions, . . .ce que le Saint-Siège a approuvé par les bulles de notre institution" #3.
    62. G. Battelli,mccj, in *Religious Life in the light of the new Canon Law* (Africa: St. Paul Publications, 1990, 1993), p. 43 states:

> To Vincent goes the credit of having realized a new form of consecrated life (*even if not strictly religious, from a juridical point of view*), that will be followed by the majority of feminine religious institutes: religious women going about the world in search of their brothers and sisters in need.

Undoubtedly, Vincent would be the first to assert that in justice, credit must be given to Louise for her major role in the collaborative foundation, education and direction of the Company. It was to her that the Holy Spirit gave a spiritual vision of the charism of the community and it was her visionary gift coupled with her practicality that enabled many of the works undertaken by Vincent to come to fruition. Truly, Louise and Vincent could certainly be adopted in our Church today as models for collaborative ministry between clergy and women religious. Perhaps this is one of the gifts of the Double Vincentian Family to the Church.
    63. SWLM, p. 707. A.46; p. 705. A.51; p. 720. A.53; p. 722. A.52.
    64. Gobillon (Fiat Edition,1886), *Louise de Marillac*, I, 68.
    A letter from Vincent to Louise between 1636-39 gives instructions regarding the retreat format among which is the following: "They can take their spiritual reading from the *Imitation of Christ* . . .,something from Granada . . .and a few chapters of the gospels" (V. de P.,I, 372).
    In her "Draft of the Rule" for the Charities before 1645, Louise wrote: "Once a year, the said women shall make a spiritual retreat" (SWLM, A.54, p. 728).
    Regarding Vincent's retreat work, Coste states: "The annual total of persons on retreat in the house of Saint-Lazare alone mounted up to seven or eight hundred" (Life & Works, III, 1).
    65. Koch, p. 75. He also noted : "She had nothing to envy in the Ladies of the Cenacle who, much later, through the influence of the Jesuit Fathers, directed spiritual retreats, and she deserves that we should make her better known" p. 74.
    66. Dirvin, p. 153.

67. SWLM, p. 113. L.104B.

68. SWLM, p. 468. L.424.

69. SWLM, p. 515. L.531B.

70. SWLM, p. 696. A.38-ON THE END OF THE CONGREGATION OF THE MISSION.

71. Might there be slight echoes of a Catherine of Siena here, challenging the clergy to live up to their calling?

72. *Documents*, p. 779. Doc.682.

73. The errors of Cornelius Jansen regarding keeping the commandments and the resistance of grace were condemned in 1642 by Pope Urban VIII and again in 1653 by Pope Innocent X. Vincent de Paul kept abreast of the continuing development of the theories and was instrumental in sending a letter to the Pope requesting action. He was also active in having three theologians from the Sorbonne go to Rome for the hearings. Vincent was staunch in protecting his Company of Priests and the Daughters from these errors. However, the spirit of Jansenism continued to spread and in 1713 Pope Clement XI condemned 101 propositions of Pasquier Quesnel.

At this time the state of the clergy in France was desperate. The priests were uneducated, untrained and in many cases living scandalous lives. In 1643 a Bishop sought Vincent de Paul's assistance thus: "The extreme desolation I encounter in the clergy of my diocese and my powerlessness to remedy it have obliged me to have recourse to you, so well known for your zealous dispositions and strong propensity to restoring priestly discipline in the places where it is found to be lax or entirely broken down" (V. de P., II, L.649, p. 411).

74. *Documents*, p. 992. Doc.847-Testament de Louise de Marillac. Cf. SWLM, p. 202. L.179.

75. Gobillon (Fiat),I, 152: "I beg the Father, the Son and the Holy Spirit by the power he has given to fathers and mothers to bless their children, that he give you his blessing, and detach you from earthly things, and attach you to him. Live as good Christians."

76. Gobillon (Fiat),I, 153: "My dear Sisters, I continue to ask God to bless you, and I beg him to give you the grace to persevere in your vocation to serve him in the way he asks of you. Take great care of the service of the poor; . . ."

77. For a fuller discussion of Louise's ecclesiology see the article by Corpus Juan Delgado, C.M., "Luisa de Marillac y la Iglesia," CEME, pp. 281-312.

78. SWLM, p. 820. A.26.

79. CCC, #461: "Taking up St. John's expression, 'The Word became flesh', the Church calls `Incarnation' the fact that the Son of God assumed a human nature in order to accomplish our salvation in it. . ."

80. That Louise's spirituality was timeless is seen in the current teaching of the Church in CCC, #520: "In all of his life Jesus presents himself as *our*

model. He is 'the perfect man,' who invites us to become his disciples and follow him." Cf. #517.

81. SWLM, p. 689. A.1.

82. SWLM, p. 718. A.8. Cf. SWLM, p. 700. A.7, 1628. One sees similarities between the ideas of Louise and Thérèse of Lisieux who in her autobiography wrote about the birth of Jesus thus: "By becoming weak and frail for me, he gave me strength and courage" The Autobiography of Saint Thérèse of Lisieux, trans. John Beevers (New York: Image, Doubleday, 1957, 1959), p. 61.

83. SWLM, p. 703. A.9.

84. SWLM, p. 732. A.21B.

85. SWLM, p. 140. L.303B. Perhaps Louise's honoring of the pre-natal life of Jesus and the pregnancy of Mary could serve as a model for the dignity and rights to life of unborn children.

86. SWLM, p. 140. L.303B.

87. SWLM, p. 142. L.137.

88. SWLM, p. 736. A.45.

89. SWLM, p. 774. A.14B. Louise's sense of awe at the mystery of the birth of Jesus has been shared by all true Christians and is still the challenge for us today. In CCC, # 563, one reads: "No one, whether shepherd or wise man, can approach God here below except by kneeling before the manger at Bethlehem and adoring him hidden in the weakness of a new-born child."

90. SWLM, p. 674. L.651.

91. This theological thought finds expression in CCC, #517: "Christ's whole life is a mystery of redemption. Redemption comes to us above all through the blood of his cross, but this mystery is at work throughout Christ's entire life: . . ."

92. SWLM, p. 666. L.647.

93. It is interesting that over two hundred years later, Thérèse of Lisieux incorporated the aspects of both the Infancy and the Passion in her name, Thérèse of the Infant Jesus and the Holy Face. Cf. Jones et al., *The Study of Spirituality,* p. 395.

94. *Documents,* p. 991. Doc. 846 (n.d.). Poème à Jèsus Naissant écrit par Louise de Marillac.

95. This invitation is open to all and continues to be placed before us in current Church teaching. CCC, #533 reads: "The hidden life at Nazareth allows everyone to enter into fellowship with Jesus by the most ordinary events of daily life: . . ." and #531 states: "During the greater part of his life Jesus shared the condition of the vast majority of human beings: daily life spent without evident greatness, a life of manual labor. His religious life was that of a Jew obedient to the law of God, a life in the community."

Bringing Jesus into the ordinary situations of life may well have been one of Louise's contributions to the simplification of the spirituality of the French School.

96. SWLM, p. 713. A.15.

97. SWLM, p. 718. A.8.

98. SWLM, p. 701. A.7, Seventh Day.

99. SWLM, p. 715. A.5. Here Louise resolved to make Jesus the model of her life in all circumstances. How interesting to read in CCC, #563: "By his obedience to Mary and Joseph, as well as by his humble work during the long years in Nazareth, Jesus gives us the example of holiness in the daily life of family and work."

100. SWLM, p. 660. L.642.

101. SWLM, p. 833. A.100, 1660.

102. SWLM, p. 719. A.8.

103. SWLM, p. 689. A.1-RULE OF LIFE IN THE WORLD, c. 1628.

104. SWLM, p. 714. A.5-RETREAT c. 1632:

"3. On the excellent way in which Our Lord joins the contemplative to the active life; a summary of my meditation."

"4. On the life of Our Lord in Nazareth and the temptations to which he was subjected in the desert; a summary of my meditation."

"5. On the evangelical counsels which Our Lord set forth in the Sermon on the Mount; their excellence and the high perfection to which they call us; a summary of my meditation."

p.715: "He did not teach us to practice it on account of our lowliness but in imitation of him who is himself humble of heart."

105. SWLM, p. 777. A.36:

. . .the Son of God came in person as a pilgrim, his life being one unending pilgrimage. This should be the example for our lives. Therefore, I have resolved to meditate profoundly on his life and to try to imitate it. I spent a great deal of time reflecting on the title of Christian which we bear, and I came to the conclusion that we must, indeed, truly conform our lives to the life of Our Lord Jesus Christ.

This aspect of conformity to Jesus was a recurring theme in Louise's writings. Perhaps this too helped to bring the theological principles of the French School within the practical reach of all.

106. SWLM, p. 726. A.55, Order of the Day, 1633.

107. SWLM, p. 540. L.513, Feb.10,1657.

108. SWLM, p. 821. A.26, 6th med.,1657.

109. The phrase of "changing the ordinary into the extraordinary" is frequently used by Dr. Susan Muto in her lectures and video series: "Becoming Spiritually Mature," Epiphany Association, Pittsburgh, PA, 1991.

Perhaps this harkens to Francis de Sales who wrote: "Des choses communes, mais pas de façon commune." (Ravier, "St. François de Sales," *Mission et Charité*, 29-30, Janvier-Juin 1968, p. 25.)

Often one tends to focus on the spectacular in the life of Jesus when it is the "ordinary" that, with the help of his grace, is usually within our grasp of imitation. Truly, Louise brought the actions and spirit of Jesus into the everyday lives of her Sisters and in this way added her own nuance to the "states and mysteries" of Jesus found in the spirituality of the French School.

110. SWLM, p. 773. A.85, 1647.

111. SWLM, p. 717. A.8-RETREAT, Monday: 2nd Meditation c.1633.

112. SWLM, p. 20. L.11,1639.

113. SWLM, p. 129. L.121, June 27,1645.

114. SWLM, p. 260. L.217, August 29,1648.

This summons of Louise is also the challenge given to Christians today. One reads in *CCC*, #544: "Jesus identifies himself with the poor of every kind and makes active love towards them the condition for entering his kingdom."

It must be noted that the imitation of Jesus in his mission to the poor was central to Vincent de Paul who continually encouraged Louise in this ministry.

115. SWLM, p. 372. L.328, 1651. Cf. Mt. 5:48 and "Lumen Gentium" #39, Flannery, I, 396: "Therefore all in the Church, whether they belong to the hierarchy or are cared for by it, are called to holiness, . . ."

116. SWLM, pp. 477-8. L.447, August 19,1655.

117. SWLM, p. 713. A.15-CONFORMITY TO THE DIVINE WILL, c.1632.

118. SWLM, p. 711. A.29-ON CHARITY.

119. SWLM, p. 711. A.29-ON CHARITY.

120. SWLM, p. 417. L.415, March 26,1653.

121. SWLM, p. 260. L.217, August 29,1648.

122. SWLM, p. 741. A.91.

123. SWLM, p. 17. L.9, 1639: " . . .I am in the love of Jesus crucified. . ." From 1639 this closure became a hallmark of Louise's letters and as well frequently appeared throughout the texts of them.

124. The seal of the Congregation was (and is) the cross of Christ crucified encircled by flames of fire and surrounded by the words: "La Charité de Jésus Crucifié Nous Presses." Louise's headstone was a cross bearing the words: "Spes Unica."

125. SWLM, p. 570. L.545B, September 22, 1657.

126. Calvet in his biography of Louise notes that "The movement of admiration and love which the mystery of the resurrection inspired in her is an original feature of her devotion which I have not encountered in other spiritual writers" p. 174.

127. SWLM, p. 720. A.12-RENUNCIATION OF SELF, c. 1633. Cf. SWLM, p. 600. L.580, July 5,1658.

128. SWLM, p. 732. A.21B.

129. SWLM, p. 286. L.246, May 5,1649. "Please greet warmly for me all our good gentlemen and ladies and our Sisters whom I embrace warmly and lovingly in the love of our crucified and risen Master."

130. SWLM, p. 196. L.174, May 8,1647.

131. At the Motherhouse of the Daughters of Charity at rue du Bac, Paris, there are three paintings of Jesus authenticated to be painted by Louise de Marillac. In each of these paintings, Jesus is represented as the glorified Christ:

A small medallion painting of the glorified Christ bears on the right the inscription: "Learn of me for I am meek,. . ." and on the left: "Come, the blessed of my Father. . . ."

A second large painting, *The Lord of Charity*, presents the glorified Christ with his heart ablaze. This painting according to the art critic M. Ed. Didron, is the first representation of the Sacred Heart to be known with certitude and predates the visions of Margaret Mary Alacoque by fifty to sixty years (Ed. Didron, "Louise de Marillac & Le Sacré Coeur," *Bulletin of Saint Vincent de Paul*, #4, Avril, 1900). This painting bears the inscription: "Ce tableau a été peint par Mlle Le Gras, nostre honoré mère et institutrice."

A third painting by Louise represents the glorified Christ, above which are the words, "God is Love." To the left of Christ, a priest administers Viaticum to a dying person and to the right of Christ a Daughter of Charity waits with a glass containing some wine to give to the person after Communion, in accordance with the directions of Louise de Marillac to her Daughters ("Louise De Marillac & Le Sacré Coeur," Anon., *Petites Annales de Saint Vincent de Paul*, Juin 1900).

132. SWLM, p. 704. A.10, c.1630.

133. CCC, #655.

134. SWLM, p. 1. A.2-LIGHT, June 4,1623; p. 704. A.50-Reference to Spiritual Espousal, February 5,1630.

135. SWLM, p. 697. A.17.

136. Coste, in *Life & Works*,I, 197 states: "She used to go to Holy Communion three times a week, on Sundays, Tuesdays and Saturdays and also perhaps on Fridays; to these may be added Holy Days and certain anniversaries. . ."

137. SWLM, p. 689. A.1: "At eight-thirty in the summer and at nine o'clock in the winter, I shall go to holy Mass."
p. 746. A.88: "The Daughters of Charity shall hear Mass every day." This may have been somewhat unusual for the times.

138. SWLM, p. 834. A.49-PRAYER BEFORE COMMUNION.

139. SWLM, p. 831. M.5B-THE VIRGIN MARY, CO-REDEMPTRIX.

140. SWLM, p. 821. M.72-ON HOLY COMMUNION.

141. SWLM, p. 768. A.75-ON THE CONDUCT OF DIVINE PROVI-DENCE. Cf. p. 1. A.2-LIGHT, June 4, 1623, Feast of Pentecost and p. 127. L.118; p. 128. L.120.

On the Vigil of Pentecost, June 7, 1642, the ceiling fell in the meeting room in the Motherhouse; Louise and the Sisters in the room narrowly escaped death. This plus Louise's earlier experience of God's spiritual favor

at Pentecost were two touchstones of the providence of God in her life; thus Louise frequently associated Pentecost with the providence of God.
142. SWLM, p. 768. A.75-ON THE CONDUCT OF DIVINE PROVI-DENCE.
For Louise the Holy Spirit was the ongoing gift of God's providence to the Church's children.
143. Regarding "fasting from Communion," Louise wrote: "With permission, they shall be deprived of Holy Communion so as to do penance for their failings in the reception of the Blessed Sacrament during the course of the year and to obtain from God better dispositions for the future" (SWLM, p. 769. A.75).
144. SWLM, p. 769. A.75.
145. SWLM, p. 689. A.1-RULE OF LIFE IN THE WORLD, c.1628.
146. SWLM, p. 339. L.118B. Cf. p. 199. L.101 (June 1647): "I forgot to ask your permission to receive Communion throughout the novena of Masses to the Holy Spirit."
147. SWLM, p. 339. L.118B.
In true humility, Louise realizes that without God's grace she is incapable of accomplishing her greatest desire to be at one with the will of God.
148. SWLM, p. 716. A.5-RETREAT, c.1632.
149. SWLM, p. 74. L.102. Although "joy" is traditionally recognized as a "fruit of the Holy Spirit" rather than one of the "seven gifts," one wonders whether or not Louise, because of her serious personality and struggle with feelings of depression saw "joy" in her own life as a great gift of the Spirit and thus expressed it as such. However, it may also have been a misnomer.
It is interesting to note that Pope Paul VI in his Apostolic Exhortation, *Gaudete In Domino*, also speaks of joy as a "gift of the Holy Spirit":
p. 5: "At this time,. . .when believers are preparing to celebrate the coming of the Holy Spirit, we invite you to implore from him the gift of joy."
p.6: "Yes, it is for us too an exigence of love to invite you to share this abounding joy which is a gift of the Holy Spirit." Pope Paul VI, Apostolic Exhortation, *Gaudete In Domino* (Rome: Vatican Polyglot Press, May 9, 1975).
Louise understands and does not deny or negate "attacks of sadness or depression" but she also cautions her Sisters not to be bound by them.
Cf. p. 742. A.91: "Often they should invoke the Holy Spirit in order to purify their thoughts, words and actions."
p. 761. A.91B: "At precisely eight o'clock, she shall go to the school and kneel down to ask for help of the Holy Spirit for herself and for her pupils, that they be taught purely for the glory of God."
150. SWLM, p. 642. L.622, June 2,1659.
151. The reception of the Holy Spirit to which Louise refers here is not synonymous with the reception of the Holy Spirit in baptism but rather refers to a special outpouring of the graces of the Holy Spirit at the Feast of Pentecost. In a meditation in preparation for Pentecost, Louise wrote:

"One of the greatest losses that a soul can experience by not participating in the coming of the Holy Spirit is that the gifts infused at baptism do not have their effect. . ." SWLM, p. 817. A.26.

152. SWLM, p. 802. A.25-THE PURITY OF LOVE NECESSARY TO RECEIVE THE HOLY SPIRIT; and p. 817. A.26-REASONS FOR GIVING ONESELF TO GOD IN ORDER TO RECEIVE THE HOLY SPIRIT, 1657.

153. SWLM, p. 802. A.25.

154. SWLM, p.350. L.345, May 19,1651. Cf. p. 353. L. 429, May 1651; p. 640. L.621, May 26,1659.

155. Calvet, p. 181. Calvet calls Louise "the disciple and mystic of the Holy Ghost." He "ventures to use the word 'pneumatocentric' to characterize the spirituality of Louise."

156. SWLM, p. 785. M.33-DEVOTION TO THE BLESSED VIRGIN.

157. SWLM, p. 830. A.31B-THOUGHTS ON THE IMMACULATE CONCEPTION OF THE VIRGIN MARY:

The Immaculate Conception of the Blessed Virgin leads us to realize and adore the omnipotence of God because grace totally vanquished nature in her. She was saved without ever having been lost, not only through mercy but also through justice, since this was essential for the Incarnation of the Son of God in the eternal plan for the Redemption of mankind.

Calvet, p. 178 states: "Not all of the theologians contemporary with her (Louise) held the belief in the Immaculate Conception, and devotion to Our Lady at that time did not stress this mystery."

Louise appeared to hold a minority view but one of which she was convinced. She had received a dream on the Eve of December 8 between 1633-47 depicting Mary as one Transfigured. Regarding this dream, Louise wrote: ". . .this one has always remained in my mind as a representation of the first grace of the Blessed Virgin who is the beginning of the light which the Son of God was to bring to the world" (SWLM, p. 735. M.35B).

Elsewhere Louise wrote: "Would to God that I could fully express the thoughts that, in his goodness, he has granted me on the subject of the Immaculate Conception of the Blessed Virgin, so that the true understanding that I possess of her merits and the desire that I have to render her fitting homage may remain always in my heart" (SWLM, p.830. A.31B).

Calvet, p. 178 also states that the Daughters may have been the first Society to be consecrated to the Immaculate Conception of Mary. Louise requested this Consecration for December 8, 1658 and it has been renewed annually since. As sharers in the spiritual tradition of Vincent and Louise, we in our own Congregation also make this dedication annually.

158. SWLM, p. 831. M.5b-The Virgin Mary, Co-redemptrix, August,1659: "Considering her in this light, I congratulated Mary on her excellent dignity which unites her to her Son in the perpetual sacrifice of the cross, reenacted and offered on our altars."

Was Louise ahead of her time? Pope Benedict XV said: "Together with

Christ, Mary has redeemed the human race." For this reason, Pius XI called her "Co-redemptrix" and Pius XII called her "auxiliatrix of the Redeemer"' Matthias Premm, *Dogmatic Theology for the Laity* (Rockford, Ill.: Tan Books and Publishers, Inc., 1977), p. 193.

As Co-Redemptrix, Mary is not *equal to* Jesus in the work of redemption but she is united *with* him in it; CCC, #964 states: "This union of the mother with the Son in the work of salvation is made manifest from the time of Christ's virginal conception up to his death; it is made manifest above all at the hour of his Passion."

159. SWLM, p. 785. M.33-Devotion to the Blessed Virgin. It is interesting to note the similarity between the points in this short reflection by Louise and those developed in *Marialis Cultus*.

160. SWLM, p. 695. A.4, Oblation to the Blessed Virgin, c. 1626:

I am entirely yours, most Holy Virgin, that I may more perfectly belong to God. Teach me, therefore, to imitate your holy life by fulfilling the designs of God in my life. I very humbly beg you to assist me. You know my weakness. You see the desires of my heart. Supply for my powerlessness and negligence by your prayers.

161. SWLM, p. 695. A.4-OBLATION TO THE BLESSED VIRGIN, c.1626: "Most Holy Virgin, deign to take my son and me into your care. Welcome the choice I make of you as our protectress."

p. 121. L.111-Account of the Pilgrimage to Chartres, 1644: ". . .I offered to God the designs of his providence on the Company of the Daughters of Charity. . . .I asked for it, through the prayers of the Holy Virgin, Mother and Guardian of the said Company,the purity of which it stands in need." Cf. p. 621. L.602, December, 1658.

p. 835. SPIRITUAL TESTAMENT: "Pray earnestly to the Blessed Virgin, that she may be your only Mother."

162. It is interesting to note that Catherine Labouré and Thérèse of Lisieux also lost their mothers early in life.

163. SWLM, p. 775. A.14B-TO THE VIRGIN MARY.

164. Raymond Deville, "St. Vincent and St. Louise in Relation to the French School of Spirituality," states that Louise "exactly like Bérulle and less like Vincent held that the feast of the Annunciation — Incarnation was *the* great feast" *Vincentian Heritage*, 11:1, 1990, p. 42.

165. SWLM, p. 801. A.13B. Cf. p. 831. M.5B.

166. SWLM, p. 815. A.32-ON THE VIRTUES OF THE MOST HOLY VIRGIN.

167. SWLM, p. 785. M.33- DEVOTION TO THE BLESSED VIRGIN.

168. SWLM, p. 800. A.13B-ON THE MYSTERY OF THE INCARNATION.

169. SWLM, p. 820. A.26.

170. Sr. Regnault, noted:

For Louise de Marillac as for Catherine of Siena, the love of God and love of neighbor were inseparable. The foundress frequently quoted God's words to this ardent soul to her first Daughters of Charity: A soul who truly loves Me also loves his neighbor, since love for Me and love of the neighbor are one and the same (Regnault, p. 114).

Cf. Thomas Aquinas, IIa, Q.44:2,8. Msgr. Paul J.Glenn, *A Tour of the Summa* (Rockford, Ill.: Tan Books, 1978), pp. 214-215.

171. SWLM, p. 821.

172. SWLM, p. 431. L.292.

173. SWLM, p. 541. L.513. Cf. p. 355. L.347; p. 434. L.383; p. 726. A.55.

174. This counsel was often given to the Daughters by Vincent de Paul. In his first Conference to them on July 31, 1634 while explaining the Rule, Vincent said: "My daughters, remember that when you leave prayer and holy Mass to serve the poor, you are losing nothing, because serving the poor is going to God and you should see God in them" (Leonard, *Conferences*, I, 4).

Serving with compassion, from the Mission Statement of the Sisters of Providence of St. Vincent de Paul, Kingston, Canada. (1989)

175. SWLM, p. 468. L.424: "We must respect and honor everyone: the poor because they are the members of Jesus Christ and our masters; . . ."

176. SWLM, p. 261. L.217.

177. Leonard, *Conferences, II,* 204.

178. Leonard, *Conferences, II,* 206. In his Conference of February 9, 1653, Vincent said to the Sisters: "And there, my dear Sisters, you have in general the essence of affective and effective love; to serve Our Lord in his members both corporally and spiritually and to do so in their own homes, or indeed in whatever place to which providence may send you."

179. Thomas McKenna, C.M., *Praying with Vincent de Paul* (Winona, MN: St.Mary's Press, 1994), p. 26.

Specific Characteristics of the Spirituality of Louise de Marillac

Today one often hears of a 'call within a call.' In reflecting on Louise de Marillac's life one could say that she had a 'call within her call' and that was to imitate the spirit of the suffering of Jesus. Within the General Characteristics of the Spirituality of Louise de Marillac one finds the recurring theme of the desire to do the will of God combined with trust in God's providence. This motif is evident within all of Louise's life but especially in her call to suffer in union with Jesus. It is the specific characteristics of this call that will now be explored.

Imitation of the Sufferings of Jesus Crucified

Throughout her life, Louise felt called to imitate the life of Jesus Christ. This she did by emulating the hidden life of Jesus through her humility and contemplation and his public life by following his example of service to his neighbor. Particularly, Louise experienced a strong call to imitate Jesus in his sufferings. She united herself to his sufferings and found in them a source of strength and hope. This is evidenced in her writings wherein she expressed her call to be united to the sufferings of Jesus in her life. In a reflection on the Passion of Christ, Louise wrote the following:

143

> Fidelity to Jesus Christ on the cross, who willed to fulfill the Scriptures. When Jesus knew that he had endured all the pain which the Scriptures had foretold, he increased his own sufferings saying,"I thirst." . . . his afflicted body, like a deer sought the relief of water. He suffered a double thirst:that of his body and of his spirit. . . .His third cry expresses his thirst to apply his merits to all souls created for paradise.[1]

In this passage one sees Louise's reference to scripture both in recounting the Passion and in her allusion to the psalms. Using the image of the deer, "Like a deer, longs for water" (Ps. 42:1), Louise saw Jesus as longing to be "reunited to the Father and to the Holy Spirit." She saw him "thirsting to apply his merits to all souls created for Paradise" and she challenged herself: "Listen to him, O my soul, as if he were speaking to you alone, 'I thirst for your faithful love.'"[2] How these words bespeak Louise's intimate relationship with Jesus and reflect the words of the *Imitation of Christ*, "It is the cry of an ardent soul deeply in love with God."[3]

Continuing this reflection, Louise surrendered herself to be united to the sufferings of Jesus:

> I gave myself to God to accept the designs of his providence if he willed me to continue, for the remainder of Lent, in a state of interior abandonment and even affliction so as to honor the sufferings of Jesus Christ which the Church places before our eyes.[4]

Herein one sees that Louise suffered interiorly and experienced to some degree the feeling of abandonment of Jesus on the cross when he cried out: "My God, My God, why have you forsaken me?" (Ps. 22:1; Mk. 15:34) United with the suffering Jesus and praying with the Church, Louise journeyed through her Lent, accepting the interior suffering as part of the provident will of God and trusting that a resurrection experience would follow. She lived the contemplative prayer spoken of in the *Catechism of the Catholic Church* which states:

Contemplative prayer is a communion of love bearing Life for the multitude, to the extent that it consents to abide in the night of faith. The Paschal night of the resurrection passes through the night and agony and the tomb — the three intense moments of the Hour of Jesus which his Spirit (and not "the flesh [which] is weak") brings to life in prayer. We must be willing to "keep watch with [him] one hour."[5]

Both in her reflections and her letters, Louise also encouraged her Sisters to unite their sufferings with those of Jesus. In a reflection on the "Pure Love Vowed to God," Louise wrote:

Let us take the first step in following him which is to exclaim, "I desire it thus, my dear Spouse, I desire it thus. As proof thereof, I am going to follow you to the foot of your cross which I choose as my cloister."[6]

It is noteworthy that Louise refers to the cross as "her cloister." She who had so desired to be a cloistered nun finds that aspect of her Christian life in a spiritual way at the foot of the cross. It was in this "cloister" of the cross that Louise was schooled and granted the grace to surrender herself to be united with and to be transformed by the will and love of the suffering Jesus.[7]

The cross was the ultimate sign of Jesus' love for humankind. Jesus had said: "And when I am lifted up from the earth, I shall draw all people to myself" (Jn. 12:32). Louise, as a devoted disciple of Jesus, desired to follow him even to the solitude of the cross as a sign of her love for him.[8]

There, I shall leave behind all earthly affections because your voice has called me and urged my heart to forget my people and my father's house so as to be open to your great love. Therefore, at the foot of this holy, sacred and adored cross, I sacrifice everything that might prevent me from loving, with all the purity you expect of me, without ever aspiring to any joy other than submission to your good pleasure and to the laws of your pure love.[9]

As Jesus had sacrificed everything for love of humankind, so too Louise, in response to his call of love was willing to sacrifice all to be one with him. This text presents an allusion to Ps.45:10 which is the "Royal Wedding Song."[10] As Jesus found joy in doing the will of God, Louise's joy was to do the will of Jesus in her life. She had learned that in this is true happiness.[11]

It is interesting to note Louise's ongoing rootedness in scripture and the frequency of 'love language and spousal allusion' that are present in her thoughts in relation to the Passion of Jesus which is the essence of love.[12]

In counselling and comforting her Sisters in their sufferings, Louise in her letters encouraged them to be united with the sufferings of Jesus. To one Sister, she wrote in 1648:

> Our good God is truly making you a participant in his sufferings by permitting you to be seriously ill. . . . I beg his goodness to give you the consolations that he usually gives to souls he wishes to sanctify in this way. . . . Rest assured that it is a sign of God's love for you since it is through this that he makes you somewhat like his Son. Suffer then, in his same spirit, through submission to all that God wills of you, and use every means given to you to recover your health.[13]

Similarly, to other Sisters she wrote in 1657:

> I hope that Our Lord will grant the prayers of his Charity and of M. Portail, to whom I conveyed your very humble greetings yesterday, and that by means of them, your sufferings will be changed into consolation because of the crosses you are privileged to bear. Yes, my dear Sisters, the greatest honor you can receive is to follow Jesus Christ carrying his cross.[14]

These counsels to her Sisters indicate acceptance of the crosses in life as part of the acceptance of the permissive will of God, but Louise also wished that the Sisters experience consolation and take every means to improve their situation. Thus Louise manifested her strong faith combined with a practical spirituality.[15] She knew well that there are times when faith alone is the mainstay of one's life; but, she knew also that God could not be outdone in generosity and that God expected persons to use the resources available to them to improve their lot. This too was an aspect of trusting in providence. One must actively participate with God to bring about change where possible.[16]

Louise's Attitude Towards the Call to Suffer

Throughout her writings Louise frequently spoke of her own call to suffer and in doing so manifested the attitude of dependence on Jesus and unity with him.[17] Louise's attitude towards suffering was not that of a masochist who enjoyed suffering for suffering's sake. Rather, she saw suffering in the permissive will of God as a means of atoning for her sins and as a way of being united with the suffering Jesus. In baptism she had been baptized into the death of Jesus and for Louise this was a lived reality. In a reflection on baptism, she wrote the following:

> . . . we who are baptized in Jesus Christ are baptized in his death. . . . Moreover, this death in which we are baptized is the result of the love which Our Lord has had for us from all eternity. . . .

> Let us live, therefore, as if we were dead in Jesus Christ. Henceforth, let there be no further resistance to Jesus, no action except for Jesus, no thoughts but in Jesus![18]

In this passage one sees again Louise's emphasis on love. Jesus' death was the result of his steadfast love and one's death in Jesus through baptism opens one to total immersion in his lifegiving love. In this depth of love, one's will desires to be in union with the will of Jesus and one's whole life desires to be focused on Jesus, "to live no longer for oneself but for him who died and was raised to life for them"(2 Cor. 5:15). Truly, Louise possessed a keen awareness of the infinite love of Jesus and a deep realization that as her model and way to the Father, he was the center of her heart and love. This fact is epitomized in the motto she chose for herself and her Company: "The love of Jesus crucified urges us." Interestingly the scriptural reference for this motto links the love of Jesus with his sufferings and death and also the Christian's call to live for him.

> The love of Christ urges us on, because we are convinced that one has died for all; therefore all have died. And he died for all, so that those who live might live no longer for themselves, but for him who died and was raised for them (2 Cor. 5:14-15).

Similarly, the seal of the Company, a heart encompassed by flames with a crucifix superimposed is a pictorial representation of this theme. Here Louise chose the two most significant symbols of Jesus' love for his people: the heart on fire with love and the crucifix. Both symbols are central to Christian spirituality as they point to the deeper reality of God's limitless love for humankind in having his only Son live, die and rise to reconcile the divine-human relationship.

Imitation of the Specific Qualities of the Suffering Jesus

In her call to follow the suffering Jesus, Louise endeavored to imitate two specific qualities of Jesus — his desire to do the will of God and his trusting abandonment to the providence of God. These particular characteristics were the hallmarks, not only of Louise's attitude towards suffering, but also of her entire spirituality.[19]

Louise's Desire to do the Will of God and to Trust in Providence

Throughout Louise's life the desire to do the will of God and to trust in providence was the fundamental impetus of her existence.

In her fidelity to this desire, Louise found her life unfolding in ways that she least expected. The providence of God often works in mysterious ways and for Louise it was through the "crosses"[20] in her life and her gradual growth through them that the Lord led her to a deeper union with him and to her total dedication to the poor.

From her earliest years, Louise desired to follow the call which she believed the Lord had given her to religious life. In her wish to enter the Franciscan Daughters of the Passion, Louise was deeply disappointed by the provincial's rejection of her on the basis of her delicate health.[21]

In keeping with the advice of her relatives, Louise accepted following God's will elsewhere and for several years found peace and happiness in her marriage. However, the cross pressed heavily upon her and her family through financial stress, sickness and death until eventually, overcome by exterior and interior trials, Louise questioned not only her fidelity to God's will but also her state in life. She was tempted to leave her husband in order to fulfil what she thought was an earlier commitment to God. In the depths of her darkness of spirit, Louise was reassured by the grace of a spiritual light from God that confirmed her in her married life and presented to her a mysterious but hopeful picture for the future.[22]

Compassionately devoted to caring for her ill husband, Louise poured out her love, her time and her energy in nursing him for nearly three years and in assisting him in his final journey. In deep faith they shared this most special of experiences. Louise recounted that she was alone with Antoine to help him on this final passage. In his last illness and agony, Louise believed that God wanted Antoine to share in the imitation of the death of Jesus because he suffered in all his body, lost his blood and was almost always meditating on the passion of Christ.[23] When he could no longer pray himself, Antoine begged Louise to intercede for him.[24] She wrote to Antoine's cousin that this would forever be imprinted upon her heart.[25] One might say that this was a "sacrament of the moment," a graced remembering for Louise which would remain with her for life.

As Mary at the foot of the cross beheld her Son pour forth his blood and give up his spirit in obedience to the Father's will (Jn. 19:25-27), so too, Louise at the bedside of her husband beheld him pour forth his blood and give up his spirit to God in death.[26] Being the woman of faith that she was, Louise must have united herself to Mary at the foot of the cross and experienced in some measure the pain of the Mother of Sorrows. Undoubtedly this would enkindle another facet of Louise's ardent devotion to Mary as the Mother of Compassion.[27] Like Mary, Louise knew that to love was to suffer. The two were inseparable.

In her bereavement Louise experienced the loss of one she loved but she "did not mourn as those who have no hope" (1Th. 4:13). Seeking the will of God and trusting in providence, Louise, with the help of Vincent de Paul, began to reconstruct and re-direct her life. She endeavored to continue her works of charity with the poor and to deepen her prayer life. Obedient to the inspiration of God, Louise, who was initially unattracted to Vincent de Paul, submitted herself totally to his direction. Vincent, who encouraged and directed her, recognized her abilities and soon drew on her expert qualities of organization, public relations, and generosity to assist in the country Charities. Through this relationship God led both of them to accomplish exceptional deeds for the poor of Paris and beyond. The providence of God had brought them together and they in turn would be "providence" for others. Now as then, the mysteries of the providence of God unfold with the co-operation of God's creatures.[28]

From 1626-1634, Louise's writings manifested her great desire to do the will of God and to trust in God's providence. The sufferings of these years were marked by her economic insecurity, her grave concern for her son Michel, family problems and her frail health. In many ways, Vincent de Paul became a father figure for Michel and also became the faithful friend and greatest support for Louise.[29] Vincent's all-consuming desire to follow the will of God and to trust in providence was always shared with Louise and undoubtedly this united their hearts to God and to one another.[30] Hence it is not surprising that in fidelity to the will of God and in utter trust in God's providence, Louise and Vincent won many hearts and souls for the kingdom and service of God.[31]

The theme of desiring to do the will of God and of trusting in providence echoed in Louise's writings throughout the years. In these first years of her association with Vincent de Paul and the works of Charity, the following text written c. 1626 represented this motif:

> Promising never again to offend God by any of my being and to abandon myself entirely to the designs of divine providence and to the accomplishment of his will in me, I sacrifice and dedicate myself to God and to the fulfillment of his holy will which I choose as my supreme consolation.[32]

It is significant that in these earliest years of her association with Vincent de Paul, Louise had already realized that her "supreme consolation" was rooted in the accomplishment of the will of God. At the age of 35 she seemed to have interiorized the words of Jesus: "Anyone who does the will of my Father in heaven is my brother and sister and mother" (Mt. 12:50). Louise had passed through her spiritual darkness of purgation and had come, through her primary Pentecost event, to a spiritual light and deeper union. In this contemplative union with Jesus and abandonment to divine providence she found her true peace and joy.[33]

Throughout the years 1634-1650, Louise, encouraged by Vincent, labored indefatigably to nourish the seeds of the young congregation of women that God had sent to them. Vincent was involved in their formation through his spiritual conferences and in the administration of the community in conjunction with Louise. However, to Louise fell the main responsibility for the daily training of the Sisters and the organization of their works. She nurtured them spiritually through her instruction and example and she educated them in the skills of serving the sick poor and teaching the young. Always seeking and obedient to the will of God, Louise continued her own growth toward union and identification with Christ and in so doing guided her Daughters along a similar path, inculcating in them the virtues of true followers of Christ.[34] In all of their undertakings and decisions the Daughters were counselled to seek the will of God and to find it in a special way in obedience to their legitimate authority, be it the Sister Servant, the Medical Doctors or their Pastors. In imitation of Jesus, "their food was to do the will of the one who sent them and to complete his work" (Jn. 4:35).[35] During these years, Louise was not without suffering. Her physical ailments were inevitably with her; anxiety over her son was ever present and community crosses were always close by.[36] In all of her adversities and trials, whether personal or communal, Louise went to the foot of the cross which was *her cloister*.[37] Here she sought the will of God and trusted in providence for direction in finding resolutions to the difficulties.[38] This way of life and prayer, Louise also taught her Sisters. She frequently wrote advising them to take their troubles to the foot of the cross and there to be united with Jesus while seeking the answers to their problems. In 1648, Louise wrote the following advice to Sr. Jeanne Lepintre:

> It is much better to love one's distress when one experiences it, and carry it to the foot of the cross, or to let the Sister Servant know of it than to look for a way to be rid of it that could cost so dearly. I beg Our Lord to teach you this truth, and I am in his most holy love. . .[39]

Always this union with Jesus on the cross was to be with an attitude of submission to God's will and trusting in his loving providence. The following excerpt from a letter of Louise to the Sisters exemplified this:

> I leave you so that you may conform yourselves entirely to the most holy will of God by the pact that we all made together never to complain about the guidance of divine providence, but to abandon ourselves entirely to it.[40]

Louise knew that abandonment to divine providence required a great leap in faith and that such a surrender was possible only when one perceived God as one who loves, journeys with and cares for his people. In emphasizing the tremendous love of God, Louise encouraged her Daughters to place their ultimate trust in God and to abandon themselves to him. Louise had learned to trust God especially in her crosses. She had come to know in her heart the meaning of the words of Paul: "The life I now live in the flesh I live by faith in the Son of God, who loved me and gave himself for me" (Gal. 2:20).

In a letter of 1649, regarding Michel's marriage, Louise spoke very clearly about the cross of her poverty and its painful effects:

> I would like to say that the whole thing is a great affliction for me, but as a Christian I must embrace the scorn which normally accompanies poverty which is the only reason why our cause is not being advanced.[41]

For a proud Marillac, such a decline in social status could be cushioned only by regarding it in light of Christian principles. The splinters of the cross were ever present for Louise.

Discussing this same situation with Vincent de Paul, Louise said: "If we were not being led in this matter by divine providence, I would be most apprehensive."[42] Again Louise faced her trials in the spirit of trusting in providence.

In 1650 after many years of worry about her son Michel, Louise finally was able to come to peace when he married and settled down. Many years prior she had, on the advice of Vincent, abandoned Michel to God's care in order to overcome her own overprotectiveness and anxiousness about him.[43] Yet, perhaps one of her greatest and longest struggles was the inability to let go of Michel and her concern for him. Her ties of motherhood were strong and her desire for his well-being, both spiritual and temporal, was ever present.[44] This, of course, was not without reason as Michel's youth and early adult life were marked by great instability and discord. Hence Louise was not exempt from the trials of parent-child conflicts and these caused her immense suffering. When this primary worry was laid to rest with Michel's marriage in 1650 a deeper sense of peace was hers.

From 1650—1660 Louise entered the final decade of her life. These years continued to be marked with great physical suffering and community difficulties; yet, as Louise's physical strength persistently declined, her interior strength and abandonment to providence increased.[45] Ever seeking the will of God in her life and trusting herself to his loving providence, Louise continued to be a light to her Daughters as she consoled and counselled them through her letters and prayers. In these final years the gems of her spiritual counsels and insights regarding the value of suffering in light of the sufferings of Jesus were evident in her letters, particularly in those to her Sisters of which the following are excerpts:

A letter of 1653 read:

> I beg her most earnestly to do the same, to give herself to God for the accomplishment of his most holy will, and to see her suffering in the light of this admirable will and the guidance of divine providence.[46]

And also a letter of 1658 containing a gem of wisdom read thus:

> We must love the good pleasure of God in all the events directed by his providence. It is true that you are in great difficulties and suffering. If I were not convinced that the Spirit of God would provide you with the assistance and guidance you need, I would be very much afraid that this work would not succeed. Let us, from this very moment, my dear Sisters, be submissive to God to accept whatever it pleases his goodness to allow to happen. . . .Do the little you can very peacefully and calmly so as to allow room for the guidance of God in your lives. Do not worry about the rest.[47]

This same idea was reiterated three months before her death when Louise wrote:

If you completely entrust everything to the guidance of divine providence and love the most holy will of God, this will contribute greatly to your peace of mind and heart. In fact, this is one of the most essential practices I know of for growth in holiness.[48]

These citations represent the lessons Louise learned through a lifetime of ongoing development in holiness and wholeness. She knew what it was to grow through and beyond her natural tendencies to hastiness, to anxiety and to seriousness. As friend and guide, St. Vincent had frequently exhorted St. Louise to be joyful and to "honor Our Lord's cheerfulness of heart."[49] Thus the joy and peace of spirit that Louise manifested here were the fruits of her lifelong journey in the way of the cross, the will of God and trust in providence.[50] In light of Louise's writings on providence, it is interesting to catch the similarity of tone with that of the loving Father speaking to Catherine of Siena:

> Do you know, dearest daughter, how I provide for these servants of mine who put their trust in me? In two ways, for all my providence for my rational creatures is for both soul and body. And whatever I do to provide for the body is done for the good of the soul, to make her grow in the light of faith, to make her trust in me and give up trusting in herself, and to make her see and know that I am who I am and I can and will and know how to assist her in her need and save her.[51]

Surely in her years of schooling with the Dominican nuns in Poissy, Louise would have been exposed to Catherine of Siena's spiritual theology. Perhaps the seeds of Louise's trust in providence were sown then, later nourished through Vincent's gentle guidance and brought to fruition through her own openness to the Spirit of God working within her heart and her life.

In March of 1660, with Jesus as her model, Louise faced the last days of her life and her impending death.[52] She bade farewell to her family members and to her Daughters. To Michel, his wife and daughter she gave her final parental blessing and to her spiritual Daughters she gave her farewell counsel "to have great care for the poor, to live in harmony and to take the Blessed Virgin as their only Mother."[53]

Continually surrendering to the will of God and trusting in his providence, Louise had to relinquish the one earthly consolation she requested: that of a visit or a letter from Vincent. All that was forthcoming was a message through another priest: "You go ahead, and I hope to see you soon in heaven."[54] Thus Louise had been stripped physically of her strength, emotionally of her greatest earthly support, and spiritually of his consolation. All was taken. As in life, so in death she would surrender in obedience to the will of the Father. She would lay down her life in humble, grateful submission, trusting in providence that God would raise her up on the last day. Then, she would be reunited to all those she loved.

Knowing that her hour was near, Louise wished solitude with Jesus and had the curtains drawn, assuring her Sisters that she would let them know when the time had come, which she did.[55] In her last agony she suffered excruciating pain, some of which was the result of the three incisions made into the gangrous tumor under her left arm.[56] At one point while agitated by a violent fever she said: "Take me away from here." The attending priest whom Vincent had sent held up a crucifix before her showing her that Jesus had not asked to leave the cross. She responded: "Oh! no, he remained there;" then added: "Let us go, since my Lord has come for me."[57] And so it was, on March 15, 1660, Louise, like Jesus on the cross, surrounded by a devoted friend and companions and having entrusted her followers to his Mother Mary, could say: "Father, into thy hands I commit my spirit" (Lk. 22:46).[58] How fitting that she should die on the Monday of Passion Week.[59] She, who in her life's sufferings, had tried to emulate the spirit of Jesus in his sufferings and who had such devotion to the Church's liturgical feasts was given the gift of entering eternal life during the season of his Passion. With Paul, Louise could say: "We believe that Jesus died and rose again, and that it will be the same for those who have died in Jesus: God will bring them with him" (1 Th. 4:14). Throughout her life, the passion and cross of Jesus was Louise's strong hope. Her Friday and Lenten devotions to the death of Jesus, she completed with the words, "Hail O Cross, our only hope."[60] In keeping with this deep devotion,

Louise requested that the marker for her grave be a wooden cross bearing the words, "Spes Unica."[61]

". . .Unless a grain of wheat falls into the earth and dies, it remains just a single grain; but if it dies, it bears much fruit" (Jn. 12:24). Often and in many ways Louise died while she lived; but now, in her final death to earth and her birth to heaven, the "fruits of love" of which Vincent had spoken blossomed.[62] For a period after her death the aroma of violets and irises came from her tomb and was noted by those who visited. The Sisters who went there to pray frequently carried this beautiful scent on their clothes to the infirmary Sisters and their other patients.[63] Thus even after death Louise consoled others.

The fruits of her labors, as exemplified in the training of her Sisters, spread far beyond the borders of France. The social services which she implemented brought solace, care and dignity to countless numbers of the poor. Yet, as she had desired in life to remain hidden, likewise she remained so after death. It was not until this present century, that final ecclesial recognition was given either to Louise's great works of mercy or to her heroic Christian virtue.[64] There may be various reasons for this, but the fact remains, that for nearly three hundred years the greatness of this valiant, little woman remained in the shadows. During that time however, her spirit lived on in her inspiration of thousands of her Daughters of Charity.[65] Today, the challenge is to retrieve the legacy of Louise de Marillac for contemporary Christians; to re-discover her secret to "finding life in the dying" and "compassion in the suffering."[66]

The journey of her spirit and life, as that of all saints, must speak to Christians of the comforting challenge of living in God's will and the confident hope of trusting in God's providence. For Louise de Marillac this was one of the essential means for growth in holiness to which all Christians are called. The cross of Christ which for many has been and is "a stumbling block" and "foolishness" (1 Cor. 1:23), was for Louise her hope and strength. Her life epitomized the message of the *Imitation:* "If you join him in suffering, you will join him in glory."[67]

Truly, with the grace of God and the intercession of Mary, Louise succeeded in living out her "Devotion to the Will of God" and her "Abandonment to Divine Providence" which she expressed in the following words:

> I must practice great humility and mistrust of myself; abandon myself continuously to the Providence of God; imitate insofar as I am able, the life of Our Lord who came on earth to accomplish the holy will of God his Father; assist my neighbor to the best of my ability both corporally and spiritually for the love which God has for all of us equally; carry out my spiritual exercises carefully.[68]

In these words lay Louise's secret to sanctity. May all contemporary Christians discover in her faith, vision and prophetic witness to the gospel of Jesus an authentic model for Christian holiness. May she who embraced and mirrored in her life the paschal mystery of Christ obtain for all the grace of saying with her and with Paul: "I have been crucified with Christ; and it is no longer I who live but it is Christ who lives in me" (Gal. 2:20).

Concluding Remarks

The author of the *Imitation*, ends the chapter "Of the Royal Road of the Holy Cross" with these words:

> If there had been anything better, anything more suited or more useful to our salvation than suffering, Christ surely would have pointed it out to us by his word and example. For the disciples who followed him and for all those who wish to follow him, he clearly urges carrying the cross, saying: "If anyone would come after me, let him deny himself and take up his cross and follow me." So, let all your

reading and studying end on this note: to enter the kingdom of God, we must endure many hardships.

Here End Suggestions Drawing One toward the Inner Life.[69]

Truly, Louise who had no doubt meditated frequently on this Chapter, had made her own this message of the gospel and the spiritual writer A Kempis. Within her life, the words of this Chapter on the "Royal Road of the Cross," "took flesh." She came to know in the core of her being: that "there is no other road to life and to true inner peace than the road of the holy cross and of our daily dying to ourselves;"[70] and that "No one feels in his heart what Christ felt in his Passion, except the person who suffers as he did."[71] Coupled with this, Louise also knew from her lived experience the truth of the following words of A Kempis:

It is not our strength but Christ's grace which can and does accomplish such great things in us. Christ's grace enables us to embrace warmly those things from which we naturally recoil. It is not in our nature to bear the cross, to love the cross, to discipline ourselves, to avoid seeking praise, to suffer insults willingly, to think humbly of ourselves, to appear humble to others, to endure adversity and loss, and not to seek prosperity as our first goal. If you take a look at yourself, you will see that you can do none of this alone, but if you confide in the Lord, he will give you heavenly strength and all that you have chosen to do will become easier. You will not even fear your enemy, the devil, if you are armed with faith and sealed with the cross of Christ.[72]

These excerpts from the *Imitation* capture the specific qualities of Louise's spiritual journey through which she grew to the deep interiorization of the knowledge of the "privilege of the cross,"[73] of the desire to conform herself to God's will and of the absolute need for her confidence in God's providence. These three streams of grace watered the spiritual landscape of the life of Louise de Marillac.

Notes

1. SWLM, p. 701. A.21-THOUGHTS ON THE PASSION OF OUR LORD.

2. SWLM, p. 701. A.21. Thérèse of Lisieux makes a similar reference in her autobiography when she describes her response to a picture of Our Lord on the cross: "The cry of Jesus on the cross — 'I am thirsty' — rang continually in my heart and set me burning with a new, intense longing" (Beevers, p. 63).

3. Thomas A Kempis, *Imitation of Christ,* William C. Creasy (Notre Dame, In.: Ave Maria Press, 1989), p. 90, Bk.3, Ch.5. Hereinafter cited as "Imitation."

Sheedy in *Untrodden Paths* (p. 8), states that Louise "acquired an intimate knowledge of the *Imitation of Christ,* which he (her Uncle Michel) was translating about this time (prior to her marriage)."

4. SWLM, p. 701. A.21-THOUGHTS ON THE PASSION OF OUR LORD.

5. CCC, #2719.

6. SWLM, p. 828. A.27.

7. Frequently in *The Dialogue* of Catherine of Siena one reads of the importance of coming to the cross of the crucified Christ. The cross of Jesus is described as a table (p. 140) and Catherine is told: "Find your delight with him on the cross by feeding on souls for the glory and praise of my name" Susanne Noffke, O.P., *Catherine of Siena: The Dialogue* (New York: Paulist Press, 1980), p. 201.

The idea of dwelling in a personal cloister is also found in Catherine's writings. In a letter to her cousin in speaking of union with God's will, she wrote the Father's words: "Dearest children, if you want to discover and know the fruit of my will, dwell always in the cell of your soul" Catherine of Siena as cited by Mary O'Driscoll, O.P., in *Catherine of Siena: Passion for the Truth, Compassion for Humanity* (New York: New City Press, 1993), p. 24.

8. Frequently throughout her writings, Louise counselled her Sisters to go to the cross to seek refuge in times of trouble or sorrow. p.416. L.363.

9. SWLM, p. 828. A.27.

10. Ps. 45:10: "Hear, O daughter, consider and incline your ear; forget your people and your father's house, and the king will desire your beauty."

11. Louise had no doubt read, prayed and integrated into her life the words of the *Imitation of Christ,* Bk.4, Ch.8:
> So, if you wish to achieve a free spirit and gain my grace, everything you do must be preceded by a spontaneous offering of yourself into the hands of God. . . .If you wish to be my disciple, give yourself to me with your whole heart (Creasy, p. 177).

12. Louise's freedom to use "love language" is indicative of her intimate, affective life of union with God. Martinez indicates that Louise had experienced "mystical prayer" before her Vincentian influence ("The Prayer of St. Louise," *Echoes,* March 1983, p. 127). Certainly Louise spoke of her

Communion experience of February 5, 1630 as a spousal union with God. The use of "love language" in her writings also situate her within the stream of the French School of Spirituality.

13. SWLM, p. 251. L.88.

14. SWLM, p. 535. L.393.

15. Louise understood the "mind-body connection," leaving to providence the healing of the soul/spirit but taking responsibility to do what was in one's scope for the body.

16. Robert Maloney in his article, "The Cross in Vincentian Spirituality," *Vincentiana XXXVII(1-2,1993),* pp. 25-47 states that Vincent and Louise "recognized that not every 'cross' should be carried, since sometimes the sufferings involved could be remedied."

17. Calvet (p. 14) writes thus of Louise's call to suffer: "But in her youth, and for long after, she was bowed down by a weight of a mysterious dispensation of providence."

18. SWLM, p. 786. A.23. This passage presents a definite allusion to Paul's Letter to the Romans, 6:3: "You cannot have forgotten that all of us, when we were baptized into Christ Jesus, were baptized into his death. So by our baptism into his death we were buried with him, so that as Christ was raised from the dead by the Father's glorious power, we too should begin living a new life."

19. Although a study could be done on each of these characteristics individually, for the present they will be addressed together as they so frequently appear in Louise's writings.

20. Robert Maloney, in the draft of the article, "The Cross in Vincentian Spirituality," speaks of "a metaphorical use of the word 'cross', referring to the sufferings that the followers of Jesus experience" (p. 4).

21. Is it only coincidence that the Order Louise desired to enter was called the "Daughters of the Passion" and that later Vincent would address her as a "Daughter of the Cross"? Leonard, *Conferences,* I, 333. L.234.

22. SWLM, p. 1. A.2. In her spiritual "Lumière," Louise received confirmation of her marriage, the knowledge that in the future she would vow poverty, chastity and obedience, would be in a small community and would serve her neighbors by going to and fro among them.

23. Gobillon (Fiat), I, 19: "I think that in this last illness, God wanted him to share in the imitation of the pains of his death, because he suffered in his whole body, entirely lost his blood, and his mind was almost always occupied in meditation on the Passion." Cf. Gobillon (Collet Edition,1862), p. 30.

24. Gobillon (Fiat), I, 19: "Pray to God for me, I am no longer able.:" Letter of Louise to Antoine's cousin Père Hilarion Rebours, Chartreux. Cf. Gobillon (Collet), p. 31.
Sheedy states: "Antoine Le Gras owes his happiness, after God, to his saintly wife. He was the first to ask and benefit by her intercession" (p. 20).

25. Gobillon (Fiat), I, 19: "words which will be forever engraved on my heart." The sorrowing heart of a loving wife must have been pierced by these final words which became like a seal on her heart. That Louise was faithful to Antoine's plea was confirmed on her deathbed when she requested her son Michel to pray always for his father.

26. Gobillon (Fiat), I, 19: "Blood poured abundantly from his mouth seven times, and the seventh took his life in an instant." Cf. Gobillon (Collet), p. 30.

27. Sheedy speaks of Louise's devotion to Our Lady thus: "A lonely girl of fifteen, with a marked attraction for silent prayer, a great devotion to the Passion and the Sorrows of Our Lady — as Louise had — could be expected to turn her thoughts in the direction of the new community (Daughters of the Passion- Capuchin nuns)" (p. 5).

28. *CCC*, #306:
God is the sovereign master of his plan. But to carry it out he also makes use of his creatures' cooperation. This use is not a sign of weakness, but rather a token of almighty God's greatness and goodness. For God grants his creatures not only their existence, but also the dignity of acting on their own, of being causes and principles for each other, and thus of cooperating in the accomplishment of his plan.

29. V. de P.,I, 67. L.40, February 19,1630:
As for your son, I shall see him, but put your mind at rest. . . . But what shall we say about this excessive affection? I certainly think, Mademoiselle, that you have to try before God to rid yourself of it. All it does is weigh upon your spirit and deprive you of the peace Our Lord wishes in your heart and the detachment from love of everything that is not himself. Do so, therefore, I beg you, and you will give honor to God Who is responsible for the sovereign and absolute care of your son. . .

30. V. de P.,I, 172. L.119. Vincent wrote the following to Louise before 1634:
Thank you for the book (you) sent me and please take care of your health. It is no longer yours since you destined it for God. And my heart is no longer my heart, but yours, in that of Our Lord, Whom I desire to be the object of our one love. Please remember to offer to God a matter that affects us.

31. Vincent frequently counselled others that "grace had its moments and one should not run ahead of providence." Early in their relationship (c.1629), Vincent exclaimed to Louise: "Mon Dieu, my daughter, what great hidden treasures there are in holy providence and how marvelously Our Lord is honored by those who follow it and do not try to get ahead of it!" V. de P., I, 59.

32. SWLM, p. 692. A.3-ACT OF CONSECRATION.

33. In a letter of 1634, Vincent wrote to Louise: "Our Lord is a continual Communion for those who are united to what he wills and does not will" (V. de P.,I, 233. L.161).
This idea is echoed in *CCC*, #2712: ". . .Contemplative prayer is the poor and humble surrender to the loving will of the Father in ever deeper

union with his beloved Son"; and in *CCC*, #2713: "Contemplative prayer is a *communion* in which the Holy Trinity conforms man, the image of God, `to his likeness.'"

34. The main virtues which constituted the spirit of the Daughters of Charity were: humility, simplicity and charity (SWLM, pp. 406, 532, 668).

35. SWLM, p. 662. L.643: "Remember always, my dear Sisters, that it is the most holy will of God which put you where you are, and that it is for the accomplishment of his will that you must work there as would an ambassador for a King." Cf. p. 772. A.85.

36. SWLM, p. 195. L.166, c. April 1647: "However, I had not yet recovered from my illness of this past winter when I suffered a relapse which was more dangerous still, and I am just beginning to recover from it."

p. 224. L.190, August 1647: "My poor health continues."

p. 134. L.109, To Vincent, 1645: "Please do me the kindness of sending someone from your house to find out what he (Michel) did and whether he said anything, without revealing my apprehensions or the dispositions of which he informed you. It would be a great comfort to me to learn something."

p. 288. L.433, May,1649: "I expect much from the establishment at Nantes since persecutions are one of the signs of the value of a work. . ." Cf. p. 287. L. 247.

37. SWLM, p. 828. A.27.

38. Vincent frequently counselled Louise not to let her crosses overtake her, but "to be happy at the foot of the cross. . .and to fear nothing" (V. de P., I, 155. L.103).

39. SWLM, p. 269. L.271. Sister Servant is the term used for the Superior. Regarding this passage, R. Maloney states that there are times when crosses "should be borne with courage since to lay them aside would cause greater pain for others" ("The Cross, Yesterday and Today," *Review for Religious*, Vol.53, No.4, July-August, 1994, p. 550).

Louise's counsel seems to offer a wisdom regarding integrating pain and distress rather than denying it or focussing on ridding oneself of it.

40. SWLM, p. 153. L.144. How this passage echoes the words of the *Imitation* : "I want you to learn to abandon yourself perfectly to my will, without grumbling or complaining" (Bk. 3, Ch. 56, p. 155).

41. SWLM, p. 308. L.274.

42. SWLM, p. 309. L.267.

43. V. de P., I, 34. L.22, January 17, 1628; p. 37. L.24, February 1628.

L.22: "Leave him alone then, and surrender him completely to what Our Lord wills or does not will. It rests with him alone to direct these tender souls."

L.24: "However, I am telling your heart in advance that I praise God because it has freed itself from the excessive attachment it had to the little one (Michel) and because you have made it correspond to reason."

44. V. de P., I, 108. L.69, To Saint Louise, May 1631:

Regarding little Michel, is that not another temptation for you to get upset because of anxiety over your obligation to take care of him? Oh! Our Lord most certainly did well not to choose you for his Mother, since you do not think you can discern the will of God in the maternal care he demands of you for your son.

45. The *Imitation* cites this truth thus: "At the same time that he bends under the weight of his cross, his burden is changed into divine comfort, for he knows that God will reward him for his efforts. And the more a person's body is weakened by affliction, the more his spirit is strengthened by inner grace" (Bk. 2, Ch. 12, p. 80).

46. SWLM, p. 424. L.338.

47. SWLM, p. 614. L.519.

48. SWLM, p. 662. L.643, December 23, 1659.

49. V. de P., I, 162. L.109. Cf. p.146. L.97; p.147. L.98.

50. The will of God was of paramount importance to Louise. It was a recurrent theme throughout her life and she directly mentioned it approximately 59 times in her letters. In many of her letters, the will of God, the cross and providence are united as one theme. Louise endeavored to see all things in her life in the light of the will of God and of God's loving providence. To both she abandoned herself.

51. Noffke, *The Dialogue*, p. 293. D.142.

52. *Documents*, p. 917. Doc. 800.

In a letter of June 1660, Sister Barbe Bailly recounted for the Sisters the last illness of Louise which lasted for six weeks. Barbe who assisted her related that Louise suffered great pain with great patience and resignation to the will of God.

53. Gobillon (Fiat), I, 154. Cf. *Documents*, p. 917; SWLM, p.835; Gobillon (Collet), pp. 167, 169.

54. Gobillon (Fiat), I, 158. Cf. Gobillon (Collet), p. 171.

Dirvin presents an interesting commentary on this scene speaking of "Vincent's physical inability to come, his possible fear of trusting his emotions to paper and the unspoken volumes contained in the spoken message" (p. 388).

This may very well be accurate in light of an earlier letter of Vincent to Louise when she was ill in 1636. He wrote:

I earnestly beg him to let you feel the joy in my heart with as much tenderness as I experienced because of your letter. Certainly, it is not that any thought came to me that Our Lord intended to dispose of you with this blow, because I could not have seen you in that state and not run to you, whatever might be the condition in which a slight tertian ague has placed me. May God be praised once again! I could not say that to you enough, or tenderly enough, to my liking (V de P, I, 356. L.253a).

Dirvin continues: "Louise accepted the message with complete tranquillity: no one has recorded that the least shadow of regret crossed her face" (p. 388).

55. A palliative care worker described this action of Louise as "the wisdom of dying." She also noted Vincent's final message as "his loving granting her permission to die."

56. Elisabeth Charpy, noted author on Louise, indicated, in a personal interview, that Louise likely suffered from breast cancer. In the museum at the Motherhouse at rue du Bac there is on display a chemise of Louise which has a large triangular insert under the left arm. (Interview with Elisabeth Charpy, rue du Bac, Paris, April 24, 1993.)

57. Gobillon (Fiat), I, 158.

These words of Louise have echoes of Jesus' cry in Gethsemane: "Abba, Father, for you everything is possible. Take this cup away from me. But let it be as you, not I, would have it" (Mk.14:36).

58. Louise's devoted companion was the Duchesse de Ventadour; her companions and followers were her Daughters.

59. Gobillon (Fiat), I, 160.

60. Gobillon (Fiat), I, 70.

CCC, #617 cites the following: "The Council of Trent emphasizes the unique character of Christ's sacrifice as "the source of eternal salvation: and teaches that this most holy Passion on the wood of the cross merited justification for us. And the Church venerates his cross as its sings: "Hail, O Cross, our only hope."

61. A replica of that cross still stands today in Louise's parish Church of St. Laurent in Paris to mark the spot of her first burial site.

62. V. de P., I, p. 46. L.27: "May you be forever a beautiful tree of life bringing forth fruits of love, and I, in that same love, your servant."

63. Gobillon (Fiat), I, 163.

Dirvin, p. 390:

...a mist was frequently seen to rise from the tomb, accompanied by the delicate but unmistakable odor of violets and irises. . . . The most touching and beautiful aspect of it was that the fragrance clung to the Sisters' clothes and was carried into the confraternity halls and the hospital wards where the patients inhaled it with joy.

Spiritual authors identify this as an extraordinary phenomena called *sweet odor* in which the body or tomb of a saint emits a sweet odor. Pope Benedict XIV declared that any sweet perfume that proceeds from a dead body would have to be produced by supernatural powers and classified as miraculous (Aumann, p. 438).

64. Louise de Marillac was canonized a saint in 1934 and in 1960 was named *Universal Patroness of all devoted to Christian Social Works.*

65. Sr. Margaret Flinton, D.C., noted author on Louise's Social Work, says: "The current cult to Louise began to sprout in the 1950's and blossomed in

the 70' and 80's, particularly through an awakening of the Daughters of Charity" (Related in a personal conversation at Emmitsburg, July 1994).

66. In so many ways Louise exemplified the words of Paul:

We are afflicted in every way, but not crushed; perplexed but not driven to despair; persecuted, but not forsaken; struck down, but not destroyed; always carrying in the body the death of Jesus, so that the life of Jesus may also be made visible in our bodies (2 Cor. 4:8-10).

67. *Imitation* (Bk. 2, Ch. 12, p. 78): "Of the Royal Road of the Holy Cross."

68. SWLM, p. 784. M.40B-ABANDONMENT TO DIVINE PROVIDENCE.

69. *Imitation*, Bk. 2, Ch. 12, p. 81.

70. *Imitation*, Bk. 2, Ch. 12, p. 78.

71. *Imitation*, Bk. 2, Ch. 12, p. 79.

72. *Imitation*, Bk. 2, Ch. 12, p. 80.

73. SWLM, p. 775. A.20-THOUGHTS ON THE CROSS. Cf. p. 535. L.393.

Louise De Marillac—Her Legacy to Contemporary Spirituality

Introduction

In 1991, Pope John Paul II wrote the following words to the Daughters of Charity: "Welcome anew the grace he (the Lord) granted his Church in giving it Saint Louise! Draw from her actions and writings the nourishment you need for your journey!"[1]

These words of Pope John Paul II may very well be spoken to all Christians of our time. Each person is called to live one's Christian life in a particular time and in a particular way; and, amidst the common journey, each has an unique path to God. The legacy of some, though never forgotten in the annals of paradise, may fade somewhat with the passage of time. The legacy of others, like waves on the shore flow in and out of relevance; while still others remain constant beacons to those who seek their guidance on the way.

To this latter group, Louise de Marillac surely belongs. Her unique way to God has an universal legacy for all who wish to grow in an integrated Christian spirituality that is rooted in the depths of solitude with God and reaches to the heights of human solidarity with the suffering poor, whomever they may be. This Chapter will endeavor to illustrate that Louise de Marillac, schooled in suffering became a prophetic witness of Christian faith, hope and compassion in her day, and as such, remains a model, teacher and guide for contemporary Christians.

Louise De Marillac :
Christian Woman—Prophetic Witness

By baptism every Christian is called upon to be a prophetic witness to the values of Christ. In every age, God raises up men and women who live these values to such a degree that they become models and teachers for others. By her decree of "sanctity", the Church has officially recognized Louise de Marillac as a woman of this calibre: a model and teacher for others in the Christian faith.

Louise de Marillac: Woman of Hope—Witness of Hope

> We have this treasure in clay vessels, so that it may be made clear that this extraordinary power belongs to God and does not come from us (2 Cor. 4:7).

Louise de Marillac would have been the first to apply these words to herself as she knew her own fragility and frequently spoke of her own powerlessness. In deepest humility, any apparent good fruits of her work and those associated with her were attributed to God.[2]

By current sociological and psychological standards, Louise de Marillac probably would have been seen as an unlikely candidate for success in life because of the apparent odds against her. Yet, in this current era of radical feminism and social analysis, Louise shines through as a woman who experienced many kinds of personal alienation, but who through her deep Christian faith was raised to the heights of sanctity as well as being a major change agent amidst the unjust social structures of her day.

As has been seen in her life story, Louise definitely faced deep personal challenges with which many people of today might identify. Louise was born out of wedlock, recognized by her father but unaccepted by her relatives and stepmother. She was an orphan at 13 and hence thrust into greater personal responsibility. She was thwarted in the first dream for her life and thus followed a second choice which did bring happiness. However, this bliss was fairly short-lived and after nursing a terminally-ill spouse, Louise, widowed at 32, became a single parent. She knew the struggles of raising a somewhat "slowly-developing and fragile" teenage son with all the inherent ramifications. On a personal level she struggled with her own personality traits, her emotional difficulties, her frail health, her financial problems and her spiritual sufferings. In addition she carried broader family burdens resulting from deaths and executions. Was Louise caught in the circle of a seemingly recurring negative life pattern? Could anything positive come from such a combination of personal historical factors? Is there an echo of: "Can anything good come from Nazareth?" (Jn. 1:46) Given the material of raw clay that composed the spiritual, emotional, psychological and physical makeup of the woman Louise, God the Potter, with the pliability of this media could in time fashion an exquisite work of timeless human art. The finished object, Louise de Marillac is a testament to the powerful ongoing creativity of God within the life of one who desires to grow in love with and for God and who surrenders sufficiently to permit the Potter to mold and fashion one into God's image. Within the raw material lies the qualities, however hidden, to manifest certain aspects of the artist's genius.[3]

In and through her life's circumstances, Louise became a champion of the poor and a change agent of social strategies and structures even within the Church. Through her expert training of her Daughters of Charity, the major social ills of Louise's time were confronted in some positive manner which gave dignity to those involved: the sick poor, the elderly, the orphans, the galley slaves, the soldiers in the battle fields, and young homeless girls. Her skills in administration and organization, her expertise in teaching and nursing combined with her compassionate caring in these works led the Church to proclaim Louise "Patroness of all Those Devoted to Christian Social Works." It is reported that even Florence Nightengale went to Paris to study Louise's writings and works on healthcare.[4]

For a woman who seemed to have so many forces working against her, Louise de Marillac through her faith and trust in God while using her own talents in co-operation with God's grace, became an example of one who not only overcame the odds but surpassed the imagination. In this lies the witness of hope that Louise offers today.[5] In the words of scripture: "God working in us can do infinitely more than we can ask or imagine" (Eph. 3:20). Louise de Marillac is a testimony to the reality of these words. She is a sign of hope for all who struggle with apparent insurmountable odds. From her one learns that by surrendering to God, trusting in God's loving providence and co-operating with God's grace, somehow in the mystery of God's plan all will work for good.[6]

In and through the crucial circumstances of her daily life as child, youth, wife, mother, widow, and foundress, Louise grew to be a woman of deep hope who saw unfold before her eyes the reality of the words of the prophet Jeremiah:

> For surely I know the plans I have for you, says the Lord, plans for your welfare and not for harm, to give you a future with hope. Then when you call upon me and come and pray to me, I will hear you. When you search for me, you will find me; if you seek me with all your heart, I will let you find me, says the Lord. . . (Jer. 29:11-13).

Truly, Louise sought the Lord with all her heart and she found him. She found him not only in her prayer but also in his poor and suffering members to whom she in turn brought hope and love.

Louise de Marillac: Woman of Faith—Witness of Faith

In this you rejoice, though now for a little while you may have to suffer many trials, so that the genuineness of your faith, more precious than gold which though precious is tested by fire, may redound to praise and glory and honor at the revelation of Jesus Christ. (1 Peter 1:6-7)

That Louise was a woman of faith cannot be denied. That her faith was tested by the fire of her life's circumstances, and that it redounded to the praise and glory of God is indisputable. The mainstay in all of Louise's difficulties, whether interior or exterior, was her faith. Louise's strong desire to remain united to the will of God kept her steadfast in imploring the grace to do so. In her early adult life frequent uncertainty, depression and discouragement were hers; yet, even in the midst of her darkest doubts, she clung to God and was rewarded with the light of faith and special graces from the Spirit.[7] Louise knew only too well that in the present she "saw in a mirror dimly" ; but she trusted that one day "she would see face to face" (1 Cor. 13:12). It was Louise's deep faith that kept the fire of love burning in her heart and the light of love shining in her life.[8] A woman of the gospel, Louise sustained her faith life through prayer, the sacraments and a life of charity.

Prayer was the lifegiving source of Louise's faith. From her youth she spent time pondering God.[9] One of her earliest paintings depicts herself seated by a river painting, the subject of which was the name of Jesus, the one she loved.[10] Prayer, the relational link between herself and God, took many forms. Louise meditated on the gospels and entered into the life of Christ. Praying the Prayer of the Church and living in harmony with the liturgical feasts, Louise also developed her own special devotions to Jesus and Mary some of which she submitted to Vincent's approval. These devotions flowed from the springs of Louise's prayer life: the Trinity, Christ and the Blessed Virgin Mary.[11]

Louise's faith was deeply nourished by her contemplation of the Incarnation and the Annunciation of the Blessed Virgin Mary. In the words of Fr. Jean Gonthier, C.M.:

The Incarnation appeared to Louise as a work of love. In the radiance of this fundamental truth, . . . she perceived the love of which God gives proof in the creation of man, and, still more, in his intention of sending his Son in person to set man back again on the road to true happiness. . . .Louise de Marillac grasps particular aspects of the love of this God, such as "in some way, he can never be able, nor wish to be separated from man."[12]

Louise perceived the relationship of God and humankind: God invited Mary to take part in the Incarnation and her response initiated the unfolding of God's plan. Louise always seemed to be cognizant of the relational aspect of God with humanity and she exclaimed with emotion this great love of God and the empowerment of humanity through it:

O admirable love! In creation you made a man, who by his consent lost all human nature; and wishing to re-establish it by way of redemption, you desire the consent of Mary for the making of the Man-God, so as to enable a God to become man. O man, how your lowliness is exalted! O human weakness, how powerful you are! O God, your secrets are truly inscrutable! You could have no counsel other than yourself for the carrying out of so powerful a love![13]

Received in the sacrament of baptism, and nourished with the eucharist, the Bread of Life, Louise sacramentally cultivated the seed of her faith. Although the other sacraments were mentioned throughout Louise's writings, these two sacraments received the most attention as central to the regular sustenance and growth in the inner life. For Louise, the graces of baptism must be drawn upon and activated through the power of the Holy Spirit if the Christian were to be effective in the world.[14]

A contemplative woman who actualized her prayer in the compassionate service of her neighbor, Louise knew that "Faith without good works is dead" (Jas. 2:17).[15] Louise labored diligently and trusted in the providence of God to bring her efforts to fruition.[16] In the words of Paul, "she groaned inwardly" (Rom. 8:23) to bring to birth new life in the spirit.[17] From her personal experiences Louise knew that in general, the things of God, like those of nature, took time to grow and often that growth could be painful.

Louise's letters to her Sisters are replete with examples of her personal pain and her compassionate solidarity with the Sisters in their daily labors and in establishing new houses. In a letter of 1652 to Sr. Cecile Angiboust at Angers, Louise wrote:

> Your account of all the afflictions and losses that have occurred at Angers is a source of great sorrow to me because the poor will suffer as a result. I beg the divine goodness to comfort and assist them in their needs.

> My very dear Sisters,you have indeed suffered great trials. However, have you stopped to consider that it is only right that the servants of the poor should suffer with their masters?[18]

Only a woman of authentic faith could speak thus to her Sisters to encourage and challenge them on their road of faith-filled service. Louise's great faith was the font of her lively trust in providence. She had learned that "faith is the assurance of things not seen" (Hb. 11:1).[19] She knew also that like a sapling, faith must be tended and nurtured so that it might develop and mature in order to bring forth good fruit. Louise matured to become "a beautiful tree of life bringing forth fruits of love";[20] as such, she, the fragile, tiny woman, stands as a stalwart, giant witness to the power of God working in and through a faithful servant.

Louise de Marillac:
Woman of Love—Witness of Compassion

For a person of faith, the seeds of suffering generally yield fruits of compassion. Having travelled the way of the cross, one comes to a deeper understanding of and feeling for the sufferings of others and hence is usually better able to accompany them on their journey: to support, to encourage, to challenge and to be for them. Such companioning requires forgetfulness of self, openness to the Spirit, to others, and to risk. Such were the dispositions of Christ, the Suffering Servant, the Compassionate One. Such were the dispositions of Mary, the Mother of Sorrows, the Mother of Compassion. Such were the dispositions of faithful disciples throughout the ages; and such were the dispositions of Louise de Marillac. Pruned and purified through personal sufferings, Louise through her deep identification with the sufferings of Jesus interiorized his attitude toward suffering so that instead of the apparent cruelties of life paralyzing and embittering her, they became lessons in the lived reality of faith, hope and love which in turn empowered Louise to walk with others on their way of the cross in their daily lives.

Louise's compassionate love for others was evidenced throughout her life in her attitudes, her actions and her writings. Whether as the young teenage girl organizing the boarders to assist the poor woman of the pension, the young wife carrying food and comfort to the poor of her parish, the family comforter in times of tragedy, the faithful wife lovingly caring for a terminally-ill husband, the collaborator of Vincent de Paul concerned for his health and the works entrusted to him, or the foundress and mentor of the Daughters of Charity, Louise de Marillac owned and transcended her personal sufferings to faithfully serve others with compassion while trusting in providence.

The legacy of Louise's compassionate actions towards those in need are recorded in biographies and accounts of her social works. These witness to the outward manifestation of her loving heart in response to the call of God to serve the poor. Yet, another avenue to the compassionate heart of Louise is to share her own words and feelings expressed in her writings. Through these insights one walks with this servant of compassion; one feels the love that was at the core of her being; one enters the privileged place where God dwells within her.

Through her own words one hears the compassionate heart of a mother, a sister, a friend. The relationship of love and suffering that she shared with the Incarnate Jesus flowed through her as a balm of healing to the brokenness and pain of others.

Louise understood and had compassion for those who suffered physically. To Sr. Julienne she wrote: "I beg Sr. Françoise to show great charity to our poor sick Sister with whom I suffer. Spare nothing to alleviate her suffering."[21] Knowing the pain of illness, Louise also rejoiced in the gift of restored health as the following letter to Sr. Jeanne Lepintre indicates:

> I praise God with all my heart for having restored your health. I must tell you that I was so sorry for you, dear Sister, suffering as you were from such a long illness in addition to your other troubles.[22]

Mental anguish was not a stranger to Louise and hence she could be a compassionate counsellor as an ensuing letter to Jeanne attests:

> My dear Sister, your great trials and mental turmoil, in all this confusion, do not arise so much from the uncertainty of events, opposition and conflicting reports, as from the fact that you have no one reliable to comfort you and give you advice. But, please believe me, my dear Sister, if I were in your place, I would ask God to grant me a great spirit of indifference and the realization that it is not up to us to act in this situation; rather I would ask him to put us in the disposition to listen and to endure all that is said for or against us so that none of it troubles us.[23]

Not only was Louise sensitive to the feelings of others in their sufferings but also in recognition of the kindnesses they did for her. She was always aware of the graciousness of a grateful heart. To Sr. Charlotte and Françoise she wrote in June of 1650: "I am completely flabbergasted that I have gone so long without writing to you. I would never have thought it possible, if someone had not assured me that I had not thanked you for your beautiful lace."[24]

Louise was not content only to suffer with her Sisters; she also endeavored to alleviate the situation as this letter to L'Abbe de Vaux indicates:

> If she has returned to Nantes, she has found a letter from me in which I assured her that I was suffering because of the trial I felt she was undergoing. I beg you most humbly, Monsieur, in your charity, to let us know if we can do something to relieve her, as well as what you have learned about the entire situation in Nantes relative to our Sisters.[25]

In her correspondence with her Sisters, Louise exhibited an awareness and understanding of human nature and of the Sisters' daily life situations. Affirming and encouraging them in their ministry, she counselled them with common sense and a warm loving heart. Following the death of one of the Sisters whom Julienne Loret had nursed, Louise advised her:

> Now I beg you to slow down a bit and to look after your health. For this, I think that you need exercise. If we are to believe Sr. Philippe, she would willingly undertake anything without taking time out to be sick. This is why I beg you, my dear Sister, to take turns teaching school, looking after the house and nursing the sick in the villages.[26]

A letter to Sr. Jeanne Lepintre in 1652 shows Louise's understanding of a heart removed from home and reveals her realization of the relationship between a person's emotional and physical wellness. It illustrates also Louise's ease in expressing her own deep emotions of caring and her desire to be united with those she loves:

> I have great compassion for our dear Sister Louise. Please tell her that her mother and sisters are well. Try to determine

whether her illness may be caused by some displeasure in being separated from them. . . .I beg you to let all our Sisters know that they are always most dear to us and that I see them very often in spirit, although I do not write to them individually. When you write to me, please ask each of them whether they have anything to tell me, and let them know that they would please me greatly by writing to me.[27]

What compassion and comfort Sr. Barbe Angiboust must have experienced in receiving the following words from Louise!

My heart aches with yours because of all the suffering that has befallen you from all sides. God be praised for the strength he has given you to work where you now are and to have completed the work at Chalons! . . . I cannot tell you, my dear Sister, with what joy we will welcome you! I know that your poor body sorely needs this rest so that you may employ it elsewhere for the glory of God. . . .I urge you not to tell them all the difficulties you have had especially with our dear Sr. Jeanne whom I have asked to go to Montmirail. Part company, I beg you, gently and cordially. We joyously await your arrival.[28]

What simple, gentle and sincere expressions of heartfelt love, understanding and counsel! What Sister even today would not be heartened to receive such a welcome home at the end of an arduous assignment! Louise was truly a woman of compassionate understanding for all. The poor were always the recipients of the fruits of her loving heart; yet, for Louise, first among the poor were her own Sisters.

Vincent de Paul also received Louise's compassionate concern. Particularly in his illnesses, Louise was eager to share possible remedies. One such occasion is thus cited:

The state of suffering and submission to which it pleases Our Lord to subject you increases the boldness I always show in expressing my puny thoughts to you. The latest one that occurred to me to bring you some relief is to suggest that you bring both legs to a sweat by using M. l'Obligeois' steam bath. But do not do this without consulting two doctors. Tea may be taken between the early-morning bouillon and dinner. Experience has shown me that it must not be taken as a substitute for other food, but that it is an excellent way to prepare the stomach to take food.[29]

Louise's ongoing care is expressed in a final letter to Sr. Jeanne Delacroix, in which Louise requested prayers for Vincent's condition:

Redouble your prayers for our Most Honored Father. His legs are so painful that he cannot walk. Because they are so weak, he cannot even say holy Mass except on rare occasions.[30]

Louise's concern was also extended to those in dire straits, particularly women who might be tempted to accept unsavory offers to alleviate financial distress. In one such situation, Louise wrote to Vincent:

I do not recall ever having seen anyone more worthy of compassion than a young woman who went to see you on two successive days last week. . . .If the Ladies are willing to assist her, I will see to it that they are not deceived. Although I do not know her, I recommend her to you with all my heart for the love of God. . .[31]

Having suffered her own pain of emotional poverty through unacceptance in childhood and death of family members, physical poverty through chronic frail health, psychological poverty through bouts of anxiety and depression, plus economic poverty, Louise de Marillac had been duly prepared to comprehend the pain of others. Her comprehension, however, was not limited to an intellectual reality; rather, it manifested itself in an affective compassion which concretized itself in deeds of love.

The ways of providence are, of course, always mysterious. The way of the cross that Louise trod led to the path of passionate caring for the sick, the poor, the depressed and the oppressed. Louise's personal experiences and growth into the Passion of Christ fashioned her into a woman of great compassion; indeed, one could say she was transformed by the Passion into a model of Compassion. Totally Christ-centered, Louise became totally other-centered. As such she was a prophetic witness, announcing in word and deed the love of God. Louise proclaimed the love of Christ to her world and continues to proclaim it to ours. Her life and ministry of compassion is a challenge to all to behold the suffering and the poor as Christ's legacy and to respond to the gospel command: "Love one another as I have loved you" (Jn. 15:12).[32]

Louise de Marillac:
Christian Woman — Teacher and Guide

The statue of Louise de Marillac found in St. Peter's Basilica in Rome bears the caption: "Puellarum a caritate mater et magistra." Louise de Marillac may be "Mother and Teacher" not only to her own spiritual Daughters of Charity, but also to any Christian who desires to live a committed, prayerful life of service devoted to Christ and to neighbor. In Louise one may find a loving mother and an understanding teacher, an authentic model and guide in the Christian life.

Louise de Marillac: Woman of Prayer—Guide in the Interior Life

The witnesses who have preceded us into the kingdom, especially those whom the Church recognizes as saints, share in the living tradition of prayer by the example of their lives, the transmission of their writings, and their prayer today.[33]

The different schools of Christian spirituality share in the living tradition of prayer and are essential guides for the faithful. In their rich diversity they are refractions of the one pure light of the Holy Spirit.[34]

These words are true of Louise de Marillac. As a saint and as a representative of the French School of Spirituality, Louise shares a living tradition of prayer and serves as a guide for the faithful.[35] Louise's spirituality and prayer were characterized by the theological principles of the French School of Spirituality and the mystical quality of its leaders but nuanced by her own charism of an active, compassionate service to the poor combining a deep integration of the contemplative and active stance.[36]

Louise desired to be a devout Christian woman.[37] She wanted to be holy as every Christian is called to be, having no grandiose plans for herself but to do the will of God in her life. The journey of Louise's inner life is expressly the witness of her openness to the will of God, her attempts to discover and to follow it through prayer and direction and her struggles amidst daily life as youth, wife, mother, and foundress.

A cursory reading of Louise's prayer reflections may indicate no exceptional mystical phenomena but a closer examination reveals that God indeed guided her and gifted her with the deep love and union of mystical prayer.[38] For most Christians, major mystics such as John of the Cross, Teresa of Avila or Catherine of Siena may be restrictive models because of their state in life or extraordinary experiences. In Louise however, one finds a witness and model who, in a sense, bridges all states of life, performs ordinary duties, becomes involved in charitable works, and then, encouraged by Vincent de Paul and empowered by God becomes "one of the most active women in the history of the Church."[39] In her spiritual dynamism, Louise is a witness to the reality that "what I am unable to do on account of my powerlessness or other obstacles in me, God will do by his kindness and omnipotence."[40] The source and the summit of Louise's Christian life was her lifelong relationship with God, notably with the Incarnate Jesus. This affiliation Louise nurtured by her fidelity to prayer. She knew the secret of becoming "his" as she wrote:

> Willingly must I allow Jesus to take possession of my soul and reign there as King. Thus, I shall preserve the joy I experience in realizing that each of us individually may desire and, indeed, has the power to become his well-beloved.[41]

Prayer is one's unique relationship with God; yet, certain fundamental attitudes, practices and developmental features mark the phases of growth in prayer. In reflecting on the prayer life of Louise de Marillac, one finds not only inspiration and hope, but also one finds in her, a companion, friend and guide who shares light for the inner journey.[42]

In this brief study it is not feasible to illustrate in detail Louise's development through the purgative, illuminative and unitive ways of the spiritual life as described by John of the Cross,[43] nor her growth in prayer according to the nine grades of prayer as explained by Teresa of Avila.[44] Rather, this short sketch will present the three expressions of prayer as outlined by the *Catechism of the Catholic Church,* and will then show that Louise by faithfully practicing these forms of prayer and by being open to the Holy Spirit working in her, simultaneously grew through the three stages of the inner life to arrive at a deep union of love with God.[45]

In the Section on Prayer, the *Catechism* speaks of three major expressions of prayer which Christian Tradition has retained: vocal, meditative, and contemplative.[46] The article continues that "these forms of prayer have one basic trait in common: composure of heart." It further states that " Vigilance in keeping the Word and dwelling in the presence of God makes these three expressions intense times in the life of prayer."[47]

Vocal prayer which employs words audibly or silently with an attentive mind and a devoted will is an ongoing expression of prayer throughout life whether in a personal form or in a liturgical mode. The body and soul unite in vocal prayer to adore, thank, praise and make supplication to God. Vocal prayer is a form of mental prayer since for the words to be prayer, the mind and heart must be focused on them, on their meaning and on God to whom they are addressed. Through this interiorization, vocal prayer initiates one into meditative and contemplative prayer, into knowledge of God and knowledge of self.[48]

In meditation one seeks through reflection to deepen one's faith, to strengthen one's will to follow Christ and to respond to his graces with affections such as gratitude, sorrow or love. One uses the imagination, the memory, the emotions and the will to consider the topic of meditation, to apply it to one's life, to make acts of affection and to take practical resolutions.[49] In the prayer of meditation, the book of Scripture and the book of one's life intersect. Jesus comes to illumine and to challenge, to invite and to encourage one to grow deeper, to come to a more profound knowledge of him. This personal knowledge of God lies at the heart of contemplation.[50]

The journey of the inner life is embarked upon through fidelity to prayer. The person devoted to prayer, both vocal and meditative, eventually creates a sacred space within the heart where God can be entertained at any time. It is the cultivation of this friendship relationship with God that opens one to a deeper loving union with the Holy Spirit which expresses itself in contemplative prayer.

The prayer of contemplation is a natural progression for one who has faithfully persevered in vocal and meditative prayer. One begins to pass from a more thinking form of prayer to a prayer of greater affection.[51] Then, because of an increased desire for God or because of a dryness of the senses,[52] one is led into a more simplified prayer consisting of a "simple interior gaze"[53] of "loving attentiveness to God" which maintains the soul in peace.[54] This "prayer of simplicity"[55] which gathers together the faculties of the intellect and the affections[56] prepares one for deeper contemplative prayer wherein the Holy Spirit with the gifts of wisdom and understanding will act within the soul. Thus begins the transition to the phase of "infused or passive contemplation"[57] which is not within the power of the individual to attain but is total gift from God.[58] Within this phase of prayer are varying degrees of intensity of the effects of one's union with God.[59] The first stage of infused prayer is identified as the "prayer of quiet" in which the will is united with God and the soul, enjoying a "generalized loving knowledge of God", desires to be in silence and repose.[60] While the will is focused on God, the intellect and memory are free; hence, other subjects are not excluded from thought but are secondary. Distractions too are possible and hence effort is required to curtail them.[61] This prayer of quiet, prepares the soul for a deeper union with God in the "prayer of union."[62] Herein one enters more fully the mode of mystical prayer. The prayer of union unites the soul with God in such a way that the interior faculties of the will, intellect and imagination are focused directly on God and the soul experiences not only a presence of God but a possession of him.[63] This prayer exhibits an absence of distractions, minimal personal effort and a greater certainty of God's presence in the soul.[64] In the degree of conforming union, the soul, through the power of the Holy Spirit, is given a deeper intuitive knowledge and understanding of God in which it seems "to peer into the very essence of God and discover divine secrets."[65] The soul is absorbed in God and longs for full and perfect union with God which of course is only attainable in eternity. Thus those who experience this stage of union may even long for death to be with God.[66] The highest degree of contemplative prayer which is a prelude to the Beatific Vision is transforming union in which the soul is conscious of the communication of the divine life and is transformed through a union of mind and will with God. Thus the soul is divinized by a divine union, living almost in a permanent state of union with God.[67] In this state the soul experiences the Trinity with a vivid awareness, lives in constant recollection of God, desires to serve God and to help any soul.[68] Rather than longing to die to be with God, the soul sees glory in helping Christ on earth. Herein is the perfect union of the contemplative and active stance.[69] The transforming union is the ideal of Christian perfection to which all are called.[70] The degree of prayer that one attains is dependent on one's fidelity to prayer, one's co-operation with God's graces and the mystery of God's gifts. One can only do the best one can by readying oneself for God's action and then leaving the results to God. What is most important is that one's prayer life expresses itself in a life of virtue and loving service of one's neighbor.[71] For many centuries this has been the true test of the effectiveness of one's prayer.

From the foregoing description one sees that contemplative prayer offers the gift of union with God. It is the deepened love relationship which through purification of the total self and loving surrender of one's will to God allows the Spirit to lead one into mystical prayer which unites one more fully with God and transforms one into the true person which God intended from the beginning. Such union and transformation is the call of every Christian. It is the command of Jesus, "Be ye perfect as your heavenly Father is perfect" (Mt. 5:48).[72] Inherent in this command is the perfection of charity—the love of God and love of neighbor. This relationship of love is rooted in prayer which leads one through the "mansions", the "gardens" and the "nights" of the inner life.

Following Jesus means to be in relationship with him, to come to know him. This is initiated by the power of the Holy Spirit through baptism and responded to in faith through prayer.[73] Louise's prayer led her into a deep ongoing relationship with Jesus who revealed to her both God and herself. Through her life of prayer, Louise models for Christians today the reality that all are called to deep union with God and that through fidelity to one's relationship with God rooted in faith-filled prayer, in a spirit of humility and confidence in God, the heights and depths of love are offered to all.

Louise de Marillac did not analyze the progression of her prayer or spiritual life; rather she described, as best she could, some of her experiences of prayer in order to share them with Vincent de Paul to whom she had entrusted the direction of her soul. These records offer insight into the depths of Louise's prayer and the transforming journey of her inner life and person. There is no doubt as to the lasting effects of Louise's prayer life as manifested in her loving service of God and her neighbor.

Little is recorded of Louise's early prayer life. The only direct reference is related by her sisters and attests to Louise's own account of her devotion to prayer from an early age which led her to practice mental prayer from fifteen or sixteen years of age.[74] This call to prayer was reflected in Louise's desire to be a contemplative nun, which obviously was not God's plan for her. As well as meditative prayer, Louise certainly would have practiced vocal prayer and other acts of devotion. One might wonder whether the later prayer directives given for the children under her Sisters' care were reflective of Louise's own training in the Convent at Poissy.[75] Certainly, there she would have been schooled in prayer and encouraged to develop a spirit of attentiveness to God.

Louise's personal records of her spiritual life begin around 1621 with accounts of her interior trials.[76] At this point Louise would have been living a meditative prayer life for fourteen years. She had married at 22 in 1613 and within her social status lived a life of simplicity, charity, prayer and penance.[77] Louise's first biographer describes her as a young wife and mother whose life was centered on God and manifested in charity to her poor neighbor.[78] Her inner life was the center of her spiritual conflicts wherein she was assailed with a great fear of sin and an excessive consideration of her own faults.[79] It is in this setting that we enter into Louise's personal accounts. In a notation of c. 1621, Louise relates an interior trial describing an experience of "discouragement, annihilation of self and desertion by God merited by her infidelities." She relates that her "heart was so depressed that the force of her emotions sometimes resulted in physical pain." A few days later "still experiencing the same trial", she found some peace in accepting the reality that she was the object of divine justice and that all God's graces to her were a means of revealing God's goodness in carrying out this justice.[80] Louise's account of the last week of January of c. 1622 first presents the inspiration to give herself to God to fulfill his holy will for the remainder of her life. It then indicates a great confusion caused by the awareness of her own faults, the suffering of great interior trials, and great painful sensations on her reflection of the conversion of St. Paul. Her meditation on the last Sunday of January indicates her desire to sow in the heart of Jesus all the actions of her heart and soul that they might grow by sharing in his merits. Louise concludes the meditation thus: "Henceforth, I shall exist only through him and in him since he has willed to lower himself to assume human nature."[81] The year 1623 was a focal point in Louise's spiritual life. It was during this year that she received the grace to make a Vow of Widowhood to give herself entirely to God should her ill husband die, that she experienced her darkest spiritual trial, even doubting the existence of God and that she received her most profound spiritual illumination from God — her *Lumière*. These events occurred within one month from May 4—June 4, 1623.[82]

In reflecting on the content of these notations it would seem that in the years of 1621-3 Louise experienced passive purgation of the spirit and perhaps had already entered into a level of mystic union with God in which the trials of the spirit effected physical responses within her.[83] Her *Lumière* was certainly a mystical experience of God's illumination of her spirit and it exhibits the characteristics which Teresa of Avila outlined in Mansions VI as marking a true mystical experience.[84] Concerning her incredible anguish of soul, Louise wrote that she was "instantly freed of all doubt, was advised as to her future, and was given an inner assurance that it was God who was teaching her these things."[85] This experience and this message Louise kept for the rest of her life, not only in her heart but also on her person. Louise wrote the message on a small piece of paper which she folded in four and carried with her thereafter.[86]

Louise's *Lumière* was a special "awakening of her soul"[87] in preparation for a closer union with God. This desire to be more completely united with God was doubtlessly ongoing in Louise's spiritual life but is seen verbalized in her next notation around 1626. Herein Louise made an "Act of Consecration" to God in which she abandoned herself to divine providence and to the accomplishment of God's will in her, dedicating herself to the fulfillment of his will which she chooses as her supreme consolation. Louise completed this consecration with the following words:

> Since you inspired me to present these gifts to you, grant me the grace of perfecting them. You are my God and my All. I recognize you as such and adore you, the one true God in three Persons, now and forever.[88]

Specific references to her prayer forms begin in 1628 with her "Rule of Life in the World".[89] At this point, Louise was a widow, a single parent and under the direction of Vincent de Paul. Her "Rule of Life" outlines a framework of spiritual practices which give some insight into the development of her inner life. From a modern stance, one realizes that the lives of saints are not meant to be duplicated but the example they give lends itself to modifications with time and culture without destroying the underlying traditional principles of the interior life that remain valid for growth in the Christian life.

A study of Louise's "Rule of Life" c. 1628 indicates that at the age of 37, her daily horarium was integrated with prayer practices aimed at keeping her united with God. Her spirit of prayer permeated her actions and her prayer times were interwoven with her household duties, her family obligations and her charitable works.

At this point, Louise's prayer life consisted of directing every part of her day towards God and God's will in her life. From rising until retiring, prayer focused her on God. Louise's "Rule" indicates that on rising, she adored, thanked, abandoned herself to the will of God and invoked the Holy Spirit to know that will. Each morning, she devoted three-quarters to an hour for meditation on the gospel and finished with a practical application from the life of a saint. Mass, spiritual reading, the Office of the Blessed Virgin and the Rosary were part of Louise's daily prayer. Two shorter periods of meditation, fifteen minutes at noon in honor of the Incarnation and thirty minutes in the later afternoon directed her thoughts to God. It was also her custom to frequently remember the presence of God. Before retiring, Louise would make an examination of conscience wherein she humbly thanked God for the graces of the day and asked forgiveness for the faults she had committed, trusting in the goodness and mercy of God, her only hope.[90] To borrow from a modern spiritual writer, Louise's prayer seemed to be "an all-encompassing orientation, a basic mood of being with him in love,. . ."[91]

In addition to the above forms of vocal and meditative prayer, Louise, in her "Rule of Life", indicated a life of penance which included fasting on Fridays, in Advent and Lent as well as on other days appointed by the Church. When not fasting and when circumstances allowed, she took only two meals a day. In endeavoring to overcome her passions of vanity and precipitousness Louise used the discipline and the hairshirt.[92]

Periodically, Louise examined herself on the Commandments, her obligations as a Christian and as a Catholic. She also desired to make two retreats a year: one during Advent and one during the season between Ascension and Pentecost.[93]

Examining this blueprint for Louise's spiritual life, one recognizes that it is basically simple, is generally within the scope of a devoted Christian, and contains the traditional means for growth in the Christian life: prayer and penance.[94] Louise knew that one could pray at any time and in any place. She knew that in order to follow God and to grow in the Christian life, prayer and openness to the Spirit were vital. These remain valid principles for today. It is possible to pray at any time and in any place by turning one's heart and mind to God, by recalling the "presence of God" as Louise was wont to do. The street, the bus, the car, the chapel, the house, the fields — any place can be a place of prayer when one opens one's heart to God.[95]

Times of formal reflective prayer in which one seeks to be receptive to the Spirit and to discern God's will for each day are also necessary for growth in the Christian life.[96] In her time periods for meditation, Louise modelled this prayer form as well.[97]

Louise's prayer forms present a beneficial paradigm but one must venture further into her prayer life to discover the spirit which animated it.

Louise's letters and reflections indicate that her prayer was grounded in humility, faith, hope and love. Humility was a primary virtue of Louise. She recognized and acknowledged her need for God and thus was able to truthfully present herself before her Lord in acts of adoration, praise, thanksgiving and supplication. Louise's faith was the source of her great trust in God's loving providence, and her active love for her neighbor was the consequence of her deep love for God which she nurtured in prayer. These virtues of humility, faith, hope and love were characteristic, not only of Louise's prayer but of her whole person. Both Vincent de Paul and her Sisters attested to this.[98] How Louise's life mirrored the words, "We pray as we live; because we live as we pray."[99]

The tradition and challenge of prayer is ever old, ever new. What nourished and challenged Louise's prayer life can still challenge and nourish today's Christian. The model thus presented seems simple; so, where is the great challenge?[100] The great challenge lies in fidelity or perseverance in prayer. Good intentions may be most inspiring on paper and even in one's heart but unless they come to fruition, they remain only intentions without blossoming into the virtues or good deeds God intended. The lesson that Louise de Marillac places before the modern Christian is that fidelity to God in little things and openness to God's will in one's life can render the unimaginable in prayer and in good works. The test is to risk accepting the ongoing invitation to conversion with its inherent path of self-denial and taking up one's daily cross.[101] Louise is a witness to the effects of total trust in a loving God who brings light from darkness, glory from humility, spiritual riches from poverty and eternal life from dying to self in loving service. The journey of Louise's prayer life into the mystery of her inner life unfolds as she abandoned herself to the loving God, whose Spirit seized her and transformed her into a radiant reflection of Jesus.

A brief survey of some of Louise's experiences in prayer will illustrate that she did indeed ascend to the heights of deep union with God and that her life manifested the resultant virtues of an heroic Christian life of charity.

It is evident that throughout her life Louise was faithful to vocal and meditative prayer. This was evidenced in her own "Rule of Life In the World" c.1628, the rule which she drafted for her Sisters in 1633[102] and her constant encouragement to her Sisters to remain faithful to prayer and to develop an interior attitude of prayer.[103]

Louise's various notations for Vincent de Paul from 1628-1660 indicate that she experienced the prayer of union. Since the effects of this unitive prayer vary only according to the intensity of union with God, it is sufficient to illustrate only some of Louise's experiences of union with God to show that God blessed her with the gift of mystical prayer. For this purpose several Communion experiences and a few retreat notes will be cited.

Around 1628 Louise relates a Communion experience which reflects the conforming union phase of "betrothal" in which Jesus draws the soul to prepare it for himself. Louise wrote:

> On the Feast of All Saints, I was particularly overwhelmed by the thought of my lowliness, when my soul was made to understand that my God wanted to come to me. However, he did not wish to come into some temporary dwelling but to a place that was rightly his and belonged entirely to him. Therefore, I could not refuse him entrance. As a living soil, I had to welcome him joyfully as the true possessor of my soul and simply acquiesce to him, giving him my heart as the throne of his Majesty.[104]

In this notation, Louise expresses an awareness of her own lowliness, the gift of an inner understanding of God wanting her entirely for himself, her acceptance of his offer and joyful welcoming him as the "possessor of her soul", her acquiescence and gift of her heart as his throne.[105]

Although Louise was being courted by God, a letter from Vincent de Paul c. 1629 indicates that she was also experiencing inner trials. Vincent wrote the following to Louise:

> But do not think that all is lost because of the little rebellions you experience interiorly. It has just rained very hard and it is thundering dreadfully. Is the weather less beautiful for that? Let the tears of sadness drown your heart and let the demons thunder and growl as much as they please. Be assured, my dear daughter, that you are no less dear to Our Lord for all that. Therefore, live contentedly in his love and be assured that I shall be mindful of you tomorrow at the sacrifice. . .[106]

Louise's retreat reflections prior to 1630 indicate her great desire to be united to God. Some of these desires she expressed thus:

> I must depend completely upon God and show no greater resistance to him now than I did when he created me. . . .

> I desired no longer to subsist of myself. After having been continuously sustained by the grace of God, it seemed to me that all that I am is but grace. I implored God to draw these graces to himself and thus I would be totally his.[107]

On May 6, 1629, Louise had made her first apostolic mission to visit the Confraternities of Charity which initiated her as the collaborator of Vincent de Paul.[108] The following February as she undertook another visit she experienced the power and the presence of God in a most striking manner. Louise was in poor health before the journey but faith in God saw her through. The day of departure at Holy Communion she was "moved to make an act of faith, and this sentiment stayed with her a long time." Louise wrote: "It seemed to me that God would grant me health so long as I believed that he could sustain me, despite all appearances, and that he would do so if I often reflected on the faith that enabled Peter to walk on the waters." She continued: "Throughout my trip, I seemed to be acting without any contribution on my part; and I was greatly consoled by the thought that God wished that, despite my unworthiness, I should help my neighbor to know him."[109]

During this trip, on February 5, 1630, Louise received another special grace from God. She recounted her experience thus:

> At the moment of Holy Communion, it seemed to me that Our Lord inspired me to receive him as the Spouse of my soul and that this Communion was a manner of espousal. I felt myself more closely united to him by this consideration which was extraordinary for me. I also felt moved to leave everything to follow my spouse; to look upon him as such in the future; and to bear with the difficulties I might encounter as part of the community of his goods.[110]

At this point in her life, prior to her full insertion into the apostolate with Vincent de Paul, it is evident that Louise was experiencing mystical contemplative prayer and this was the source of her strength and dynamism in her life of charity. It was God's revelation to her of mysteries of the humanity of Jesus, her desire to imitate his life and her gradual awareness of his identification with the poor that impelled Louise to serve them.[111] From her earliest records Louise spoke of the humanity of Jesus but through the years this focus intensified and she received from God a deep understanding of Jesus. In the 1630's, Louise wrote the following:

> It is then that the invention of his divine love teaches me and permits me to attach myself to the greatest means he has given me for reaching my end, the most holy humanity of his Son. With the help of his grace, this sacred humanity shall be the only example for my life.[112]

A retreat note c. 1630 indicates Louise's desire to serve God as long as he willed. She wrote:

> To consider the Blessed Virgin accepting to be deprived of her Son and remaining on earth for the good of Christians, with the desire to remain here myself so long as it is the good

pleasure of God for me to accomplish his holy will in this life. [113]

In a spirit of true humility, Louise was most conscious that God would accomplish his designs within her. In 1633 she recorded the following:

> I shall, therefore, have great confidence in him who has assured me that, despite my misery and powerlessness, he will accomplish all that he desires in me. . . . One means to attain my goal is that, without there being anything in me to indicate it, others see me as having received graces from God. This humbles me but, at the same time, gives me courage.

> No desires—no resolutions. The grace of my God will accomplish whatever he pleases in me.[114]

Around this time, Louise, in an Easter meditation realized that in order to rise with Christ she must die to herself by deadening her disordered passions and desires; she knew this was beyond her own powers but that God was asking this of her and so she acquiesced thus: "Therefore, I gave him my full consent to operate in me by his power whatever he willed to see accomplished."[115]

Louise experienced many other spiritual favors from God during the ensuing years. In the center of her being, she remained united with God while also experiencing great interior and exterior trials, which through suffering, molded her more into the likeness of Jesus. Proceeding to the last decade of her life, one continues to find in Louise's notations, simple descriptive passages which denote her unitive relationship with God. One such passage is that of August 24, c. 1650 when Louise exuberantly wrote to Vincent to share a joyous intuitive experience of God. Her letter read:

> My heart is still overflowing with joy on account of the understanding which, I believe, our good God has given

me of the words, "God is my God", and the awareness I
had of the glory which the blessed render to him as a
consequence of this truth. Therefore, I cannot help communicating with you this evening to ask you to assist me
to profit from this excess of joy . . .

Vincent responded:

Blessed be God, Mademoiselle, for the tenderness with
which his divine Majesty honors you! You must receive it
respectfully and devoutly and in view of some cross which
he is preparing for you. His goodness generally prepares
those he loves in this way when he wishes to crucify
them.[116]

In 1651 during her retreat, Louise, misunderstanding a reading
on sin in the *Memorial* by Louis of Grenada, was oppressed by
the punishment it depicted and seemed to be "immersed in a
generalized terror." She reported that God came to her help thus:
"The words 'God is he Who is' filled me with peace even though
I discovered within myself sins against his goodness."[117]

In 1657, Louise's meditation notations again indicate an
intuitive understanding of the humanity of Jesus coupled with
his relationship with the poor. She wrote:

My meditation was more reflective than reasoning. I felt
an attraction for the holy humanity of Our Lord and I
desired to honor and imitate it insofar as I was able in the
person of the poor and of all my neighbors. I had read
somewhere that he had taught us charity to make up for
our powerlessness to render any service to his person. This
touched my heart very particularly and very intimately.

. . . the fact that the neighbor has been given to me in the
place of Our Lord, by means of a love which his goodness
knows and which he has revealed to my heart, although I
am unable to put it into words.[118]

For Louise, love of God and love of neighbor were inseparable: love of God, especially in the person of Jesus, and love of neighbor, particularly in the person of the poor.[119]

Of an August 1658, Communion experience Louise wrote: "I suddenly felt moved by the desire that Our Lord should come to me and communicate his virtues to me."[120]

Around this time, Louise wrote a prayer reflection for her Sisters on John 12:28-35 in which she emphasized the phrase, "and I, if I be lifted up will draw all men to myself" as being the call to the "Pure Love of God". Her introductory paragraph is significant in that she is speaking not only to her Sisters but also to all who desire a deep union with God. Louise accepts that this unitive love is possible for all:

> My very dear Sisters and all souls that aspire to the perfection of pure divine love, these are the words of our beloved Master and Spouse who teaches us thereby that we may hope for this and that such aspirations are in keeping with his plan as seen in the attraction that he will exert when he is raised up from the earth.[121]

Within this reflection one finds several points confirming that Louise is indeed speaking of mystical prayer in the unitive way. The following are of note:

> Therefore, let us love and we will thereby grasp its endlessness since it depends in no way on us. Let us often recall all the actions of the life of our Beloved so that we may imitate them. Not content with the love that he bears for all chosen souls, he wishes to have some very cherished ones raised up by the purity of his love.
>
> My Lord, I received a kind of new light concerning the uncommon love that you wish to receive from those whom you choose to exercise the purity of your love on earth.[122]

Coming to the closing years of Louise's life there appear two passages which reflect her deep union with God. The one of 1657 on the Holy Spirit presents many inferences to the highest mystical union. This passage will speak for itself:

Is there anything more excellent in heaven or on earth than this treasure? (Holy Spirit) How is it possible to live a disorderly life after having given oneself entirely to be open to this infinite good? Should I not desire, O my God, to die upon receiving it? To live for as long as it pleases you, but with your life which is one of total love. May I not, beginning in this world, flow into the ocean of your divine Being? Should I be so fortunate as to receive the Holy Spirit, Oh, how I must desire this with my whole heart!

No longer to walk any path but this one; no other satisfaction but that of loving and of willing your good pleasure.[123]

You still see weaknesses in me in my desire for the affection of creatures. Consume this, O Ardent Fire of Divine Love!. . .I reject, with all my heart, my excessive abruptness which I renounce forevermore, whatever the temptation that may come to me from the world, the flesh, or the devil. At least, I shall do so if I am so fortunate that the Holy Spirit will deign, by the divine goodness, to come into my soul and to restore in it the graces with which your goodness filled it at my baptism. . . . Eternal Father, I beg this mercy of you. . . My Savior, grant me this grace, . . . Holy Spirit, operate this marvel in your unworthy subject by the loving union which you have from all eternity with the Father and the Son.[124]

A few months before her death, Louise recounted another eucharistic experience which in many ways reflected graces of her past life and epitomized the simplicity of her soul, her spirituality and her great union with God. She recorded the following:

On the Feast of Saint Geneviève, in 1660, as I was receiving Holy Communion, I felt, upon seeing the Sacred Host, an extraordinary thirst which had its origin in the belief that Jesus wanted to give himself to me in the simplicity of his divine infancy. When I was receiving him and for a long time afterward, my mind was filled by an interior communication which led me to understand that Jesus was bringing not only himself to me but also all the merits of his mysteries. This communication lasted all day. It was not a forced, interior preoccupation. It was rather a presence or a recurrent recollection, as sometimes happens when something is troubling me.

I felt that I was being warned that, since Jesus had given himself entirely to me, laden with the merits of all these mysteries, I must make use of this occasion to participate in his submission to humiliations.

One means to attain this end is to be found in the fact that, without any cause in me, I appear to others as having received some graces from God. This both humbles me and gives me courage.

No desires, no resolutions. The grace of my God will accomplish in me whatever he wills.[125]

That Louise de Marillac received special mystical graces from God is evidenced in her spiritual reflections and notations to Vincent de Paul. During their lives, the knowledge of such favors would have been within their private domain. However, the authenticity of such graced experiences is found in the resultant growth in virtue evidenced in a holy life. This Louise certainly manifested and was confirmed by those closest to her.[126] That she lived a life of deep union with God is attested to by Vincent de Paul and by her Daughters.[127] That she possessed deep humility, prudence, patience, meekness and poverty is similarly documented.[128] Of greatest general significance was Louise's virtue of charity. Her love of God manifested itself in her unceasing and selfless love of her neighbor, especially the poor. Grounded in humility and simplicity, Louise evidenced a charity that Christ alone could impel. Louise's mustard seed of her life of faith, hope and prayer blossomed into a great tree of charity. As God the Father said to Catherine of Siena and as Teresa of Avila said to her Sisters: What God wants is works.[129] It was just such works of "courageous endurance and service"[130] for the Lord and her neighbor that made Louise de Marillac such a light in the darkness of her day.

Louise de Marillac: Woman of Charity — Guide in the Apostolic Life

"THE SAINT OF CHARITY ENTERS THE VATICAN BASILICA"

These words were headlines in an Italian newspaper on 20 April, 1954 when the statue of Louise de Marillac began its ascent to the final niche for founders and foundresses in St.Peter's Basilica in Rome.[131] What joy this caption must have brought to her spiritual family as Louise, the mother and foundress, joined Vincent de Paul the father and founder, in the Mother Church of Christendom. Now, in an unique manner both saints were duly recognized as founders and as great saints of Charity. Vincent de Paul, had long been named the Patron of Charity and a similar recognition was soon to come for Louise de Marillac.[132] Six years later, Pope John the XXIII pronounced the following words on her behalf:

> Among those who have consecrated themselves to the exercise of this virtue of charity, Saint Louise de Marillac is worthy of special mention and praise. . . .Burning with this heavenly flame, she wished to give herself totally to the service of humankind. . .She had at heart . . . the throng of the suffering. For all of them she wished to show herself a mother of compassion.[133]

These words were among those in which Pope John XXIII, on February 10, 1960 proclaimed Louise de Marillac the patroness of all those dedicated to Christian Social Works. In her activities he saw what today are so specially developed and called "Christian Social Works". Hence in her abundant charity, Louise de Marillac was a prophetic leader in Christian Social Action and as such is a model and teacher for modern Christians.

The prophetic call of Louise's apostolic life can be traced back to her *Lumière* experience of 1623. In it are the seeds of a Christian life destined to blossom and bear fruit. In this foundational experience of Louise, one sees a direct call rooted in God, which was to be nurtured and developed in community and brought to fruition in mission to others.[134]

For Louise this vocation of total dedication to the apostolic life developed gradually and eventually came to bear magnificent fruit. Louise's total life was rooted firmly in her relationship with God and grew to be particularly so in the imitation of Jesus in his public life of loving service to the poor. As well, Louise's life was deeply grounded in the Church and its mission which she recognized as a continuation of that of Jesus. She always saw her baptismal commitment as the foundation of her discipleship and mission in the Church. Like Jesus, Louise desired deeply to do the will of the Father and to witness to him through her service to others. Louise was a laywoman who, following the call of God, and in communion with Jesus and others, labored in the vineyard of the Lord to bring forth fruits of love that changed the face of her society and even of the Church.[135]

Through the efforts of Vincent de Paul and Louise de Marillac, the social ills of France were embraced with steadfast love bringing about remarkable changes in that sphere and through the foundation of their Company of the Daughters of Charity, transforming forever the image of the Church.[136]

Christian Social Action may be defined as social action permeated by gospel values. As such, Louise de Marillac is aptly designated its patroness and by this title becomes an universal model for all Christians. Through their baptism, Christians are deputed to share in the mission of Jesus and the Church by going out to one's neighbor in compassionate caring and service.[137] It is on this command of love that all will be judged. "What you did to the least of my brethren, you did to me" (Mt. 25:40).[138]

As model and teacher in the sphere of Christian Social Action what does Louise de Marillac embody for modern-day Christians?

Louise exemplifies the firm belief in her baptismal call to image Jesus in her life. She illustrates that this is possible only through a deep relationship with Jesus in a stable and vital interior life. Hence, Louise's social action was rooted in her personal and communal relationship with Jesus. She knew well the importance of the words of Jesus cited in John's gospel: "I am the vine and you are the branches, whoever remains in me, with me in him bears fruit in plenty; for cut off from me you can do nothing" (Jn. 15:5).[139] She knew too that with these words, Jesus signified his Church. For Louise, communion with Jesus and with his Church was the source of her holiness and of her apostolic life of Christian Social Action. Similarly, this same communion is the source for Christians today.[140]

In 1623, Louise, the wife and mother, knew that God had called her to a special mission which would unfold in communion with others. In 1629, this apostolate began when Vincent de Paul "missioned" Louise to begin her visitations of the "Charities" in France.[141] Louise, now a widow, had time to devote herself more fully to charitable works and thus began the sprouting of the seeds of 1623. For several years they had germinated in the darkness of suffering and the warmth of prayer; now they were ready to pierce the soil of the garden that would be Louise's unique field of mission. Dedicated lay women had tried to respond to the needs of the sick and the poor. Louise, with her expertise of leadership and management skills evaluated, encouraged and revitalized their "Charities". Yet, she saw the need for another complementary group of women to work in conjunction with the Ladies of the Charities in a manner of total commitment to the poor and the sick. From this vision developed in 1633, the conception of the Daughters of Charity, who one day would be an universal symbol of charity and would extend to the four corners of the world. From this great tree many branches would flourish in their spirit and their mission of charity. Since they were not "religious" of their day, they modelled a new form of consecrated life and service in the Church. They worked hand in hand with the Ladies of Charity and as such were forerunners of an ideal that the Church seeks today wherein all members work together to fulfill the mission of the Church.[142]

Louise's *Lumière* indicated that community and mission were to be interdependent. As one was to be united with Jesus, so one was to be united with members of the Christian Community to bring compassion and service to the suffering members of Christ. For Louise this union in community came to be lived out in a special form of life totally dedicated to service of neighbor. For her the union in community was the source of strength for mission and Louise often encouraged her Sisters to make this a priority. Even on her deathbed this was one of her final exhortations: "Take good care of the service of the poor. Above all, live together in great union and cordiality, loving one another in imitation of the union and life of Our Lord."[143] For a mission to be carried out effectively a spirit of union must exist among the workers. If a mission is a Christian work, then this unity must be founded on Jesus. This principle of Louise and her Daughters is re-echoed in a current counsel to all Christians today who are called to continue the mission of Jesus in serving others according to their state in life.[144]

The mission to Christian social action carries an underlying mandate to the spiritual aspect of the person—to evangelization. It is primary to note that in Louise's own works and in the training of her Daughters she and Vincent de Paul always emphasized the spiritual aspect of their service. According to Vincent de Paul, the Daughters of Charity were founded by providence to minister to the spiritual and corporal needs of the poor. Both Vincent and Louise repeatedly stressed this. In the "Rule for the Motherhouse" one reads:

Since the Sisters of Charity are obliged to serve the sick poor both corporally and spiritually, in imitation of Our Lord who, in curing, always gave some advice for the salvation of souls, saying to some, "Go and sin no more," giving others to understand that their faith would save them, and speaking many more words of advice, our Sister Infirmarians shall take great care that the sick have great submission to the will of God and great trust in his love.[145]

This call to evangelization which is so strongly stressed today was constitutive to the mission of Louise and the Daughters. Pope John Paul II reiterated this to the Daughters in 1991 by saying:

In keeping St. Louise's spirit, you join in her spirituality of missionary action. . . . This evangelizing, charitable action places you at the heart of the church from which you radiate like a fire burning with love.[146]

Indeed this "fire burning with love" was exactly what ignited the Christian social works of Louise de Marillac. Her affective love of God necessitated her effective love towards her neighbor, especially the poor who represented Christ to her. Louise's zeal and charity were rooted in her deep interior union with God. She was consumed with the desire to do the Father's will, to imitate the life of his Son, Jesus and to allow the Spirit to lead her. Daily nourished by this loving Trinity, Louise accomplished deeds beyond the imagination which Pope Pius XI in 1934 termed "the miracle of her works".[147]

Only the power of the love of God working within Louise could accomplish the works that she did. From the earliest years of her marriage, her first biographer attests to her works of charity in her parish where she "visited the sick poor, gave them broths and remedies, made their beds, instructed them and consoled them by her exhortations, disposed them to receive the sacraments, and buried them after their death.[148] He continues that, "She attracted ladies to this service by her advice and example."[149] How God would build upon these beginnings! In later years through her numerous personal actions of social service, her initiation, organization and development of ongoing programs in health care and education, Louise's humility and compassion continued to be manifested in her attention to the individual, especially the most marginalized. Her Sisters attested to her attention to prisoners in the following witness: "I have seen her gathering poor people around her who were coming out of prison; she washed their feet, dressed their sores and clothed them from her son's wardrobe."[150] This primary focus of Louise on the dignity of the person was a prophetic witness to the Church's exhortation to all faithful today. One reads in *Redemptor Hominis* :

The person is the primary route that the Church must travel in fulfilling her mission: the individual is the *primary and fundamental way for the Church,* the way traced out by Christ himself, the way that leads invariably through the mystery of the Incarnation and Redemption.[151]

It was this dignity of the person in Jesus Christ that led Louise to minister with compassionate love to the most neglected of her society: the foundlings, the prisoners, the galley slaves, the insane, the isolated elderly, and uneducated little girls.[152] Louise however, did not stop at the individual problem. She used her abilities and expertise to enter more deeply into the social strata of her society and inaugurated works on a broader scale which tackled the various forms of poverty in a constructive and ongoing manner. It was in this spirited work that her holy genius lay. Here too she pre-figured current social doctrine which states: "Service to society is expressed and realized in the most diverse ways, from those spontaneous and informal to those more structured, from help given to individuals to those destined for various groups and communities of persons."[153] Louise lived Pope John Paul II's description of solidarity. He wrote:

Solidarity is not a feeling of vague compassion or shallow distress at the misfortunes of so many people, both near and far, . . .it is a firm and persevering determination to commit

oneself to the common good. . .to the good of all and of each
individual because we are all really responsible for all.[154]

The Holy Father continued with other aspects of Solidarity
which in the light of faith sees the neighbor in the image of God
(SRS 40, p. 75)) and cites the Church's first contribution to Social
Action as that of evangelization — offering solutions to the problems of the world by proclaiming the truth about Christ, about
herself and about the human person and applying this to concrete
situations (SRS 42, p. 82). In other words, might one not say with
Louise and Vincent, "bringing food for the body and food for the
soul"?[155] This call to solidarity with the poor and underdeveloped
has been a major thrust of recent papal social documents emphasizing particularly the role of the lay faithful in this essential aspect
of the mission of the Church.[156] Louise de Marillac remains a model
and guide for the missionary spirit which all Christians are called
to live in their own unique environment. For the myriads of unsung
faithful who share in the salvific mission of the Church, Louise is a
model of faithful stewardship and service in her deep adherence to
God and in her untiring ministry to her neighbor.

Such fidelity to mission is rooted in one's call to holiness.
Louise was ever conscious of her call to holiness and it was the
living out of this primary vocation that energized and vivified all
social action that Louise undertook. So too, for today's Christian,
the Church repeatedly echoes the importance of everyone's call
to holiness as the basis of all mission. Pope John Paul II wrote:

> Holiness, then, must be called a fundamental presupposi-
> tion and an irreplaceable condition for everyone in fulfill-
> ing the mission of salvation within the Church. The
> Church's holiness is the hidden source and the infallible
> measure of the works of the apostolate and of the mission-
> ary effort.[157]

In his Encyclical Letter *Redemptoris Missio*, Pope John Paul II
continued: "*The universal call to holiness* is closely linked to the
universal call to mission. Every member of the faithful is called to

holiness and to mission."[158] Reading the Chapter of this Encyclical entitled, "Missionary Spirituality", one sees clearly how Louise's spirituality encompassed the missionary qualities set forth for today's Christians. Such attitudes as "docility to the Spirit"; "being molded from within by the Spirit so that we may become ever more like Christ"; "gifts of fortitude and discernment"; "boldness in preaching the gospel"; "intimate communion with Christ"; "self-emptying which leads to the foot of the cross"; "apostolic charity; a zeal for souls, inspired by Christ's own charity, which takes the form of concern, tenderness, compassion, openness, availability and interest in people's problems, especially the least and the poorest".[159] The Holy Father calls for "holiness among missionaries and throughout the Christian community, especially among those who work most closely with missionaries." He strongly affirms that "The Church's missionary spirituality is a journey towards holiness."[160] How interesting to note Louise's words of exhortation and encouragement to her Daughters regarding their Mission to the service of the poor. Louise frequently reminded her Daughters of their call to holiness with such words as:

> It is only reasonable that those whom God has called to follow his Son should strive to become holy as he is holy and to make their lives a continuation of his. What a blessing that will be for all Eternity! The merits of Jesus crucified have earned this grace for us. . . .[161]

Louise was well aware that docility to the Holy Spirit was the secret to holiness and success in their endeavors. She counselled her Sisters to:

> Pray for the Company so that, in his goodness, God may send his Holy Spirit upon all in general and upon each individual Sister in order that we may all be very faithful to him.[162]

Only by becoming ever more like Christ and serving in selflessness would their mission bear fruit. Hence Louise reminded her

Sisters of the spirit of service that they needed. One example ran thus:

> It is not enough to visit the poor and to provide for their needs; one's heart must be totally purged of all self-interest, and one must continually work at the general mortification of all the senses and passions. In order to do this, my dear Sisters, we must continually have before our eyes our model, the exemplary life of Jesus Christ. We are called to imitate this life, not only as Christians, but as persons chosen by God to serve him in the person of his poor.[163]

In a life of service to others the gift of fortitude is essential and Louise knew this. She affirmed her Sisters with: "Blessed be God for the strength and courage he gives you in all your works. You are accomplishing wonders."[164] She also encouraged them thus: "Be so stout-hearted that you find nothing difficult for the most holy love of God and of his crucified Son. . ."[165]

Louise knew only too well that the cross was inherent in mission and she reminded her Sisters of this fact:

> I urge them to reflect and to recall that it is not necessary to be filled with joy and consolation in order to please God. Since the Son of God accomplished the work of salvation for the entire world through sorrow and pain, it is quite logical for us, if we wish to share in his merits, to overcome ourselves and to accept suffering.[166]

All Christians are called to apostolic charity according to their state in life. For the Daughters of Charity this was their essence for being and even when travelling Louise reminded them to be conscious of their mission:

> If they have some time, they shall go to the hospital to visit any of the sick poor who might be there, recalling that the

love and service of God and neighbor is their sole reason
for existence.[167]

Central to the spirit of the Daughters of Charity was the
dignity of the individual who was seen as a member of Christ.
This truth was never to be forgotten by the Sisters and was the
touchstone of their mission of service to the poor. How often
Louise and Vincent exhorted them thus:

> In the name of God, my dear Sisters, . . .above all, be very
> gentle and courteous toward your poor. You know that
> they are our masters and that we must love them tenderly
> and respect them deeply. It is not enough for these maxims
> to be in our minds; we must bear witness to them by our
> gentle and charitable care.[168]

The words, "It is not enough for these maxims to be in our
minds; we must bear witness to them by our gentle and charitable
care." — in other words by our lives, challenge modern Christians
to live fully the apostolic and missionary vocation to which all
are called.

Louise epitomized this call in her own life and offers to today's
faithful an authentic representation of the spirit that is necessary
to incarnate the prophetic mission of Christ in one's life. Regard-
less of one's state in life, the gospel values of: the quest for
holiness, openness to the Spirit, the dignity of the person,
selflessness, imitation of Jesus, the reality of the cross in service,
sharing one's talents, time and goods, having a concern for one's
neighbor especially the marginalized and the poor, are of permanent significance and universal application to one's social apostolate however that presents itself.[169] In Louise de Marillac, one
sees a woman who lived her apostolic and missionary call in the
Church as teenager, wife, mother, widow and finally as a woman
totally consecrated to the poor. In each stage of her life she lived
an integrated spirituality combining her primary duties of life
with an apostolic Christian social action. She models the reality

that one can be apostolic and missionary in one's family, one's parish, and one's city. Louise also attests to the power of God working within. When there is a deep union with God, a generous spirit and good will, God can work marvels. It is the power of the Risen Christ working within the fragility and the weakness of the human person that witnesses to the steadfast love of the Redeemer. It is this love that is the oil in the lamp of the Christian and becomes the light in the darkness of doubt and discouragement in the lives of one's neighbor. As for Louise, so too for all Christians, it is the love of Jesus crucified that urges one to serve one's neighbor. Only love can do such things. The fire of this love within each heart is rekindled with the breath of the Spirit who empowered the apostles to be witnesses to the ends of the world. Every Christian is called to share in this mission and Louise de Marillac stands as a witness to the fecundity of the Christian who cooperates fully with God's designs in one's life. Like the apostles after their Pentecost experience she too after her Pentecost experience, was led by the Spirit to witness to the ends of the earth, to the loving salvation of Jesus Christ. (AA 1:8)

In addressing St. Louise de Marillac as he blessed her statue in St. Peter's Basilica, Cardinal Tedeschini said: "You come to hold the place of charity, that charity to which statues do not suffice, but which requires grateful souls glorifying Christ."[170] No words would please Louise more. She who desired to remain hidden and anonymous in her life's works in honor of the humility and hidden life of Jesus would likely simply bow her head at the sight of a twelve-foot statue but would rejoice with the call for "grateful souls glorifying Christ" to be witness to his charity. She whose life radiated the light and warmth of this same love, stands today as an acknowledged saint of charity, a prototype and patroness of Christian Social Action and thus an authentic guide in the apostolic life.

Concluding Remarks

Louise de Marillac was a prophetic witness in an heroic degree to the virtues of faith, hope and charity. She was both an interior woman and an active woman — a contemplative in action. Her life confirmed her interiority and those who knew her best attested to this. However, as Vincent de Paul witnessed, the path to interiority was not always easy for her.[171] Nor may the path to interiority be easy for the modern Christian, but travel it one must if one desires to grow in union with God and to have an effective apostolate of service.

By embracing an interior life, every Christian, through the power of the Spirit, is enticed to experience the love of God and thence the God of love.[172]

An inner life nourished by prayer leads to the surrender of one's heart and will to God, with the resultant transformation of one's spirit and being. The ultimate goal of prayer is loving union with God by conformity to the divine will. Since God is love, this union of heart and will must express itself in a life of love. Yet, as one journeys in prayer and love, one experiences as a fragile human being the mixture of the near and the far, the joy and the pain, the light and the darkness of the immanent and the transcendent; but, in faith one trusts in the steadfast love of the Lord and the transforming power of the Spirit. The call of every Christian is to enter into a love relationship with God, to enjoy union with God, to live a life of loving service as did Jesus and ultimately to be able to say with Paul, "It is no longer I who live, but it is Christ who lives in me" (Gal. 2:20). This too was the call of Louise de Marillac and the witness of her life of prayer and loving service demonstrates that God indeed does transform those who actively desire to be re-formed into his likeness and image. God is always waiting to lead his people out of darkness into his radiant light so that they may reflect that light to others. Louise de Marillac was and is a reflection of that light. In her constant desire to conform herself to the divine will as did Jesus, she grew to radiate the reality of Jesus' words: "I am the light of the world, whoever follows me will not walk in darkness but will have the light of life" (Jn. 8:12).Such is the challenge she left her Daughters; such is the challenge she leaves Christians of today.

Notes

1. Pope John Paul II, Letter of July 3, 1991 to Sister Juana Elizondo on the occasion of the Fourth Centenary of the Birth of Louise de Marillac. *Echoes of the Company*, October, 1991, p. 382.

2. SWLM, p. 789. A.56-NOTES ON THE MEETINGS OF THE LADIES OF CHARITY: "It is very evident, in this century, that divine providence willed to make use of women to show that it was his goodness alone which desired to aid afflicted peoples and to bring them powerful helps for their salvation."

3. In a current Video Series , "Becoming Spiritually Mature", Dr. Susan Muto, Ph. D. speaks of one's "outline of limitations and because of one's dignity in God, one's treasure of possibilities." This we see actualized in the life of Louise and we see it as a hope for our own lives. "Becoming Spiritually Mature", A Video Series by Adrian van Kamm, C.S.Sp., Ph.D. and Susan Muto, Ph.D., Epiphany Association, Pittsburgh, PA, 1991.

4. Portal, F., *Les Filles de la Charité De Saint Vincent de Paul et De La Bienheureuse Louise de Marillac* (Paris: Gigord, Ed.,1921), p. 48.

5. Francis de Sales speaks of the "indifferent heart like a ball of wax in God's hands, ready to receive all the impressions of his will" (Francis de Sales, trans. by John K. Ryan, *Treatise On The Love Of God*, Vol.II (Rockford,Il.: Tan Books and Publishers, Inc.,1975), p. 106).

Openness to the will of God in one's life allows God to fashion and form us, to lead us to deeper union with the Transcendent who then becomes more immanent to us.

6. "We know that all things work together for good for those who love God" (Rom. 8:28). Julian of Norwich so frequently spoke this truth in her oft-cited words of "All will be well" (Julian of Norwich, *Revelations of Divine Love*, ed. Halcyon Backhouse with Rhona Pipe (London: Hodder and Stoughton, 1987, 1992), p. 55).

7. This was particularly evident in Louise's *"Lumière"* experience of 1623.

8. SWLM, p. 542. L.513, Feb. 10, 1657. To the Sisters at Nantes, Brittany, Louise wrote: "Courage my dear Sisters! This life is so short for so many! And as you know, the recompense for our interior and exterior sufferings is eternal. But it will be given only to those who have fought valiantly. I wish victory to all of you, my dear Sisters. . ."

9. Calvet, p. 166: "She said herself that from her early youth she had had a great facility in meditation. . ."

10. This small painting is in the Museum of the Daughters of Charity at rue du Bac in Paris.

11. Louise's prayer life was in harmony with the rhythm of prayer that is expressed currently in the *Catechism of the Catholic Church.* Herein # 2698, reads: "The Tradition of the Church proposes to the faithful certain rhythms of praying intended to nourish continual prayer. Some are daily . . . Sundays, centered on the Eucharist,. . . The cycle of the liturgical year and its great feasts. . ."

As to the uniqueness of one's prayer the *Catechism* continues: "The Lord leads all persons by paths and in ways pleasing to him, and each believer responds according to his heart's resolve and the personal expressions of his prayer. . .." (#2699). As seen, this reality too was present in Louise's prayer life.

12. Jean Gonthier, C.M., "Listening to Saint Louise : The Mystery of the Incarnation", *Echoes of the Company*, No. 2, February 1983, pp. 82-83.

13. Gonthier, "Listening to Saint Louise," p. 82. A. 13B, trans. by Jean Gonthier, C.M.

14. SWLM, p. 817. A.26. How in tune Louise is with today's teaching. CCC, #2044 states: "The fidelity of the baptized is a primordial condition for the proclamation of the holy gospel and for the *Church's mission in the world*"; and (#2047): "The moral life is a spiritual worship. Christian activity finds its nourishment in the liturgy and the celebration of the sacraments."

15. CCC, #'s 2716, 2719. Given that contemplative prayer is "the obedience of faith, the unconditional acceptance of a servant and the loving commitment of a child, participating in the 'Yes' of the Son become servant and the *Fiat* of God's lowly handmaid" (#2716); that "it is a communion of love bearing Life for the multitude, to the extent that it consents to abide in the night of faith" (#2719); then, in truth Louise was a contemplative.

16. Calvet remarked that "Louise was a staunch Christian woman whose love had borne fruit" (p. 184).

17. Regarding the slow beginnings of a new foundation, Louise wrote: "This is painful for persons who would like to see the designs of God succeed immediately and who desire to work incessantly for him to whom they have wholeheartedly dedicated themselves" (SWLM, p. 605. L.578).

18. SWLM, p. 391. L:341, Feb.17, 1652.

In a letter of 1640 to the Sisters at Angers, Louise wrote: "Courage then, my dear Sisters! Let us serve with hearts filled with the pure love of God which enables us always to love the roses amidst the thorns. How short is this life of pain" (SWLM, p. 36. L.426).

Similarly in May of 1649, Louise wrote to Sr. Jeanne Lepintre:

I expect much from the establishment at Nantes since persecutions are one of the signs of the value of a work. . ..We should reflect upon all that has happened only to praise God for having saved from shipwreck those who remained steadfast, and to recognize the occasions that he has given us to suffer for his love. I beg him with all my heart to take complete possession of all that we are on this holy feast day (Feast of Pentecost); (SWLM, p. 288. L.433, May 22, 1649).

19. Louise's faith was active. Prior to a trip she was fearful of making because of her ailments she wrote: "It seemed to me that God would grant me health so long as I believed that he could sustain me, despite all appearances, and that he would do so if I often reflected on the faith that enabled Peter to walk on the waters" (SWLM, p. 704. A.50).

20. Coste, V. de P., I, 46, L.27.

21. SWLM, p. 278. L.241, April 1649.

22. SWLM, p. 296. L.253, August 18, 1649 (Nantes).

23. SWLM, p. 320. L.284, Jeanne Lepintre, May 4, 1650.

24. SWLM, p. 323. L.277.

25. SWLM, p. 373. L.329, Sept.27, 1651.

26. SWLM, p. 375. L.354, Julienne Loret (Chars) Oct.6,1651. Was Louise a forerunner to modern "job sharing"?

27. SWLM, p.393. L.210, Jeanne Lepintre, March 27, 1652. This letter indicates that the Sisters knew how to write. This in itself is a credit to Louise's concern for her Daughters as many people of the day were illiterate.

28. SWLM, p. 441. L.398, Feb.16,1654-(Brienne).

29. SWLM, p. 495. L.463, December 1655.

30. SWLM, p. 678. L.656, February 2,1660.

31. SWLM, p. 540. L.512, February 1657.

32. Georgette Blaquiere, in her book, *The Grace to Be a Woman*, trans. Robert Wild (New York: Alba House, 1983), p. 97 states: "Compassion is prophetic because, beyond the present suffering, in the light and power of faith, it proclaims the hope that God is present and victorious."

33. CCC, #2683.

34. CCC, #2684.

35. Modern spiritual writers contend that the French School of Spirituality has greatly shaped modern Christian spirituality; hence, tenets of the theological principles may have been evident in Christian spirituality until recently and perhaps now it is opportune to reclaim some of them.

36. Louise seems to have been gifted with the authentic blend of the "Martha and Mary" of the gospels or even the spirit of Jesus which she had an impassioned desire to imitate.

37. SWLM, p. 689. A.1-RULE OF LIFE, c. 1628. Louise spoke thus of herself: "As a woman desirous of becoming devout."

38. A point of interest is that both Louise and one of her Daughters made reference to her possible ability to "read hearts" which is a supernatural gift identified by J. Aumann (*Spiritual Theology*, p. 430) as an extraordinary phenomenon observed in the lives of saints and mystics.

In one of her retreat notes Louise wrote: "Am I mistaken when I think that I clearly perceive the interior motives of others, particularly my Sisters in the Company?" (SWLM, p. 782 A.11- NOTES DURING A RETREAT.)

During one Conference with Vincent de Paul on Louise's virtues after her death, one of the Sisters recounted: "Father, Mademoiselle was most prudent in all things and it seemed as if she knew the failings of everyone, because she told us about them before they were mentioned to her" (Leonard, *Conferences,*IV, 311).

In studying Louise's prayer notes it is most interesting to see how frequently the descriptions of her spiritual experiences echo the reflections of Teresa of Avila and John of the Cross.

39. Benito Martinez, C.M., "The Prayer of Louise", *Echoes of the Company,* #3, March 1983, p. 130.

40. SWLM. p. 714. A.5-RETREAT, c. 1632. What a consoling and encouraging thought in the struggles of life! These words are a gem of wisdom from the heart and pen of Louise.

41. SWLM. p. 714. A.5-RETREAT, c. 1632.

The image of a reigning King is often not kindly looked upon today but the spiritual truth behind the imagery is totally valid. Only in submitting one's heart and life to the gentle power and will of God can one experience the depths and heights of this unique love relationship. In this text Louise reflects the "universal call to holiness" and her "well-beloved" imagery is indicative of the contemplative expression of prayer. Teresa of Avila often spoke of God as "his Majesty". An image used today which carries a similar connotation is "Jesus as Lord of one's life."

42. Louise did not journal her prayer but because of her sharing with her spiritual director, Vincent de Paul, sufficient records of her prayer life are available to permit us to perceive how her prayer and interior life unfolded as she matured as a Christian woman. These personal notations enable us to acknowledge Louise de Marillac as a genuine "Guide in the Interior Life."

43. An excellent summary of John's doctrine is presented by Keiran Kavanaugh in *Christian Spirituality: Post-Reformation and Modern*, eds. Louise Dupré and Don E. Saliers (New York: Crossroad, 1991, pp.81-84). The following points are taken from this source:

John of the Cross speaks of the Trinitarian God communing with human persons, transforming them and assuming them into his divine personal life. The union, goal of the spiritual life, is a union of love brought about through a long process of interiorization and purification of all the activities of the human faculties. In this process, through the theological virtues, the soul becomes like to God. The union of love is a union of likeness.

John of the Cross condenses this lifelong journey into three characteristic phases, representing a particular way of living and responding to the reality of God's self-communication. The first phase is life in the senses wherein the love of Christ is felt with sensible fervor helping the beginner to take solid steps forward. The next phase is a dark night and negation leading to a more sober and genuine relationship with God. This phase unfolds gradually in an active and passive manner in both the sensory and spiritual parts of a person's makeup. The third phase is full union or likeness of love (pp. 82-83). Traditionally these three phases have been termed purgative, illuminative and unitive.

For a thorough treatment of the ways of the inner life as explained by John of the Cross the following may be consulted: Keiran Kavanaugh, O.C.D., *John of the Cross, Selected Writings*, The Classics of Western Spirituality (New York: Paulist Press, 1987); Susan Muto, *John Of The Cross For Today: The Ascent* (Notre Dame, Indiana: Ave Maria Press, 1991).

For a briefer handling of this topic see: J. Aumann, *Spiritual Theology*, Ch.6, "Christian Perfection and Mystical Experience", pp. 125-134 and Ch.8, "Progressive Purgation", pp. 177-207.

44. These degrees of prayer refer to those described by Teresa of Avila in the *Interior Castle*.

For a synopsis of these stages see J. Aumann, *Spiritual Theology*, pp. 317-357.

Briefly the grades of prayer as cited by Aumann are: vocal prayer, meditation, affective prayer, prayer of simplicity, prayer of quiet, prayer of union, prayer of conforming union, and prayer of transforming union. The first four belong to the predominantly ascetical stage of the spiritual life; the other four grades of prayer are infused and belong to the mystical phase of the spiritual life. (*Spiritual Theology*, p. 316.)

The ascetical stage of the spiritual life refers to the process in which the person can attain through personal effort, with the help of grace the level of prayer described. Thus with the help of grace and personal work, it lies within the power of the Christian to pray vocally, to meditate and to experience affective prayer and the prayer of simplicity.

The mystical stage of the spiritual life refers to the phase in which the Holy Spirit predominantly acts upon the soul. This level of prayer is not within the natural power of the Christian but is totally gift of God in the varying degrees to which God wishes to grant it. One may be disposed for God's graces of prayer by endeavoring to conform one's will to the divine will and to grow in love for God. This creates a receptivity for the deeper relationship of mystical prayer. All Christians are called to this phase of prayer but the degree to which God grants this union lies in the mystery of God.

For a fuller treatment of this topic the following texts may be consulted: Teresa of Avila, *Interior Castle*, Trans. and Ed., E. Allison Peers (New York: Image Books, 1961); *The Collected Works of St. Teresa of Avila*, trans. K. Kavanaugh, OCD, and O. Rodriguez, OCD (Washington DC: Institute of

Carmelite Studies, 1976); Tessa Bielecki, *Teresa of Avila, Mystical Writings* (New York: Crossroads, 1994).

45. The three expressions of prayer presented in the *Catechism (CCC)* -vocal, meditative and contemplative appear to be based on the grades of prayer identified and explained by Teresa of Avila in her book, *The Interior Castle.* It is to be noted that Teresa's description of and guidance for the spiritual life and that of John of the Cross are congruous and complementary; hence, the interrelatedness of the grades of prayer and the three stages of the spiritual life. Of note as well is the fact that in the spiritual journey the grades of prayer and the stages of the spiritual life are not always distinctly differentiated or successive but are often interrelated with one or other predominating.

For a fine summation of the complementary doctrines of Teresa and John see "Teresa of Jesus and John of the Cross", E.W. Trueman Dicken in *The Study of Spirituality*, Jones et al., pp. 363-376. A fuller treatment of their doctrines of the mystical life are found in *The Graces of Interior Prayer*, A. Poulain, S.J. (1910) trans. Leonora L. Yorke Smith (Westminster, Vt.: Celtic Cross Books, 1950, 1978).

An indepth study of the mystical life is also presented by Francis de Sales in his Treatise *On The Love of God.* This is the work with which Louise would have been most familiar. Louise does not mention having read either the works of Teresa of Avila or John of the Cross but in a letter to a Sister, she does refer to "the great Saint Teresa" (SWLM, p. 427. L.370). In his Conferences to the Sisters, Vincent occasionally cites Teresa of Avila.

Part Four of the *Catechism* offers an excellent and very helpful synopsis of the topic of Christian Prayer.

46. CCC, #2699.

47. CCC, #2699.

48. *CCC,* #'s 2700-2704. See also J. Aumann, *Spiritual Theology*, p. 316.

Catherine of Siena in her *Dialogue* attests to this. She recounts the words of Jesus to her: "The soul should season her self-knowledge with knowledge of my goodness, and her knowledge of me with self-knowledge. In this way vocal prayer will profit the soul who practices it and it will please me. And if she perseveres in its practice, she will advance from imperfect vocal prayer to perfect mental prayer." Noffke, *The Dialogue*, p. 125. Cf. Prof. Fabio Giardini, O.P., *The Varieties and Unity of Christian Prayerlife* (Rome: PUST, 1994), p. 257.

49. John of The Cross describes meditation as "a discursive act built on forms, figures and images, imagined and fashioned by these senses [intellect and imagination]" (*Ascent of Mount Carmel*, II, 12, [3]). Classics of Western Spirituality: *John of the Cross, Selected Writings*, Kieran Kavanaugh, O.C.D. (New York: Paulist Press, 1987), p. 106. Hereinafter cited as *CWS:John of the Cross.*

Teresa describes mental prayer as "an intimate sharing between friends; it means taking time frequently to be alone with him who we know loves us" (Teresa of Avila, *The Book of Her Life*, 8,5 in *The Collected Works of St. Teresa of Avila*, trans. Kieran Kavanaugh, O.C.D., and O. Rodriguez, O.C.D. (Washington: ICS Publishers, 1987) I, 96). See also: CCC, #'s 2705-2709 and J. Aumann, p. 318.

Vincent de Paul describes meditation thus:

Mental pray is made in two ways: one by way of the understanding, and the other with the will.

By way of the understanding, when after something has been read the mind wakes up in the presence of God and then occupies itself in seeking to know the meaning of the mystery proposed, in seeing its suitable lesson, and in arousing the affections to seek God and avoid evil. And although the will produces these acts, yet it is called prayer of the understanding, because its chief function, which is to seek out the truth, is exercised by the understanding, which is occupied primarily with the subject put before it. This is what is ordinarily called meditation. Everybody can make it, each according to his ability and the lights which God may bestow (Leonard, *Conferences*, II, 52).

50. CCC, #2712: "Contemplative prayer is the poor and humble surrender to the loving will of the Father in ever deeper union with his beloved Son."

51. According to Poulain, meditative prayer is identified as "affective prayer" when affections such as praise, love and thanksgiving predominate over intellectual considerations. A. Poulain, S.J. *The Graces of Interior Prayer*, p. 7.

52. John of the Cross identifies this process as "the dark night of the senses". It is a stage of purification in preparation for deeper entry into the inner life. If the soul is to reach divine union, it must empty itself of its intellectual imaginings, leaving this interior sense in darkness. *Ascent,*II, 12, 3, *CWS:John of the Cross*, p. 106.

It is not within the scope of this brief topic to detail the stages of purification as described by John of the Cross which appear to be prerequisites for growth in union with God. However, every praying person intent on this path of inner life will experience in some degree both the purification of the senses and of the spirit —the dark nights. Through active and passive purgation the soul is often painfully purified in preparation for union with God.

53. This phrase is used by Bossuet and cited by Poulain, p. 10. It is interesting to note that the English word "contemplate" comes from the French verb "contempler" which means to "gaze at".

54. John of the Cross, *Ascent*, II, 12, [8], *CWS:John of the Cross*, p. 108. CCC, #2715: "a *gaze* of faith, fixed on Jesus. . . . This focus on Jesus is a renunciation of self and the gaze of Jesus purifies the heart."

55. The term "prayer of simplicity" was used by Bossuet. Poulain used the expression "simple regard" and Teresa of Avila called this prayer, "the

prayer of acquired recollection" to distinguish it from infused recollection which is the first grade of mystical prayer. (Aumann, p. 327).

According to Poulain, the prayer of simplicity or *simple regard* is a mental prayer wherein to a great degree intuition replaces reasoning, affections and resolutions expressed in few words show little variety and a thought or sentiment returns incessantly and easily among many other thoughts. It is a slow sequence of single glances cast upon one object. (Poulain, p. 8).

56. CCC, #2711. The *Catechism* expresses this idea as follows: "gathering up one's heart, recollecting one's being under the prompting of the Holy Spirit, abiding in the dwelling place of the Lord which we are, awakening our faith in order to enter into the presence of him who awaits us." Once there, "we let our masks fall, turn our hearts back to the Lord who loves us, so as to hand ourselves over to him as an offering to be purified and transformed."

57. Infused Contemplation is termed passive because the predominant action is on the part of the Holy Spirit acting upon the soul. It is not within the power of the individual to produce the effects of the Spirit.

In his book *The Mysticism Debate*, Paul Murray, O.P., describes infused contemplation as "nothing other than a loving and quasi-experimental knowledge of God which, because it cannot be obtained by our own personal efforts, requires a special illumination and inspiration of the Holy Spirit." *The Mysticism Debate* (Scotdale, Penn.: Herald Press, 1977) p. 38.

It is interesting to read Vincent de Paul's description of contemplation which he gave to the Sisters: "The other sort of prayer is called contemplation. In this the soul, in the presence of God, does nothing else but receive from him what he bestows. She is without action, and God himself inspires her, without any effort on the soul's part, with all that she can desire, and with far more" (Leonard, *Conferences*, II, 52).

58. Teresa of Avila says that God gives the gift of mystical prayer, "when he wills and as he wills and to whom he wills" (Mansions IV, 1, Peers, p. 73).

In discussing infused contemplative prayer, Vincent de Paul questioned the Sisters: "Have you ever, my dear Sisters, experienced this sort of prayer? I am sure you have, and in your retreats you have often been astonished that, without doing anything on your part, God himself has replenished your soul and granted you knowledge you never had before" (Leonard, *Conferences*, II, 52).

59. Poulain, p. 55. Poulain posits that degrees of prayer should not be exaggerated and that the soul may pass imperceptibly from one type of prayer to another. In the prayer of union, degrees may not be successive. Cf. *Ascent*,II, 15, 1, *CWS:John of the Cross*, p. 118.

60. John of the Cross describes the prayer of quiet thus: "At the moment it [the soul] recollects itself in the presence of God, it enters on an act of general, loving, peaceful, and tranquil knowledge, drinking wisdom and love and delight" (*Ascent*, II, 14, 2, *CWS:John of the Cross*, p. 112).

Teresa of Avila compares the "prayer of quiet" to a basin being filled with water directly from the source which is God. Mansion, IV, 2. *Interior Castle,* Peers, p. 81.

Elsewhere Teresa of Avila speaks of the experience of the "prayer of quiet" as follows: "I sometimes experienced . . .even while reading, that a feeling of the presence of God would come upon me unexpectedly so that I could in no way doubt he was within me or I totally immersed in him" (The Book of Her Life, 10, 1. *The Collected Works of St. Teresa of Avila,* I, 105).

61. Poulain, pp. 13-14.

62. Poulain describes the state of union thus:

> The mystic states which have God for their object attract attention at the outset by the impression of recollection and union which they cause us to experience. . . . God gives us an experimental, intellectual knowledge of his presence . . . makes us feel that we really enter into communion with him. The manifestation increases in distinctness as the union becomes of a higher order (p. 65).

The prayer of union then is one phase of prayer having varying degrees. Teresa of Avila and John of the Cross speak of the two degrees of "spiritual espousal" and "spiritual marriage". (Mansions, VII,2, *Interior Castle,* Peers, p. 213; *Canticle,* 22,3, CWS, p. 257.) To describe these two degrees of prayer, J. Aumann uses the terms "prayer of conforming union" and prayer of "transforming union". It would seem that *CCC* also employs this latter terminology.

The *Catechism* speaks of contemplative prayer as "an attentiveness to the word of God, and a silent love which achieves real union with the prayer of Christ to the extent that it makes us share in his mystery (#2724), celebrated in the Eucharist so that our charity will manifest it in our acts" (#2718).

63. Poulain, p. 66. Mystic union is a union with God by love. This love is called forth by a known, experimental possession of God.

64. Poulain, p. 237.

65. Aumann, p. 346.

The intuitive knowledge which the soul receives is the result of the Holy Spirit's gifts of knowledge and wisdom acting upon the soul's virtues of faith and charity. See Aumann, p. 331.

CCC, # 2713: "Contemplative prayer is a *gift,* a grace . . ., a covenant relationship established by God within our hearts. . . a *communion* in which the Holy Trinity conforms man, the image of God, 'to his likeness.' "

66. Teresa of Avila in Mansions VI, 6, describes this intense longing for God as an effect of the mystical espousals wherein the soul is awakened to a keen awareness of God's loving presence in the soul and an acute knowledge of the mysteries of God. She wrote: "Having won such great favors, the soul is so anxious to have complete fruition of their Giver that its life becomes sheer, though delectable, torture. It has the keenest longing for death, and so it frequently and tearfully begs God to take it out of this exile" (Peers, p. 163). Cf. Poulain, p. 243 ff. See Aumann, p. 345.

67. Teresa of Avila, Mansions VII, Peers, p. 214. Cf. Giardini, *The Varieties And Unity Of Christian Prayerlife*, pp. 265-266.

68. Teresa of Avila, Mansions VII, Peers, p. 209.

69. Paul Murray speaks of the Christian mystic "as someone actively open and receptive to God." He identifies contemplation as "an immanent activity", but effected within us only by the Holy Spirit. The interior state of "passivity" in no way excludes, but rather encourages, a fully active and involved Christian life in the service of others. Paul Murray, O.P. *The Mysticism Debate*, p. 30.

70. See Poulain, pp. 283-297.

71. Teresa of Avila states the following: "Believe me, what matters . . . is whether we try to practise the virtues, and make a complete surrender of our wills to God and order our lives as his Majesty ordains: let us desire that not our wills, but his will, be done" (Mansions III, Peers, p. 65).

In Mansions VII, Teresa writes: "We should desire and engage in prayer, not for our enjoyment, but for the sake of acquiring this strength which fits us for service" (Peers, p. 231).

The Rule of 1633 for the First Daughters of Charity reads: "They shall read a passage of the holy gospel so as to stimulate themselves to the practice of virtue and the service of their neighbor in imitation of the Son of God" (SWLM, p. 726).

72. CCC, # 825: "Strengthened by so many and such great means of salvation, all the faithful, whatever their condition or state — though each in his own way — are called by the Lord to that perfection of sanctity by which the Father himself is perfect" [LG 11, #3].

In his book, *Crossing The Threshold of Hope* (p. 88), Pope John Paul II in discussing the universal call to holiness and mystical prayer writes the following:

Christian mysticism is born of the *Revelation of the living God.* This God opens himself to union with man, arousing in him the capacity to be united with him, especially by means of the theological virtues - faith, hope, and, above all, love.

Christian mysticism in every age up to our own-including the mysticism of marvelous men of action like Vincent de Paul, John Bosco, Maximilian Kolbe-has built up and continues to build up Christianity in its most essential element. It also builds up the Church as a community of faith, hope and charity. It builds up civilization. . .

73. John Paul II, *Crossing The Threshold of Hope*, p. 17. Pope John Paul II, describes the relationship of prayer thus:

In prayer, then, the true protagonist is God. The protagonist is *Christ,* who constantly frees creation from slavery to corruption and leads it toward liberty, for the glory of the children of God. The protagonist is the *Holy Spirit,* who "comes to the aid of our

Louise De Marillac—Her Legacy to Contemporary Spirituality

weakness." We begin to pray, believing that it is our own initiative that compels us to do so. Instead, we learn that it is always God's initiative within us, . . . *This initiative restores in us our true humanity; it restores in us our unique dignity.* Yes, we are brought into the higher dignity of the children of God, the children of God who are the hope of all creation.

74. Gobillon (Fiat Edition) I, 235: "Remarques sur les vertus de mademoiselle le Gras, écrites par soeur Mathurine Guérin pour soeur Marguerite Chétif." Cf. Charpy, *Documents,* p. 946, Doc.822.

75. SWLM, p. 736. A.80-RULE FOR THE SISTERS WHO CARE FOR THE CHILDREN: "They shall have the children make acts of adoration, love, thanksgiving and supplication so as to avoid offending God during the day and throughout their lives." The older children were to pray to God before going to bed and once they were in bed the Sisters were to have them give their hearts once more to God. (p. 373)

p. 811. A.81-REMARKS ON THE RULE FOR THE SISTERS WITH THE FOUNDLINGS. This record refers to such practices for the older children as visits to the Blessed Sacrament, Mass, and the Rosary.

76. SWLM, p. 691. A.13-AN INTERIOR TRIAL, c.1621. In this notation, Louise relates an experience of "discouragement, annihilation, . . .and desertion by God because of infidelities."

p. 692. A.15B-ON THE DESIRE TO GIVE ONESELF TO GOD, c.1622. This reflection presents Louise's inspiration to give herself to God to fulfill his holy will for the remainder of her life.

p. 693. A.3-ACT OF CONSECRATION, c. 1626. Herein Louise abandons herself to divine providence and to the accomplishment of God's will in her, dedicating herself to the fulfillment of his will which she chooses as her supreme consolation.

p. 695. A.4-OBLATION TO THE BLESSED VIRGIN, c. 1626. Louise dedicates herself to Mary so that she may more perfectly belong to God by imitating Mary's holy life by fulfilling the designs of God in her own life. Louise also invokes Mary to take her son and herself under her care.

In reflecting on the content of these notes it would seem that in the years of 1621-2, Louise was experiencing passive purgation of the spirit and perhaps had already entered into a level of mystic union with God in which the trials of the spirit effected physical responses within her.

77. Gobillon attests that Louise nurtured her prayer life on such works as the "Imitation of Christ", "Louis of Grenada", the works of Francis de Sales, "The Spiritual Combat" and Sacred Scriptures. Her personal penances consisted of fasts, vigils, the penitential cincture and acts of charity. In addition she had the penance of chronic poor health. Gobillon (Fiat) I, 11-12.

78. "Her practice of every virtue possible in that state was edifying. She applied herself from the first years to visiting the poor sick of the parish where she lived. She herself gave them broths and remedies, made their

beds, instructed them and consoled them by her exhortations, disposed them to receive the sacraments, and buried them after their death."

"The virtue of charity which, according to the doctrine of the Holy Spirit, is strengthened and evermore increased by helping the sick, was established in her heart with such strength and zeal, that she set no limits to her plans. She did not rest satisfied with helping the sick in their homes, but went to visit them in the hospitals to add some comforts to the basic care which was supplied there, and to render them personally the lowest and most distressing services." These accounts were attested to by Louise's servants. Gobillon (Fiat) pp. 8-9.

79. Gobillon (Fiat), I, 13.

80. SWLM, p. 691. A.13-AN INTERIOR TRIAL, c.1621.

81. SWLM, p. 692. A.15B-ON THE DESIRE TO GIVE ONESELF TO GOD, c.1622.

82. SWLM, p. 1. A.2-LIGHT.

83. Teresa of Avila, *Interior Castle,* Mansions VI, Peers.

Compare these trials with Teresa of Avila's description of interior trials in Mansions VI of *Interior Castle*:

> When we come to interior sufferings! If these could be described they would make all physical sufferings seem very slight, but it is impossible to describe interior sufferings and how they happen (p. 129).
> When Our Lord gives him (the devil) leave to test her soul, and even to make her think herself cast off by God, for there are many things which assault her soul with an interior oppression so keenly felt and so intolerable that I do not know to what it can be compared, save to the torment of those who suffer in hell, for in this spiritual tempest no consolation is possible (p. 131).
> In this tempest there is no help for it but to wait upon the mercy of God, Who suddenly, at the most unlooked-for hour, with a single word, or on some chance occasion, lifts the whole of this burden for the soul. . .(p.132).

84. Teresa of Avila, *Interior Castle*, Mansions VI, Peers, pp. 141-2.

The hallmarks of a true mystical encounter described by Teresa of Avila are: The soul knows for certain that God has acted within it. It has the inner assurance that the knowledge of an intellectual locution is from God. Frequently the results of the locution are instantaneous bringing peace to the troubled soul. The words of the locution stay within the person's memory.

85. SWLM, p. 1. A.2-LIGHT.

86. The original handwritten account on Louise's folded paper is preserved in the archives of the Daughters of Charity at rue du Bac in Paris.

87. Teresa describes the locution as a means God uses to awaken the soul (Peers, p. 139).

88. SWLM, p. 693. A.3-ACT OF CONSECRATION, c. 1626. Around this same time Louise made an "Oblation to the Blessed Virgin" in which she dedicated herself to Mary so that she might more perfectly belong to God by imitating Mary's holy life by fulfilling the designs of God in her own life. Louise also invoked Mary to take her son and herself under her care. SWLM, p. 695. A.4-OBLATION TO THE BLESSED VIRGIN, c. 1626.

89. SWLM, p. 689. A.1-RULE OF LIFE IN THE WORLD.

Louise's biographer, Gobillon does indicate some of Louise's spiritual practices prior to 1628 such as devotion to meditation, spiritual reading, reading of scripture, times of retreat, penances, fasting and charitable works. (Gobillon, [Fiat], I, 11, 12.) Herein, Bishop Camus counsels Louise to moderate her spiritual retreats as she had a "spiritual avidity that needed to be restrained" (Ibid). Vincent de Paul would continue to guide Louise in this manner of "moderation."

90. SWLM, p. 689. A.1.

91. Susan A. Muto, *Meditation in Motion* (New York: Image Books, 1986), p. 102.

92. It must be noted that the discipline, in various forms, and the hairshirt were common means of penance for many centuries for devout women such as Louise. Such practices may not be customary today but the reality of the necessity for bodily penance in conjuction with interior penance to assist in growth in virtue is valid.

93. Although lengthy retreats may not be feasible for the average Christian, a day or a weekend, once or twice a year, could offer the time to "come aside" to be with the Lord, to be revitalized and to recall who one is and where one is going. It is interesting to observe that practices, such as retreats, that for so long were the hallmark of a devout Christian life are more and more entering into the ordinary framework of the corporate business world with the aim of improving interpersonal relationships, management skills and company production.

94. The importance of prayer and penance for the Christian Life are reiterated in the *Catechism.*

Regarding prayer, CCC states: "It is always possible to pray" (#2743); "Prayer is a vital necessity" (#2744); and, "Prayer and the Christian life are inseparable. . ." (#2745).

With reference to penance, the *Catechism* asserts: "The interior penance of the Christian can be expressed in many and various ways. Scripture and the Fathers insist above all on three forms, *fasting, prayer* and *almsgiving,* which express conversion in relation to oneself, to God, and to others" (#1434).

The topic of conversion is further discussed in *CCC* in terms of "taking up one's cross daily and following Jesus as the surest means of penance" (#1435) and the source and nourishment of conversion and penance being found in the eucharist (#1436).

95. CCC, #2660: "Prayer in the events of each day and each moment is one of the secrets of the kingdom revealed to 'little children,' to the servants of Christ, to the poor of the Beatitudes."

96. CCC, #2697 states: "But we cannot pray 'at all times' if we do not pray at specific times, consciously willing it. These are the special times of Christian prayer, both in intensity and duration."

97. Of note is the fact that even though Louise had experienced God's direct intervention in her life and undoubtedly had reached a high degree of prayer, her daily prayer life still maintained the fundamental structure of vocal and meditative prayer. Louise knew that one must always prepare oneself to be open to receive the communications of God and this was her active stance therein.

Teresa of Avila also maintains that one should always meditate until God makes it impossible. She refers here especially to the prayer of "simple regard" and says: "But if it does not already meditate in this way, it will be well advised to attempt to do so; for I know that the most sublime kind of prayer will be no obstacle to it and I believe omission to practise it often would be a great mistake" (Peers, Mansions VI, p. 176).

98. Leonard, *Conferences*,IV, 309-333.

Following Louise's death in 1660, the two Conferences which Vincent de Paul held with the Sisters on Louise's virtues indicate that a major witness which Louise gave to the Sisters was that of her deep humility (pp. 318, 325-326), confidence in providence (p. 320) and great charity (pp. 319, 327).

99. CCC, #2752.

100. For the modern Christian, the time frame for prayer presented in Louise's horarium could very well be prohibitive because of the rhythm of life lived, particularly in European and North American cultures. However, the ideal presented of an integrated life of prayer is a challenge which the modern Christian is called to face. Susan Muto suggests : ". . . the challenge is to transcend the pressure of time, not to make it an excuse to neglect prayer" (*Meditation in Motion*, p. 101).

The simple prayer practices of Louise are within the range of the ordinary Christian who desires to develop a life of prayer. Such practices as a brief morning prayer, a short time of reflective prayer, a reading of scripture, the rosary, daily Mass when possible, recalling the presence of God, a nightly review of the day to thank God for graces received and to ask pardon for failures, help develop a prayer life which keeps one in tune with God and if lived in a spirit of faith will lead to deeper union as it did for Louise.

CCC, #2698 states: "The Tradition of the Church proposes to the faithful certain rhythms of praying intended to nourish continual prayer." This article outlines daily prayers, such as morning and evening, grace before and after meals, the Liturgy of the Hours. Sundays are to be centered on the Eucharist and prayer and the cycle of the liturgical year is to be a basic rhythm of the life of prayer. Louise's rhythm of prayer was certainly in tune with these principles.

101. "If any want to become my followers, let them deny themselves and take up their cross daily and follow me" (Lk. 9: 23).

102. SWLM, A.55-ORDER OF THE DAY, 1633, p. 726.

103. SWLM, p. 52. L. 388, 1641: "If some of you are worried or troubled, I beg of you, in the name of God, to turn immediately to prayer and to be very faithful to our Rules and to the practice of the virtues required by your state."

p. 825 M.73-ON THE INTERIOR SPIRIT NECESSARY FOR THE DAUGHTERS OF CHARITY:

It seems to me that our interior conversation with God should consist in the continuous remembrance of his holy presence. We must adore him every hour and make acts of love for his goodness, recalling, as far as possible, the thoughts that we received during meditation so that we may correct our faults and advance in this same holy love.

104. SWLM, p. 697. A.17-FEARS AND CONSOLATIONS EXPERIENCED CONCERNING HOLY COMMUNION.

In a Retreat note c. 1632, Louise reiterates these sentiments: "Willingly must I allow Jesus to take possession of my soul and reign there as King. Thus, I shall preserve the joy I experience in realizing that each of us individually may desire and, indeed, has the power to become his well-beloved" (SWLM, p. 715. A.5-Retreat).

105. Compare Louise's words with those of Teresa of Avila in describing the entrance to Mansions VII: "For he must needs have an abiding-place in the soul, just as he has one in heaven, where his Majesty alone dwells: so let us call this a second heaven" (Peers, p. 207).

Certainly Louise is aware of God's action in her soul. This may be described as an infused intuitive experience characteristic of the prayer of union. The point of God possessing the soul is also an aspect of union. It would appear that Louise was being led in an unitive way.

106. Coste, V. de. P., I, 62. L.36-To Saint Louise, c. 1629.

107. SWLM, p. 702. A.9-RETREAT.

In this notation Louise seems to indicate an intuitive knowledge of an awareness of a very deep union with God in which she desires to be totally his by being drawn into him. Such a union would be mystical marriage — the two becoming one. This is reflective of the union in Mansions VI and VII in Teresa of Avila's grades of prayer. Note Teresa's words in Mansions VII: ". . .those who were already prepared to put away from them everything corporeal and to leave the soul in a state of pure spirituality, so that it might be joined with Uncreated Spirit in this celestial union" (Peers, p. 216).

108. Cf. Gobillon (Fiat), I, 28; Coste, V. de P., I, 64, L.39.

109. SWLM, p. 704. A.50-VISITS TO THE CONFRATERNITIES OF ASNIÈRES AND SAINT-CLOUD.

It is interesting that in the beginning of Louise's apostolic life, and indeed throughout the future years, God supplied for her poor health and brought about marvelous fruits from her labors. In this passage it would seem that God was actually living and working in her. On two occasions in 1647 and 1660, Vincent de Paul stated that Louise "had been as good as dead for ten or twenty years and the only life she had was that which she received from divine grace" (Coste, *Life & Works,* I, 463). Cf. *St. Vincent de Paul,*III, 256; IX, 324.

Truly this suggests a unitive way of life and reflects the words of Paul: "I live now, not I but Christ lives in me" (Gal. 2:20).

110. SWLM, p. 704. A.50-VISITS TO THE CONFRATERNITIES OF ASNIÈRES AND SAINT-CLOUD. In this notation, Louise described an extraordinary spiritual experience which she accepted as a spiritual espousal. The action of God initiated the espousal and Louise's response completed it. The commitment had an implication of permanency and was ratified by the "sharing of goods".

111. It is without doubt that Vincent de Paul was instrumental in the unfolding of Louise's deep awareness of the identification of the poor with Jesus and Jesus with the poor.

112. SWLM, p. 709. A.19-ON THE LOVE WHICH GOD HAS SHOWN TO US IN THE MYSTERY OF THE REDEMPTION.

Louise believes that God has taught her about the humanity of his Son and has allowed her to attach herself to him — to enter a special relationship with him.

In a retreat note c. 1633 Louise wrote a similar resolution: "I shall calmly adore the divinity in the Infant Jesus and imitate, to the best of my ability, his holy humanity especially his simplicity and charity which led him to come to us as a child so as to be more accessible to his creatures" (ibid., p. 718. A.8-RETREAT).

113. SWLM, p. 704. A.10-RESOLUTIONS FOR THE PERIOD FROM ASCENSION TO PENTECOST, c. 1630.

This notation is reflective of the point which Teresa of Avila makes in Mansions VII regarding the soul no longer wishing to die to be with God but rather being willing to remain on earth in order to do God's will and bring glory to his name by having others praise him. *The Interior Castle,* VII, Peers, p. 220.

114. SWLM, p. 717. A.8-RETREAT c. 1633. Louise has been given an "assurance by God"; hence, a special communication had occurred between them. It is very interesting to see that Louise repeated almost the identical sentiments of humility and confidence in her final notation of 1660.

p. 719. In the same retreat Louise experienced another affirmation from God, this time in the persons of Jesus and Mary. Louise wrote:

> At holy Mass, as I was giving myself wholeheartedly to the Blessed Virgin so as to belong entirely to God according to his good pleasure, it seemed to me that Our Lord was presenting my past and future unworthiness to his Holy Mother. Believing that they both had accepted me, I asked a proof that . . .

115. SWLM, p. 720. A.12-RENUNCIATION OF SELF.

In this notation, Louise certainly surrendered herself to God's transforming action in her life. In simple terms, she gave her "yes" of espousals to spiritual marriage.

Of interest is the similarity between this passage and one which John of the Cross describes in *The Spiritual Canticle* as the union of spiritual marriage. He wrote: "You dried up and subdued in me the appetites and passions,. . .an impediment to this state. . . .that my nature now alone and denuded of all temporal, natural, and spiritual impurity may be united with you alone, with your nature alone, through no intermediary. This union is found only in the spiritual marriage . . ." (Stanza 22:7, *CWS:John of the Cross*, p. 259).

Fr. Benito Martinez, C.M., in his article, "The Prayer of Saint Louise", commenting on this text, wonders whether or not it might actually be "transforming union" (*Echoes*, #3, March 1983, p. 133). If so, God had granted Louise the highest form of mystical prayer and established her in the unitive way prior to her total dedication to the service of the poor and to the institution of the Daughters. Such union may very well be a pre-requisite for one chosen by God to be "foundress" and "educator" of a spiritual family dedicated to charity.

Of equal note is the statement of John of the Cross in *The Living Flame*, in reference to the highest degree of union: "Few persons have reached these heights. Some have, however; especially those whose virtue and spirit were to be diffused among their children. For God accords to founders, with respect to the first fruits of the spirit, wealth and value commensurate with the greater or lesser following they will have in their doctrine and spirituality" (#12, *CWS:John of the Cross*, p. 305).

Following John's premise, the great following that God destined Louise to have in her spirituality and Christian lifestyle certainly would warrant a high degree of unitive life with God.

116. SWLM, pp. 341-2. L.369 - To Monsieur Vincent, August 24 before 1650.

Louise's intuitive knowledge of God and the resultant joy are characteristic of an intellectual vision as described by Teresa of Avila in Mansions VII. Vincent's response is consistent with one of Teresa of Avila's timings of such a favor as mentioned in Mansions VI. See *Interior Castle*, Mansions VII (Peers, pp. 209, 216) and Mansions VI (p. 193).

117. SWLM, p. 352. L.305 - To Monsieur Vincent, May 1651.

118. SWLM, pp. 820-821. A.26.

Teresa of Avila frequently mentioned that in mystic prayer, infused gifts cannot be explained. Teresa also mentioned in Mansions VII that the soul is given an intellectual awareness of the Humanity of Jesus. *Interior Castle*, Peers, p. 215.

Louise's infused knowledge regarding her neighbor is reflective of the Father's words to Catherine of Siena : "Such is the means I have given you to practice and prove your virtue. The service you cannot render me you must do for your neighbors" *The Dialogue,* p. 36.

119. Here again one sees the echo of *The Dialogue,* p. 36: " Nor could she do otherwise, for love of me and love of neighbor are one and the same thing: Since love of neighbor has its source in me, the more the soul loves me, the more she loves her neighbors."

120. SWLM, p. 825. A.18-DESIRE TO IMITATE OUR LORD AT HIS DEATH.

This notation represents a passive action of God on Louise characteristic of unitive prayer. She frequently mentioned that God filled her with a desire for him.

121. SWLM, p. 827. A.27-ON THE PURE LOVE WE HAVE VOWED TO GOD.

It is interesting to compare Louise's reflections on this passage with those of John of the Cross in *The Spiritual Canticle*:

That is: beneath the favor of the tree of the cross. . ., where the Son of God redeemed human nature and consequently espoused it to himself, and then espoused each soul by giving it through the cross grace and pledges for this espousal. . . . The espousal of which we speak bears reference to perfection and is not achieved save gradually and by stages (Stanza 23:3,5, *CWS:John of the Cross,* pp. 260-261).

122. SWLM, p. 827. A.27-ON THE PURE LOVE WE HAVE VOWED TO GOD.

In this reflection Louise also wrote: "Therefore, at the foot of this holy, sacred and adored cross, I sacrifice everything that might prevent me from loving, with all the purity that you expect of me, without ever aspiring to any joy other than submission to your good pleasure and to the laws of your pure love" (p. 829).

123. SWLM, p. 819. A.26. Herein, Louise expressed thoughts similar to those written by John of the Cross in *The Spiritual Canticle,* Stanza 28:8, *CWS:John of the Cross,* p. 269: ". . .The soul in this state of spiritual espousals [or spiritual marriage — cited in footnote 14] ordinarily walks in the union of love of God, which is a habitual and loving attentiveness of the will to God."

124. SWLM, p. 819. A.26-REASONS FOR GIVING ONESELF TO GOD IN ORDER TO RECEIVE THE HOLY SPIRIT.

Characteristics of Mansions VII of the *Interior Castle,* are reflected particularly in such phrases of Louise as: "Should I not desire, O my God, to die upon receiving it? To live for as long as it pleases you, but with your life which is one of total love. May I not, beginning in this world, flow into the ocean of your divine Being?" Cf. Peers, pp. 219, 220.

" . . .no other satisfaction but that of loving and of willing your good pleasure." Cf. Peers, pp. 217, 219.

"You still see weaknesses in me in my desire for the affection of creatures. Consume this, O Ardent Fire of Divine Love! . . .I reject, with all my heart, my excessive abruptness which I renounce forevermore,. . ." Cf. Peers, p.226.

John of the Cross speaks of the conscious reception of the Holy Spirit as the sign of mystical marriage and transforming union. *Spiritual Canticle,* Stanza 38:3, *CWS:John of the Cross,* p. 279. Louise does not say that she "received the Holy Spirit" but her ardent desire, her ecstatic expressions, her total surrender to God and her conscious awareness of the resultant transforming union with the Holy Spirit indicate her preparedness for this infusion of God's love, if God so desired.

125. SWLM, p. 833. M.8B-ON HOLY COMMUNION: 1660 (Jan. 3, if liturgical calendar not changed)

Note how this communication echoes Louise's retreat resolution c. 1633 when she wrote: "I shall calmly adore the divinity in the Infant Jesus and imitate, to the best of my ability, his holy humanity especially his simplicity and charity which led him to come to us as a child so as to be more accessible to his creatures" (SWLM, p. 718. A.8-Retreat).

John of the Cross, in *The Spiritual Canticle,* states the following: "In this high state of spiritual marriage the bridegroom reveals his wonderful secrets to the soul . . . He communicates to her, mainly, sweet mysteries of his Incarnation and of the ways of the redemption of humanity, which is one of the loftiest of his works. . ." (Stanza 23:1, p. 260). Cf. Stanza 37:2, p. 276.

126. Leonard, *Conferences,* IV, 318. During the Conference of July 3, 1660 on The Virtues of Louise de Marillac, one of the Sisters expressed the following: "As for the virtues she practised, a whole book would be necessary if they were to be written down, and persons of far greater intellect than ours to report them. However, as obedience obliges me, it must be done. But when I have said all I remember, a great deal more will remain to be said."

127. Leonard, *Conferences,* IV, 314, 315, 325, 326.

On the discussion of Louise's virtues one Sister stated: "She was of a most interior spirit and her mind was much occupied with God" (p. 314). Vincent continued: "Her soul was raised up to God, and this was because she had for a very long time created a deep fund of devotion in her heart. . . .Mademoiselle Le Gras had this gift of blessing God in all things" (p.314). Vincent later remarked to the Sisters: "Well now, you must believe that your Mother had a great fund of interior spirit to regulate her memory in such a manner that she only used it for God, and only used her will to love him" (p. 315). Another Sister spoke of Louise having "a great sense of the presence of God in all her actions" (p. 325). Another remarked: "As soon as ever she was alone, she was wrapped in prayer, but when anyone approached her, she at once showed a smiling countenance and never let it be seen that she had been intruded on. . ." (p. 326). Commenting on her sufferings, one Sister remarked: ". . .during her illnesses and when in pain she had her mind constantly raised to God and always looked to his good pleasure in these circumstances. No one ever heard her complain of her infirmities; on the contrary, she was always gay and content" (p. 310).

128. Leonard, *Conferences,* IV.

The Sisters and Vincent de Paul all attested to Louise's great humility.

She was an example of humility in community life and in governance. The Sisters recounted her spirit of humility and her public acts of humility such as: confessing her faults, asking forgiveness with arms outstretched, lying on the floor, serving table, washing dishes, serving the poor, and kissing the feet of the Sisters on Good Friday (pp. 315, 318, 319, 325). Vincent stated: "I have never seen any who accused themselves of their sins with so much purity" (p. 315). The words of the Father to Catherine of Siena are an apt description for Louise: "The soul who lives virtuously sets her tree's root in the valley of true humility" (*The Dialogue*, p. 171).

Confirming the Sisters' comments on Louise's prudence, Vincent commented: "It is true that I do not know if I have ever seen anyone as prudent as she was. She had this virtue in a high degree and I wish with all my heart that the Company had it" (*Conferences*, IV, 311).

Following numerous attestations by the Sisters of Louise's spirit of poverty, Vincent exhorted them: "Blessed be God Who gave this spirit to Mademoiselle Le Gras! . . . Let us follow her example, Sisters, in the way she loved this virtue of poverty" (p. 314).

129. *The Dialogue*, p. 42 #11: "Such are the fruits of action that I ask of the soul: that virtue should prove itself in response to need. . . . What I want is many works of patient and courageous endurance and of the other virtues I have described to you—interior virtues that are all active in bearing the fruit of grace."

The Interior Castle, Mansions VII (Peers, p. 228): "This, my daughters, is the aim of prayer: this is the purpose of the Spiritual Marriage, of which are born good works and good works alone." Teresa later remarks: ". . .we should desire and engage in prayer, not for our enjoyment, but for the sake of acquiring this strength which fits us for service" (p. 231).

130. *The Dialogue*, p. 42, #11.

131. *L'Avenire d'Italia*, 20 April, 1954 as cited in *L'Echo De La Maison-Mère*, #5, Mai, 1954, Paris.

132. Vincent de Paul was proclaimed "Patron of Charity" on May 12, 1885. Cited by A. Dodin in *L'Esprit vincentian*, p. 29.

133. Pope John XXIII, February 10 , 1960 proclamation of Louise de Marillac patroness of all those dedicated to Christian Social Works. Cited in *L'Echo De La Maison-Mère*, # 4, avril 1960, Paris.

134. SWLM, p. 1. A.2-Light.

Louise was shown by God that she was to go out to her neighbor and that she would be united with others in this work.

135. It is interesting to note that the recent document on the Laity, *"Christifideles Laici,"* by John Paul II (Vatican: Polyglot Press, 1988) (Hereinafter cited as CFL), speaks of the laity's mandate as rooted in their baptismal call (#13, p. 28), their communion with Jesus and their mission of evangelization (#32, #33, pp. 92-93) which is lived out in the proclamation of the gospel through charity towards one's neighbor through contemporary forms of spiritual and corporal works of mercy (#41, p. 119).

How this resonates with Louise's understanding of her Christian call as a laywoman and as a foundress; indeed, she was prophetic.

136. Pope John Paul II, in 1991 wrote the following to Sr. Juana Elizondo, Superior General of the Daughters of Charity: "A way was opening up for a new order of things in the church. Hundreds of health care or teaching institutions for women would adopt an analogous way of life for the service of their neighbor in the world" (Pope John Paul II, Letter on the Occasion of the Fourth Centenary of the Birth of Louise de Marillac. "Echoes of the Company", October 1991, pp. 380-383).

137. CFL, #13, p. 28: "Thus with the outpouring of the Holy Spirit in Baptism and Confirmation, the baptized share in the same mission of Jesus as the Christ, the Savior-Messiah."

138. CFL, #14, p. 32:
They [lay faithful] exercise their kingship as Christians, above all in the spiritual combat in which they seek to overcome in themselves the kingdom of sin (Rom 6:12), and then to make a gift of themselves so as to serve in justice and in charity, Jesus who is himself present in all his brothers and sisters, above all in the very least (Mt 25:40).

139. CFL, #3, p. 10: "The voice of the Lord clearly resounds in the depths of each of Christ's followers, who through faith and the sacraments of Christian initiation is made like to Jesus Christ, is incorporated into the Church and has an active part in her mission of salvation."

140. CFL, #16, p. 41:
Life according to the Spirit, whose fruit is holiness, stirs up every baptized person and requires each to *follow and imitate Jesus Christ,* in embracing the Beatitudes, in listening and meditating on the Word of God, in conscious and active participation in the liturgical and sacramental life of the Church, in personal prayer, in family or in community, in the hunger and thirst for justice, in the practice of the commandment of love in all circumstances of life and service to the brethren, especially the least, the poor and the suffering.

141. Coste, *V. de P.,* I, 64. L. 39, May 6, 1629:
Go, therefore, Mademoiselle, go in the name of Our Lord. I pray that his divine goodness may accompany you, be your consolation along the way, your shade against the heat of the sun, your shelter in rain and cold, your soft bed in your weariness, your strength in your toil, and, finally, that he may bring you back in perfect health and filled with good works.

142. CFL, #20, p. 54. This passage cites the importance of all Christians working together in communion within the Church and especially notes "that what distinguishes persons is *not an increase in dignity,* but *a special and complementary capacity for service. . ."*

143. SWLM, p. 835. SPIRITUAL TESTAMENT.

Cf. p. 770. A. 85: "They shall remember that true Daughters of Charity must be united in order to fulfill God's expectations. . . . we must have but one heart and act with one mind as do the three divine Persons."

144. CFL, #32, pp. 90-91:
Communion with Jesus which gives rise to the communion of Christians among themselves, is an indispensable condition for bearing fruit. . . Communion and mission are profoundly connected with each other, they interpenetrate and mutually imply each other, . . .*communion represents both the source and the fruit of mission: communion gives rise to mission and mission is accomplished in communion.*

145. SWLM, p. 809. A.92.

Vincent discussing "The Spirit of the Company" with the Sisters (Leonard, *Conferences*, II, 204-206), emphasized the necessity of "affective and effective love" in the following remarks:
The affective love of God passes on to effective love which is the service of the poor. . . (p. 204).
The love of Daughters of Charity is not only tender, it is effective, because they serve the poor effectively, both in body and soul. You are bound to teach them how to lead a good life,. . .this is what marks you off from many religious who tend the body only. . . You should bring two sorts of food to the sick poor: food for the body and food for the soul. . . .you should speak a few words to them, the fruit of your mental prayer, for their instruction, say five or six words so that you may lead them on to fulfil their duties as Christians and to practise patience (p. 205).
And there, my dear Sisters, you have in general the essence of affective and effective love; to serve Our Lord in his members both corporally and spiritually and to do so in their own homes, or indeed in whatever place to which providence may send you (p. 206).

146. Pope John Paul II's letter to Sister Elizondo, July 3, 1991 as cited in *Echoes of the Company,* October 1991, p. 383.

147. His holiness Pius XI, Discourse at the Vatican, November 1933 as cited in *L'Echo De La Maison-Mère,* #12, December, 1933: "It is already a miracle, one could affirm it, that the number and the variety of works for which the Blessed had been prepared even by the hand of God." Quoting Louise's first biographer, Gobillon, the Holy Father continued: "One could not humanly understand how this servant of God could carry out so many offices of charity; do, and even more, go in search of so many works of charity."

148. Gobillon (Fiat) I, 8.

149. Gobillon (Fiat) I, 9.

150. Leonard, *Conferences,* IV, 310.

151. Pope John Paul II, "Encyclical Letter, The Redeemer of Man", [Redemptor Hominis] (Boston: Daughters of St. Paul, 1979), p. 26.

152. The Beatification Process of Louise lists several works which were presented in her cause: Co-Foundress of the Daughters of Charity, The Foundlings, Confraternities of Charity, The Hospital of the Holy Name for the elderly of both sexes, Schools, Patronage of Young Women, Help to the Provinces Desolated by War. (Motherhouse Archives of the Congregation of the Mission, rue de Sèvres, Paris, 1902.)

As stated earlier for a fuller treatment of Louise's social works see: *Louise de Marillac; Social Aspect of Her Work,* Margaret Flinton, D.C. (New York: New City Press, 1992).

153. CFL, #41, p. 119.

154. John Paul II, Encyclical Letter *Sollicitudo Rei Socialis* (Boston: St. Paul Publ., 1989), 38, p. 71. Hereinafter cited as SRS.

155. Leonard, *Conferences,* II, 205:
A Daughter of Charity should not only attend to the bodily wants of the poor, she is bound, and in this she differs from many, many others, to instruct the poor. . . . you seek the poor out in their own homes, which so far, has never been done, as long as they are willing to receive those whom God sends them. Accordingly, you should bring two sorts of food to the sick poor: food for the body and food for the soul. . .

156. CFL, #42, p. 124:
The lay faithful must bear witness to those human and gospel values that are intimately connected with political activity itself, such as liberty and justice, solidarity, faithful and unselfish dedication for the good of all, a simple lifestyle, and a preferential love for the poor and the least. This demands that the lay faithful always be more animated by a real participation in the life of the Church and enlightened by her social doctrine.

157. CFL, #17, p. 43.

158. John Paul II, *Redemptoris Missio* (Sherbrooke, QC: Editions Paulines, 1991), #90, p. 125.

159. *Redemptoris Missio,* VIII, Missionary Spirituality, pp. 121-124.

160. *Redemptoris Missio,* #90, p. 125.

161. SWLM, p. 372. L.328 , September 22, 1651.

162. SWLM, p. 640. L.621, May 26, 1659. Cf. p. 350. L.345, May 19, 1651: "Pray for us, my dear Sisters, that Our Lord Jesus Christ may bestow his Spirit upon us on this holy feast (Pentecost) so that we may be so filled with his Spirit that we may do nothing or say nothing except for his glory and his holy love. . ."

163. SWLM, p. 260. L.217, August 29, 1648. Cf. p. 434. L.383, November 13, 1653: "I hope that your gratitude will place you in the disposition necessary to receive the graces you need to serve your sick poor

in a spirit of gentleness and great compassion, in imitation of Our Lord who acted this way with the most unfortunate."

164. SWLM, p. 11. L.142, June 24, 1644.

165. SWLM, p. 139. L.344, October or November 1645. Cf. p. 12. L.43, c.1636: "I pray that he will grant you sufficient strength and courage to overcome the little difficulties you will encounter."

166. SWLM, p. 626. L.605B, January 4, 1659.

167. SWLM, p. 766. L.134, May 2, 1646. Cf. p. 81. L.547, c.August 1642: "Make good use of this gift (vocation),and please God by serving your masters and his dear members with devotion, gentleness and humility."

168. SWLM, p. 320. L.284B, May 4, 1650.

169. CFL, #55, p. 168:
All the states of life, whether taken collectively or individually in relation to the others, are at the service of the Church's growth. While different in expression they are deeply united in the Church's "mystery of communion" and are dynamically coordinated in its unique mission.

170. *L'Echo De La Maison-Mère, #5*, Mai, 1954, p. 142.

171. Leonard, *Conferences*, IV, 314. In speaking of Louise, Vincent said: "Mademoiselle Le Gras was such an interior woman, although by nature she had a bent in the opposite direction."

172. "Therefore, I will now allure her, and bring her into the wilderness, and speak tenderly to her" (Hos. 2:14).

Louise de Marillac—A Saint and Model for Today

The spirituality of Louise de Marillac is relevant for contemporary Christians. Three timely perspectives will confirm this: the current writings of Pope John Paul II, the present ecclesial and international focus on Women, and recent studies in the history of Christian spirituality.

Even a cursory reading of the 1994-1995 documents of Pope John Paul II indicate the significance of the lived reality of the spirituality of Louise de Marillac as model and guide in the realization of the challenges which the Holy Father is presenting to the Christian world during these years devoted to the preparation for the Third Millennium, the promotion of a "culture of life"[1] and the emphasis on the dignity and importance of women in the Church and in society.

In his Apostolic Letter, *Tertio Millennio Adveniente* issued on November 10, 1994,[2] Pope John Paul II speaks of the "old" and the "new" as always being interwoven in the history of the Church.[3] These words are certainly applicable to Louise de Marillac who from an historical and ecclesial era similar to our own comes with the fire and light of Christ's love to shine in a world that is being darkened by a "culture of death".[4] As a woman whose entire life was devoted to enhancing the lives of others, Louise de Marillac can truly speak to us today through her life and through her spirituality.

The relevance of Louise's spirituality is explicitly evident within the pages of *Tertio Millennio Adveniente*. Herein the focus expressed by Pope John Paul II for the three-year spiritual preparation for the Jubilee Year 2000 reflects the main tenets of Louise's spirituality. The main spiritual principles which the Holy Father outlines clearly echo those discussed in this study of the spirituality of Louise de Marillac. Hence Louise may serve as a model of preparation for the Jubilee of the Incarnation of the Redeemer and as a guide for contemporary Christians entering the Third Millennium.

Describing the First Phase as Ante-Preparatory, the Holy Father speaks of the commemoration of the Birth of Christ in which the Jubilee will be *"deeply charged with Christological significance."*[5] He continues:

> The Jubilee celebration should confirm Christians of today in their *faith* in God who has revealed himself in Christ, sustain their *hope* which reaches out in expectation of eternal life, and rekindle their *charity* in active service to their brothers and sisters.[6]

The Christological witness of Louise de Marillac modelled and continues to model these precise Christian virtues of faith, hope and charity which the Holy Father challenges all to renew in their lives. This study has illustrated the manner in which Louise lived this threefold call and how she may be a mentor for contemporary Christians.

The Jubilee Year is to be a *prayer of praise and thanksgiving* for the *gift of the Incarnation and Redemption*, for the *gift of the Church* and for *the fruits of holiness* in the lives of the many men and women throughout history who have welcomed the gift of Redemption.[7]

Throughout her life, Louise de Marillac praised and thanked God for these gifts of the Incarnation and Redemption and as a woman of the Church grew in those "fruits of holiness" to which the Holy Father alludes. She remains a sign of God's ongoing creativity in the lives of all.

Continuing to outline the Second Phase of Preparation which will consist of the three years of 1997-1999, the Holy Father expresses their theological and spiritual foci for Christians. In these foci, one finds reflected the spiritual heritage of Louise de Marillac as presented in this study. A summation of the principles will confirm this. Year One, 1997 is to be devoted to a *reflection on Christ*, the Word of God, made man by the power of the Holy Spirit. *The distinctly Christological character* will emphasize the Incarnation, Christ's mission of preaching the Good News, a deeper understanding of the Incarnation of Jesus and his birth from the Virgin Mary, and the necessity of faith in Christ for salvation. The means for this deeper appreciation will come through a return to scripture through the liturgy, devotional reading or instruction.[8]

This first year also calls for a renewed appreciation of one's baptism as the basis for Christian living, a strengthening of faith and of the witness of Christians, a true longing for holiness and the contemplation of the divine Maternity of Mary.[9]

Each of these theological principles was exemplified in this study of the spirituality of Louise de Marillac and her lived faith experience serves as a witness to their possibility for all Christians.

Year Two, 1998 of the Preparation is to be devoted to the Holy Spirit: his sanctifying presence within the Church, the accomplishment of the Incarnation through his power, his distribution of gifts for the welfare of the Church and particularly his agency in the new evangelization.[10] As model to be "contemplated and imitated during this year," the Holy Father presents Mary "who conceived the Incarnate Word by the power of the Holy Spirit and then in her whole life allowed herself to be guided by his interior activity."[11]

How this theme echoes Louise's great devotion to the Holy Spirit, to Mary and to the primacy of the will of God in her own life. For Louise, Mary is the model par excellence whom she chose as mother and model for herself and for her Sisters. As seen in this study, Louise too, demonstrates a devotion to the Holy Spirit, to the will of God and to Mary that serves as a paradigm for contemporary Christians.

The final year of preparation, 1999 calls all believers to see things in the perspective of Christ who came from the Father and returned to him. Hence the Christian life is to be seen as a pilgrimage to the Father requiring personal conversion and communal conversion which then extends to the whole of humanity.[12] This conversion embraces the liberation from sin and the acceptance of gospel values particularly the twofold reality of the love of God and the love of one's neighbor which encompasses the moral law of the believer.[13]

Speaking of Christ's mission to "preach the good news to the poor" (Mt. 11:5; Lk. 7:22), the Holy Father asks "how can we fail to lay greater emphasis on the *Church's preferential option for the poor and the outcast*?"[14] Again the Holy Father cites Mary as the perfect model of love towards God and neighbor.

Reflecting on the emphasis of this final year of preparation, again the relevance of the spirituality of Louise de Marillac as witness and model becomes evident. She presents to us a Christian who lived the journey to the Father's house; a journey marked by an heroic degree of love of God and neighbor, in which ongoing conversion and growth in gospel values led her to give her life to the poor and the outcast. The witness of her life serves as a mirror in which contemporary Christians may see a privileged path to follow.

Pope John Paul II speaks of the Jubilee Year itself as giving glory to the Trinity since the preparation led from Christ and through Christ, in the Holy Spirit to the Father; and he mentions also its intensely eucharistic character: the sacrament in which the Savior who took flesh in Mary's womb twenty centuries ago, continues to offer himself to humanity as the source of divine life.[15] These two emphases of the Trinity and the eucharist were very important in Louise de Marillac's spirituality and hence her experience of them can be retrieved into the present with renewed relevance for contemporary spirituality.

Concluding his Apostolic Letter, *Tertio Millennio Adveniente,* the Holy Father states: "The more the West is becoming estranged from its Christian roots, the more it is becoming missionary territory".[16] He then invokes Mary, "who two thousand years ago offered to the world the Incarnate Word, to lead the men and women of the new millennium towards the One who is 'the true light that enlightens every man' (Jn. 1:9)."[17] This study of Louise de Marillac has illustrated that her spirituality was profoundly focussed on Jesus, the Incarnate Word, embraced a deep Marian devotion, and was uniquely apostolic; hence, Louise de Marillac as mentor and guide, spans the centuries to radiate light and hope to Christians for the Third Millennium who are invited to follow a similar path.

Robert P. Maloney, C.M., describes a specific spirituality as "a governing vision, a driving force, enabling a person to transcend himself or herself. It is the specific way in which a person is both rooted in God and relates to the created world. It is insight as the source of action, a world-view that generates energy and channels it in a particular direction."[18] For Louise de Marillac this vision and driving force became the imitation of the Incarnate Jesus in his spirit and his works so that she became totally transformed by him, configured to him and devoted to her neighbor, especially the poor and suffering to offer them the dignity and love that was theirs as members of Jesus. How clearly Louise's attitude and view towards life are consistent with those expressed by Pope John Paul II in his recent Encyclical Letter, *Evangelium Vitae* on the Value and Inviolability of Human Life. Herein he states: "The Incarnation reveals not only the boundless love of God but also the *incomparable value of every human person."*[19] The Holy Father later expresses the objective of the encyclical as a *"precise and vigorous reaffirmation of the value of human life and its inviolability,* and a pressing appeal to every person in the name of God to: *respect, protect, love and serve life, every human life!"*[20] In reading this *Gospel of Life* and its call for the creation of a "culture of life" based on the dignity of the human person who shares the image of Jesus, the vocation of loving service to life as exemplified by Louise de Marillac shines as a brilliant beacon illuminating the way for those who will accept this challenge of Christ's Vicar. The personal experience of Louise de Marillac in the service of life, blazed a path of charity that is as pertinent now as it was in her day. Not only in her spiritual theology, but also in her apostolic life, Louise, the woman of yesteryear, stands as saint and model for today. In keeping with this study of Louise de Marillac, several striking points from *Evangelium Vitae* illustrate her relevance as a prototype for contemporary Christians.

In a society marked by practical materialism and the devaluing of life, the Holy Father calls for a cultural change and a new life style based on the *primacy of being over having, of the person over things.*[21] The Holy Father summons a respect for the inviolability of life in every phase from the unborn to the elderly and encourages all to: "Walk as children of light". . .to build a new culture of life. Such a cultural transformation, he maintains, is connected both to the present historical situation, and also to the Church's mission of evangelization which is "to transform humanity from within and to make it new".[22] Discussing the call to evangelization the Holy Father states:

> Evangelization is an all-embracing, progressive activity through which the Church participates in the prophetic, priestly and royal mission of the Lord Jesus. It is therefore inextricably linked to *preaching, celebration and the service of charity.* Evangelization is a *profoundly ecclesial act,* which calls all the various workers of the holy gospel to action, according to their individual charisms and ministry.[23]

From this, all have a duty to *preach the holy gospel of life,* which is the very person of Jesus Christ, to *celebrate it* in the Liturgy and in daily living through self-giving love, and to *serve it* with programmes and structures which support and promote life.[24]

The current materialistic ambience leads to supremacy of the strong over the weak and to personal dignity being replaced by efficiency, functionality and usefulness. Herein the first to be harmed are women, children, the sick or suffering and the elderly.[25]

In such an environment, the value of human suffering is rejected as useless.[26] Yet, the Holy Father states: "Looking at `the spectacle' of the cross (Lk. 23:48) we shall discover in this glorious tree the fulfillment and the complete revelation of the whole *holy gospel of life.*"[27] He continues:

. . .in the midst of a dramatic conflict between the "culture
of death" and the "culture of life",. . .the glory of the cross
is not overcome by this darkness; rather, it shines forth ever
more radiantly and brightly, and is revealed as the center,
meaning and goal of all history and of every human life.[28]

On the cross Jesus attains the heights of love "by laying down
his life for his friends" (Jn. 15:13), and in this way proclaims that
life finds its centre, its meaning and its fulfillment when it is given up.
Having said this, the Holy Father calls all to imitate Christ and
to follow in his footsteps (1 Pt 2:21).[29]

This following of Jesus in loving service to life requires, says
the Pope: "*a contemplative outlook,* arising from faith in the God of
life, who has created every individual as a `wonder' (Ps 139:14),
and seeing in every person his living image (Gen. 1:27; Ps 8:5)."[30]
Such a contemplative stance offers meaning and dignity to every
person and to every situation: the sick, the suffering, the outcast
or the dying.

The Holy Father exhorts all by virtue of sharing in Christ's
royal mission, to support and promote human life through the
service of charity, which *must be inspired and distinguished by a specific
attitude* of caring and responsibility for one's neighbor especially
the poorest, most alone and most in need. In helping the hungry,
the thirsty, the foreigner, the naked, the sick, the imprisoned—as
well as the child in the womb and the old person who is suffering
near death —people have the opportunity to serve Jesus.[31] He
continues that this is a *particularly pressing need at the present time,*
when the "culture of death" so forcefully opposes the "culture of
life", but primarily it is a need which springs from "faith working
through love" (Gal 5:6).[32]

The Holy Father reminds Christians that it was this attitude
of deep love that gave rise down the centuries to an *outstanding
history of charity,* which brought into being in the Church and
society many forms of service to life and he challenges every
Christian community, with a renewed sense of responsibility, to
continue to write this history through various kinds of pastoral

and social activity. It is precisely this challenge to Christians preparing for the new millennium that evokes the memory of the outstanding faith-filled witness of Louise de Marillac, and her superb works of charity that merited for her the title of "Patroness of all Christian Social Workers".

As wife, mother, widow and foundress Louise de Marillac devoted herself to the preservation of the dignity of life in all its phases. As mother she brought to birth a fragile infant son, devotedly cared for him and nurtured him. She anguished through his tense teen years, sought help for him and continued to seek his good throughout her life. As wife she lovingly and diligently nursed for three years a terminally-ill husband, shared with him his sufferings and the dignity and solace of a holy death, even though by human standards it was an agonizing journey. Louise had always been aware of and open to the needs of the poor, the sick, the suffering, the dying and the dead, but in her widowhood, she was guided by God to devote herself totally to the loving service of her neighbor, to the promotion of the dignity of all persons especially the most destitute and abandoned. As foundress of the Daughters of Charity she ministered to and taught her Sisters to serve the foundlings, the orphans, the prisoners, the mentally handicapped, the elderly, the plague-stricken, the wounded soldiers and the dying. In all she saw the face of Jesus and ministered compassionately to them and to him. Louise, whose own life was always fragile and beset by illness and crosses illustrated a quality of life that God continually and wondrously recreated into an "other-centered" lifestyle that enriched the lives and dignity of every person she touched. How fitting a model for the "new lifestyle" based on the "primacy of being over having, of the person over things" that the Holy Father calls Christians to adopt![33]

In the midst of every form of human suffering, Louise de Marillac found strength at the foot of the cross of Jesus. His cross was the source and symbol for Louise's charity, the sign of love and life, as she endeavored to alleviate the sufferings of others while at the same time uniting them to the sufferings of Jesus and seeing the suffering Jesus in them. Her faith-filled vision of life and of the mystery of suffering inspired her to "respect, love and serve life, every human life" as Jesus himself had done.[34] In this aspect of her personal spirituality and loving service, Louise shines as a light in the darkness of yesterday and today. For those who want to "walk in the light and to build a new culture of life", Louise has gone before.[35]

Through her own life of faith, hope and charity, Louise de Marillac preached the "Gospel of Life", Jesus Christ. She read this "good news" on her knees and preached it with her heart, hands and feet. She celebrated it in her own life and in the lives of others and she served it in compassionate charity with others. In a "culture of death" in her own society, Louise gave her life and those of her Sisters to create a "culture of life." Hence, is Louise not the saint to guide and to lead the way in this modern "Gospel of Life"? As symbol for today, the relevance of Louise's self-giving love and her contemplative, apostolic genius in the cause of the dignity of the person created in the image of Jesus, is self-evident. With Mary, Louise stands at the foot of the cross of every suffering, threatened human life, to plead the precious Blood of Jesus for the preservation and sanctity of the lives for which he died. Through his suffering, death and resurrection, these valiant women implore the birth of "a culture of life" to replace a "culture of death".

In this Encyclical, Pope John Paul II highlights the role of women in the required transformation of society. He writes:

In transforming culture so that it supports life, *women* occupy a place, in thought and action, which is unique and decisive. It depends on them to promote a "new feminism" which rejects the temptation of imitating models of "male domination", in order to acknowledge and affirm the true genius of women in every aspect of the life of society, and overcome all discrimination, violence and exploitation.[36]

The Holy Father calls women to: *"bear witness to the meaning of genuine love"*, by teaching the authenticity of human relations through openness and acceptance of others. This, he maintains "is the indispensable prerequisite for an authentic cultural change and it is the fundamental contribution which the Church and humanity expect from women."[37]

In this current year of international focus on Women, on several occasions, Pope John Paul II has addressed women on their role in the Church and in society. In his Message for the 1995 World Day of Peace, the Holy Father spoke to and of women as "Teachers of Peace". In reading this message, it is interesting to recognize how its themes connect Louise de Marillac with the women of today. The following points illustrate this:

As educators of peace, the Pope invites women to become:

teachers of peace with their whole being and in all their actions, to be witnesses, messengers and teachers of peace in relations between individuals and between generations, in the family, in the cultural, social and political life of nations, and particularly in situations of conflict and war.[38]

The Holy Father wishes that women "continue to follow the path which leads to peace, a path which many courageous and far-sighted women have walked before them!"[39] Who could be a more significant model in this area than Louise de Marillac who truly taught peace through the witness of her own life and through those she educated to be envoys of peace and compassion to all, even to the battle fields. This study of the spirituality of Louise de Marillac has shown that she knew personally the pain of family dissensions between generations, the tragic sufferings of the social and political life of her country and the horrendous results of the ravages of war. Louise and her Sisters maintained their own inner peace and calm in such situations by their trust in God's loving providence for them. It is precisely to this spirit that the Holy Father refers when he says:

In order to be a teacher of peace, a woman must first of all nurture peace within herself. Inner peace comes from knowing that one is loved by God and from the desire to respond to his love. History is filled with marvellous examples of women who, sustained by this knowledge, have been able successfully to deal with difficult situations of exploitation, discrimination, violence and war.[40]

The Pope also notes that: "Women need to help women, and to find support in the valuable and effective contributions which associations, movements and groups, many of them of a religious character, have proved capable of making in this regard."[41] Certainly Louise de Marillac exemplified such a woman of peace and her life witnessed to her dedicated support of women through the Confraternities, her Community, the retreats and the spiritual direction which she gave. This has not been forgotten and today in Paris, in a small chapel in the church of Louise's "Lumière", groups of struggling women gather to support one another, to pray and to seek the intercession and guidance of Louise de Marillac as they endeavor to reaffirm their dignity and respect.

The Holy Father stresses the need "to acknowledge and to promote the dignity of women as persons, their unique role in education for peace and their critical importance in the family and society."[42] Today in all parts of the world, Louise's Daughters continue to carry on her mission of peace and education in support of women in their rights and dignity.

Pope John Paul further asserts that "Women have the right to insist that their dignity be respected" as well as "the duty to work for the promotion of the dignity of all persons, men as well as women."[43] Perhaps these lines connect with the Pope's former statement on the creation of a "new feminism". It sometimes occurs that one who feels unfairly treated may treat others in like fashion. In some feminist movements this appears to be happening and men as well as other women are being marginalized and denied their rights and dignity. Within society and especially within the Church, women and men need to collaborate in mutuality and respect to work for peace and the promotion of the dignity of all persons. In this area too, one finds an excellent example in the relationship of

Louise de Marillac with Vincent de Paul. Rooted in God, in the gospel and in their mutual love for the poor, Vincent and Louise grew in a holy, loving friendship and brought to France and to the Church the fire and light of a charity that still blazes throughout the world. Louise and Vincent could unquestionably be a paradigm for the apostolic relationship between priests and women to which the Holy Father referred in his Holy Thursday homily to priests.[44] This study has shown that Louise de Marillac was an ecclesial woman who appropriated her baptismal dignity and mission within the Church. Living and working within her various vocations as wife, mother, widow and foundress, Louise was always a woman of character, of purpose and of compassion. She bridged the social strata of her time and walked as easily with princesses as with paupers. In everyone she saw the dignity of a child of God and sought to protect it. Louise de Marillac was an authentic Christian woman who still has much to teach contemporary men and women in both ecclesial and civil circles during these years of international focus on Women.

In recent studies of the history of Spirituality, the role of women has been gaining more attention from scholars who express the need for further study in order to present a more authentic picture of the history of Spirituality. Philip Sheldrake, in *Spirituality & History* states:

> In terms of mainstream spirituality, women have been conceived as generally marginal to its creation. . . .their absence distorts our historical mentality and causes conceptual errors. Because the process of giving meaning to the past is vital for the development of the Christian tradition, women's marginalization effectively structures them as "a minority." They are effectively excluded from the formation of theory which determines not only what history is but what spirituality is.[45]

Sheldrake asserts the need to create "as full a picture as possible of the past" in order to establish a valid "contemporary spiritual identity". He writes:

Because the past acts as a mirror for our present, a revision of our historical perspectives and an attempt to reach as full a picture as possible, is vital if our establishment of a contemporary spiritual identity is not to repeat the oppressions of the past in new ways by preventing others from having a history and, therefore, a proper identity at all.[46]

The importance of an authentic history of spirituality is important not only to scholars but to all seeking models and mentors for their spiritual life. Sheldrake expresses this idea as follows:

The presentation of the history of spirituality is not merely a scholarly issue but is of general concern. This is partly because many of us belong within living spiritual traditions which have a long history, and partly because many people today are turning to the wisdom of the past, often through the medium of spiritual classics. This issue of historical interpretation is therefore a live one. . . . Present values in spirituality demand that we seek to retrieve or revise because we believe that history has subordinated certain groups and advanced others and that it is important for our present identity and desire to live more complete Christian lives, to recover their story.[47]

In a similar vein, William Thompson speaking of the French School of Spirituality writes: "As feminist theological criticism is beginning to teach us, much of the contribution of women to theology and spirituality in general is only now beginning to receive the attention it has always deserved."[48]

From this historical stance, the study of the Spirituality of Louise de Marillac has profound relevance for the history of spirituality and for the creation of a contemporary spirituality in which she, as one of the great women of the Church, is retrieved into the present and is re-introduced as a Christian mentor for today. One cannot discount the importance of Louise de Marillac's contribution to the field of spirituality as "both an heiress of the French school and an excellent witness to the main lines of seventeenth-century French spirituality".[49] It is a recognized fact that modern spirituality has been greatly inspired by the theological principles of the French School but it is also acknowledged that minimal information regarding the influence of the feminine spiritual leaders of that time has filtered through; hence, the need to explore and to retrieve this rich heritage of Christian spirituality. This study of the Spirituality of Louise de Marillac aims to bring into greater light and clearer focus one such woman who, vivified by her *Incarnational mysticism* contributed to transforming the social, spiritual and ecclesial culture of her day, a milieu not unlike the present.[50] If one current objective of the study of the history of Spirituality is to establish women in their rightful place, then this study of the Spirituality of Louise de Marillac contributes to recovering her spirituality for the general public and to highlighting the living tradition that is hers. Further, it enhances her recognition for her role in the simplification and the transmission of the principles of French Spirituality integrated with her active stance which have, through her Daughters, influenced thousands of Christians in every part of the world. Today when the world is in desperate need of witnesses to authentic and practical Christian spirituality Louise de Marillac endures as a contemporary manifestation of the power of the Holy Spirit operative in the life and works of a soul receptive to the will of God. Through the "miracle of her life, the miracle of her works and the miracle of her posterity"[51] Louise de Marillac emerges as a courageous, compassionate and contemporary counselor in the Christian life. Her Christian witness and message is universal but includes a special significance for women of today. Louise has walked the paths of various vocations and lifestyles. Her way was often fraught with pain and struggle, but through her trust in providence, her life bore glorious fruits. Through her story and the reality of her spiritual intercession, Louise continues to be present to assist women to persevere in their Christian ideals and with hope in the Redemptive love of Christ, to reach out to others in compassion so that a transformation of the current culture may evolve. As woman of yesteryear, saint and model for today, Louise de Marillac radiates "Light in our Darkness".

Notes

1. John Paul II, *Evangelium Vitae,* (Vatican City: Libreria Editrice Vaticana, 1995), #95, p. 133.

2. John Paul II, *Tertio Millennio Adveniente*, Apostolic Letter On Preparation for the Jubilee of the Year 2000, (Vatican City: Libreria Editrice Vaticana, 1994).

3. John Paul II, *Tertio Millennio Adveniente*, #18, p. 23.

4. John Paul II, *Evangelium Vitae*, #12, p. 18.

5. John Paul II, *Tertio Millennio Adveniente*, #31, p. 36.

6. John Paul II, *Tertio Millennio Adveniente*, #31, p. 36.

7. John Paul II, *Tertio Millennio Adveniente*, #32, p. 37.

8. John Paul II, *Tertio Millennio Adveniente*, #39, p. 48.

9. John Paul II, *Tertio Millennio Adveniente*, #'s 41-43, pp. 49-50.

10. John Paul II, *Tertio Millennio Adveniente*, #'s 44-45, pp. 51-52.

11. John Paul II, *Tertio Millennio Adveniente*, #48, p. 55.

12. John Paul II, *Tertio Millennio Adveniente*, #49, p. 55.

13. John Paul II, *Tertio Millennio Adveniente*, #50, p. 56.

14. John Paul II, *Tertio Millennio Adveniente*, #51, p. 57.

15. John Paul II, *Tertio Millennio Adveniente*, #55, p. 59.

16. John Paul II, *Tertio Millennio Adveniente*, #57, p. 63.

17. John Paul II, *Tertio Millennio Adveniente*, #59, p. 65.

18. Robert P. Maloney, C.M. *The Way of Vincent de Paul,* p. 21.

19. John Paul II, *Evangelium Vitae,* #2, p. 5.
This encyclical was issued on March 25th, the Feast of the Incarnation of Jesus, the feast central to Louise's spirituality.

20. John Paul II, *Evangelium Vitae,* #5, p. 9.

21. John Paul II, *Evangelium Vitae,* #98, p. 137.

22. John Paul II, *Evangelium Vitae,* #95, p. 132.

23. John Paul II, *Evangelium Vitae,* #78, p. 111.

24. John Paul II, *Evangelium Vitae,* #78, p. 111.

25. John Paul II, *Evangelium Vitae,* #23, p. 33.

26. John Paul II, *Evangelium Vitae,* #23, p. 32.

27. John Paul II, *Evangelium Vitae,* #50, p. 69.

28. John Paul II, *Evangelium Vitae,* #50, p. 69.

29. John Paul II, *Evangelium Vitae,* #51, p. 71.

30. John Paul II, *Evangelium Vitae,* #83, p. 117.

31. John Paul II, *Evangelium Vitae,* #87, p. 122.

32. John Paul II, *Evangelium Vitae,* #87, p. 121.

33. John Paul II, *Evangelium Vitae*, #98, p. 137.

34. John Paul II, *Evangelium Vitae*, #5, p. 9.

35. John Paul II, *Evangelium Vitae*, #95, p. 132.

36. John Paul II, *Evangelium Vitae*, #99, p. 138.

37. John Paul II, *Evangelium Vitae*, #99, p. 139.

38. Pope John Paul II, "Women: Teachers of Peace, Message of Pope John Paul II for the 1995 World Day of Peace," L'Osservatore Romano, N.50, 14 December 1994, English Edition, #2, p. 1.

39. John Paul II, " Women: Teachers of Peace, Message for 1995 World Day of Peace," #2, p. 1.

40. John Paul II, " Women: Teachers of Peace, Message for 1995 World Day of Peace," #5, p. 1.

41. John Paul II, " Women: Teachers of Peace, Message for 1995 World Day of Peace," #5, p. 2.

42. John Paul II, " Women: Teachers of Peace, Message for 1995 World Day of Peace," #3, p. 1.

43. John Paul II, " Women: Teachers of Peace, Message for 1995 World Day of Peace," #10, p. 2.

44. John Paul II, "Letter of The Holy Father, Pope John Paul II, to Priests for Holy Thursday 1995," (Vatican City: Vatican Press, 1995), p. 11.

45. Sheldrake, *Spirituality & History,* p. 97.

46. Sheldrake, *Spirituality & History,* p. 102.

47. Sheldrake, pp. 99-100.

48. Thompson, CWS: *Bérulle,* p. 22.

49. Raymond Deville, "Saint Vincent and Saint Louise in Relation to the French School of Spirituality, *Vincentian Heritage,* 11 (1), 1990, p. 40.

50. William H. Thompson, *Christology and Spirituality,* (New York: Crossroad Publishing Co., 1991), p. 107. Thompson speaks of an "incarnational type of mysticism in which the mystic stays with the world even while transforming it". This he asserts is consistent with the incarnationalism of Christianity and has its ground in the Incarnation. Louise de Marillac certainly represents this form of mysticism.

51. Pope Pius XI, "Discours de Sa Sainteté Pie XI, November 1, 1933. On the Occasion of the announcement of the Decree of Sainthood of Blessed Louise de Marillac. *L'Echo De La Maison-Mère,* #12, December 1933, p. 255.

Acknowledgements

"... what I am unable to do on account of my powerlessness or other obstacles in me, God will do by his kindness and omnipotence."

Louise de Marillac

A work such as this does not come to completion without the assistance of many people. Indeed, "God by his kindness," has gifted me with community, family and friends who have encouraged and assisted me during these years. To all who have supported me in any way I extend my deepest gratitude and ask God to bless you.

Primarily significant in the ongoing process of this work has been my religious congregation, especially our General Councils, Sr. M. Joan LaFleur, and my local community by their faithful support and understanding.

Members of the double Vincentian Family have been important to the success of this work. Fr. Robert Maloney, C.M., Superior General of the Vincentians, by his support and generous permission for the use of their Library in Rome and Fr. Paul Henzman, C.M., Archivist at the Motherhouse, rue de Sèvres, Paris, by his kind and generous assistance have provided valuable resources.

Mother Juana Elizondo, Superioress General, Sr. Pauline Lawlor, General Councillor, Sr. Mildred Cheramie, Sr. Elisabeth Charpy, Sr. Maguerand, Sr. Lélandais and the Community of

Filles de la Charité at rue du Bac, Paris, welcomed me into their home and hearts, graciously shared their heritage with me and affirmed my rootedness in Vincent and Louise.

Fr. John Lawlor, C.M., Director, and the Sisters of St. Joseph's Provincial House, Emmitsburg, MD, especially Sr. Margaret Flinton, D.C., have provided me with information, materials and encouragement.

Fr. Joseph Henchey, CSS and Fr. Robert Stefanotti, O.Carm., as professors and friends have particularly contributed to this work: Fr. Henchey by empowering me to pursue doctoral studies and by his ongoing prayerful support and Fr. Stefanotti through his critiques of the primary drafts and his reassuring confidence in their future.

Several friends have read sections of this manuscript in its various stages and have offered useful suggestions. In particular Catherine Guerrasio has patiently read copy during my writing time in Rome and in addition has saved me untold hours at the I.O.R.

This study has been directed wisely and calmly by Fr. Basil Cole, O.P., who with his most efficient reading of text, concise instructions and gentle humor has guided this work to completion. Fr. Fabio Giardini, O.P., has also offered helpful suggestions and substantial encouragement.

To those named and to all those unnamed but gratefully remembered I am deeply indebted.

I thank my community, family and friends for their love, prayers and support. Ultimately I thank our provident God who, "by his omnipotence," has given me the health, time, ability and means to complete this study.

For the permission to use Congregational materials of the Double Vincentian Family, I am most grateful.

Bibliography

I. Sources Related to Louise de Marillac

1. Primary Sources

Charpy, Elisabeth, F. dl C. ed. *Louise de Marillac: Écrits Spirituels*. Paris: Filles de la Charité, 140 rue du Bac, 1983.

——————————. *La Compagnie Des Filles De La Charité Aux Origines: Documents*. Paris: Filles de la Charité, 140 rue du Bac, 1989.

Coste, Pierre, C.M., ed. *St. Vincent de Paul: Correspondance, Entretiens, Documents*. 14 vols. Paris: Gabalda, 1920 - 1925.

——————————. ed. *Conférences aux Filles de la Charité*. 1923. Paris: Soeurs de Saint Vincent de Paul, 140 rue du Bac, 1952.

——————————. ed. *The Conferences of St. Vincent De Paul to the Sisters of Charity*. 1923. Paris: Soeurs de Saint Vincent de Paul, 1952. Translated by Joseph Leonard, C.M. Maryland: Christian Classics, Inc., 1968.

——————————. ed. *SAINT VINCENT DE PAUL: CORRESPONDENCE, CONFERENCES, DOCUMENTS*. Vol. I. Paris: Gabalda, 1920. Edited by Jacqueline Kilar, D.C. Translated by Helen Marie Law, D.C., John Marie Poole, D.C., James R. King, C.M. Annotated by John Carven, C.M. New York: New City Press, 1985.

——————————. ed. *SAINT VINCENT DE PAUL: CORRESPONDENCE, CONFERENCES, DOCUMENTS*. Vol. II. Paris: Gabalda, 1921. Edited by Jacqueline Kilar, D.C. and Marie Poole, D.C. Translated by Marie Poole, D.C. et al. Annotated by John W. Carmen, C.M. New York: New City Press, 1990.

Sullivan, Louise, D.C. ed. and trans. *Spiritual Writings of Louise de Marillac: Correspondence and Thoughts*. New York: New City Press, 1991.

2. Secondary Sources

i. Biographic Works According to Chronological Order

Gobillon, M. *La Vie de Mademoiselle Le Gras*. Paris: Chez André Pralard, 1676.

——————————. *La Vie De La Vénérable Louise de Marillac, Veuve de M. Le Gras*. Paris, 1676. Revue par M. Collet. Paris: Librairie de Mme De Poussielgue-Rusand, 1862.

Gobillon, M. *Louise de Marillac, veuve de M. Le Gras, Sa Vie, Ses Vertus, Ses Lettres, Son Esprit*. Paris, 1676. 4 vols. Introduced by Fiat. Reproduced by Bruges: Société St. Augustin, 1886.

Baunard, Mgr. Louis. *La Vénérable Louise de Marillac*. Paris: Poussielgue, 1898.

——————————. *Sainte Louise de Marillac*. Édition Abrégée. Paris: Gigord, 1934.

De Broglie, Emmanuel. *La Vénérable Louise de Marillac*. Paris: Librairie Lecoffre, 1911.

De Broglie, Emmanuel. *The Life of Blessed Louise de Marillac*. Translated by Joseph Leonard,C.M. London: Burns Oates & Washbourne Ltd., 1933.

Sainte Louise de Marillac, Fondatrice et Première Supérieure des Filles de la Charité. Paris:

Église paroissiale Saint-Denys de la Chapelle, 1935.
Woodgate, M. V. *St. Louise de Marillac: Foundress of the Sisters of Charity.* London: Herder Book Co., 1946.
Calvet, J. *Louise de Marillac par elle-même.* Paris: Aubier, 1958.
——————. *Louise De Marillac: A Portrait.* Translated by G. F. Pullen. New York: P.J. Kenedy & Sons, 1959.
Guy, Jean. *Sainte Louise de Marillac: Femme au grand coeur, âme de feu.* Paris: Société Saint-Paul, 1960.
Dirvin, Joseph I., C.M. *Louise de Marillac.* New York: Farrar, Straus & Giroux, 1970.
Regnault, Vincent, D.C. *Saint Louise de Marillac-Servant of the Poor.* Translated by Louise Sullivan, D.C. Rockford, Illinois: Tan Books and Publishers, Inc., 1983.
Charpy, Elisabeth, *Petite vie de LOUISE DE MARILLAC.* Paris: Desclée de Brouwer, 1991.

ii. Major Studies

Charpy, Elisabeth, F. dl C. *Contre vents et marées.* Paris: Hallépée, 1988. English translation "Come, Wind or High Water," printed as a serial in *Echoes of the Company.* January 1987-June 1988.
——————. *Un chemin de sainteté.* Paris: Hallépeé, 1988.
——————. *A Way To Holiness.* Translated by Sister Catherine Whelan, D.C. Dublin: Mount Salus Press, 1990.
Coste, P., C.M. *La Bienheuruese Louise de Marillac, Glanes Spirituelles.* Paris: Mignard, 1924.
Flinton, Margaret, D.C. *Louise de Marillac: Social Aspects of Her Work.* New York: New City Press, 1992. Translated by the author from the original French edition of her doctoral dissertation, *Sainte Louise de Marillac, L'aspect Sociale de Son Oeuvre.* Paris, Sorbonne, 1958.
Poinsenet, M.D. *De L'Anxiété à la Sainteté Louise De Marillac.* Paris: Librairie Arthème Fayard, 1958.
Portal, F. *Les Filles de la Charité De Saint Vincent de Paul et De La Bienheureuse Louise de Marillac.* Paris: Gigord, Ed., 1921.
Sheedy, J.P., C.M. *UNTRODDEN PATHS, The Social Apostolate of St. Louise de Marillac.* London: Salesian Press, 1958.

iii. Material from the Archives Lazaristes, Maison-Mère, Paris. Motherhouse of the Congregation of the Mission, 95 rue de Sèvres, Paris.

Carron, L'abbé G.T.J. *Vies Des Dames Françaises. (Qui ont été les plus Célèbres dans le XVII.e Siècle, par leur Dévouement pour les Pauvres;...).* Louvain: Chez Vanlinthout et Vandenzande, 1826. s.v. "Vie De Louise De Marillac, Dame Le Gras."
Dictionnaire Critique De Biographie Et D'Histoire. Deuxième Édition. Edited by Henri Plon. Paris: Henri Plon, 1872. s.v. "Errata Et Supplément Pour Tous Les Dictionnaires Historiques D'Après Des Documents Authentiques Inédits." s.v.(Le Gras, Louise de Marillac, mad.) Par A. Jal.
Didron, Ed. "Louise de Marillac & Le Sacré Coeur." *Bulletin of Saint Vincent de Paul.* 4 (avril 1900): 97-102.
"Louise de Marillac." *Bulletin de Saint Vincent de Paul.* 1 (Janvier 1900): 68-79.
"Louise De Marillac & Le Sacré Coeur." *Petites Annales De Saint Vincent de Paul.* 6 (15 Juin 1900): 161-174.
Extracts from "The Beatification Process of Louise de Marillac." 1902.

De Marillac. *Documents Historiques Sur La Famille DE MARILLAC.* Receuillis Par Les Descendants De Jacques-Victor Hippolyte DE MARILLAC. Paris: Lahure, 1908.

De Marillac, Michel. *Les CL. Pseaumes De David, Et Les X. Cantiques, inférés en l'office de l'Eglise.* Traduits en vers françois Par Mre Michel De Marillac, Conseiller du Roy en Son Conseil d'Estat, et Surintendant de Ses Finances. Paris: Chez Edme Martin, 1625.

L'IMITATION DE JESUS-CHRIST. Traduction De Michel De Marillac, Garde Des Sceaux De France. (Translations:1621,1626,1630,1631). Paris: Glady Frères, Éditeurs, 1876.

iv. Articles

Delgado, Corpus Juan, C.M. "Luisa de Marillac y la Iglesia." *Evangelizare.* 30 (1991): 279-312.

Deville, Raymond, S.S. "Saint Vincent and Saint Louise In Relation to the French School of Spirituality." *Vincentian Heritage.* 11, 1 (1990): 29-44.

——————————. "The Role of Saint Vincent de Paul and Saint Louise de Marillac as Architects and as Moving Spirits behind the Spiritual and Missionary Renewal in Seventeenth-Century France." *Vincentian Heritage.* 14, 1 (1993): 1-14.

Martinez, Benito. C.M. "The Prayer of St. Louise." *Echoes of the Company.* Part I. 3 (March 1983): 125-135; Part II. 4 (April 1983): 175-183.

Roman, Fr. Jose Maria, C.M. "St. Louise de Marillac, Foundress of the Daughters of Charity: IV. Configuration of the Institute." *Echoes of the Company.* (May 1993): 226-240.

v. Related Studies

a. Books

Coste, Pierre, C.M. *The Life & Works of St. Vincent de Paul (Monsieur Vincent: Le grand saint du grand siècle).* 3 vols. Translated by Joseph Leonard, C.M. New York: New City Press, 1987.

Dodin, André, C.M. *ST. VINCENT DE PAUL et la charité.* Bourges: Tardy Quercy, 1989.

——————————. *Vincent de Paul and Charity, A Contemporary Portrait of His Life and Apostolic Spirit.* Translated by Jean Marie Smith and Dennis Saunders. Edited by Hugh O'Donnell, C.M. and Marjorie Gale Hornstein. New York: New City Press, 1992.

——————————. *L'esprit vincentien, Le secret de saint Vincent de Paul.* Paris: Desclée de Brouwer, 1981.

Maloney, Robert P., C.M. *The Way of Vincent de Paul: A Contemporary Spirituality in the Service of the Poor.* New York: New City Press, 1992.

Mckenna, Thomas, C.M. *Praying with Vincent de Paul.* Winona, MN: St.Mary's Press, 1994.

Mezzadri, Luigi, C.M. *A Short Life of St. Vincent de Paul.* Translated by Thomas Davitt, C.M. Dublin: The Columba Press, 1992.

b. Articles

Gonthier, Jean, C.M. "Listening to St. Louise: Educator in Holiness." *Echoes of the Company.* 2 (February 1983): 80-87.

———————————. "Listening to St. Louise: Educator in Holiness." *Echoes of the Company.* Part I. 5 (May 1983): 247-253. Part II. 6 (June 1983): 278-288.

Koch, Bernard, C.M. "The role of the laity in the Church according to Saint Vincent-Active participation of Saint Louise de Marillac." *Echoes of the Company.* 2 (February 1992): 69-81.

Maloney, Robert P. C.M. "The Cross in Vincentian Spirituality." *Vincentiana* XXXVII (1-2, 1993): 25-47.

———————————. "The Cross in Vincentian Spirituality." Copy of unpublished draft, 1993.

———————————. "The Cross, Yesterday and Today." *Review for Religious.* 53, 4 (July-August, 1994): 544-559.

———————————. "Providence Revisited." *Review for Religious.* 54, 2 (March-April, 1995): 207-223.

Udovic, Edward R., C.M. "Caritas Christi Urget Nos: The Urgent Challenges of Charity in Seventeenth Century France." *Vincentian Heritage.* 12, 2 (1991): 85-104.

vi. Ecclesial Testimonies According to Chronological Order

Pius XI, "Discours de Sa Sainteté Pie XI, November 1, 1933. On the Occasion of the announcement of the Decree of Sainthood of Blessed Louise de Marillac. *L'Echo De La Maison-Mère,* 12 (December 1933): 252-258.

Pacelli, His Eminence, Cardinal E. "Panegyric of Saint Louise De Marillac." Given at Rome in the Church of Saint Andre Della Valle, March 14, 1934. Copy obtained from Saint Joseph's Provincial House, Emmitsburg, Maryland.

Tedeschini, Cardinal. Installation of Statue of St. Louise de Marillac in St. Peter's Basilica. April 21, 1954. *L'Echo De La Maison-Mère.* 5 (Mai 1954): 141-144.

John XXIII. Proclamation of St. Louise de Marillac, Patroness of all those who devote themselves to Christian Social Works. February 10, 1960. *L'Echo De La Maison-Mère.* 4 (avril 1960): 157-159.

John Paul II. Letter to Sister Juana Elizondo, Superior General on the Occasion of the Fourth Centenary of the Birth of St. Louise de Marillac. *Echoes of the Company.* 9-10 (October 1991): 380-383.

vii. Interviews

Charpy , Elisabeth, F. dl C. Motherhouse of the Daughters of Charity, rue du Bac, Paris. Interview, April 24, 1993.

Flinton, Margaret, D.C. Provincial House of the Daughters of Charity, Emmitsburg, Maryland. Interviews July 24, 1993 and July 20, 1994.

Henzman, Paul, C.M. Archivist, Motherhouse of the Congregation of the Mission, rue de Sèvres, Paris. Interviews, April 26, 1993 and March 15, 1994.

Maguerand, Anne Marie, F.dl C. Archivist, Motherhouse of the Daughters of Charity, rue du Bac, Paris. Interviews April 25, 1993 and March 14, 1994.

II. Source Material Related to the French School of Spirituality

1. Major Studies

Cochois, Paul. *BERULLE et l'École française.* Paris: Éditions du Seuil, 1963.
Cognet, Louis. *La Spiritualité Moderne.* Paris: Editions Aubier-Montaigne, 1966.
——————————.*Post-Reformation Spirituality.* Translated by P.J. Hepburne-Scott from *De la Dévotion moderne à la Spiritualité française.* London: Burns & Oates, 1959.
Deville, R. *L'école française de spiritualité*-Bibliothèque d'Histoire du Christianisme. n. 11 Paris: Desclée, 1987.
——————————. *The French School of Spirituality-An Introduction and Reader.* *Translated by Agnes Cunningham. Pittsburgh:* Duquesne University Press, 1994.
Pourrat, P. *Christian Spirituality.* Vol. III Westminster, MD.: Newman Press, 1953.
Bérulle and the French School Selected Writings-The Classics of Western Spirituality. Edited by William M. Thompson. Translated by Lowell M. Glendon, S.S. New York: Paulist Press, 1989.

2. Reference Texts

Aumann, Jordan. *Christian Spirituality in the Catholic Tradition.* San Francisco: Ignatius Press. London: Sheed & Ward, 1985. s.v. Chapter 9. "Modern Spirituality."
Christian Spirituality:Post Reformation and Modern-World Spirituality. Vol. 18 of World Spirituality: An Encyclopedic History of the Religious Quest. Edited by Louis Dupré and Don E. Saliers. London: SCM Press, 1990. s.v. "Seventeenth-Century French Spirituality: Three Figures." By Michael J. Buckley.
Dictionnaire du Grand Siècle. sous la direction de François Bluche. Paris: Fayard, 1990.
Dictionnaire de Spiritualité. Paris: Gabriel Beauchesne et ses fils, 1937.
  s.v. T. I. "Bérulle (Cardinal Pierre De)." By A. Molien.
  s.v. T. IV. "État." By Fernand Jetté.
  s.v. T. V. "Française (école)." By André Rayez.
  s.v. T. IX. "Louise De Marillac (sainte)." By André Dodin.
A Dictionary of Christian Spirituality. Edited by Gordon S. Wakefield. London: SCM Press Ltd. 5th ed. 1989.
New Catholic Encyclopedia. Vol. XIII. New York: McGraw-Hill, 1967. s.v. "Spirituality, French School Of." By E.A. Walsh.
Oxford Illustrated History of Christianity. Edited by John McManners. Oxford: Oxford University Press, 1992. s.v. "The Expansion of Christianity (1500-1800)." By John McManners.
The Study of Spirituality. Edited by Cheslyn Jones, Geoffrey Wainwright and Edward Yarnold, S.J. New York: Oxford Press, 1986. s.v. "Bérulle and the 'French School'." By John Saward.

3. Articles

Deville, Raymond, S.S. "Saint Vincent and Saint Louise In Relation to the French School of Spirituality." *Vincentian Heritage.* 11, 1 (1990): 29-44.
——————————————, "The Role of Saint Vincent de Paul and Saint Louise de

Marillac as Architects and as Moving Spirits behind the Spiritual and Missionary Renewal in Seventeenth-Century France." *Vincentian Heritage.* 14, 1 (1993): 1-14.

Dodin, André, c.m. "Saint Vincent de Paul, mystique de l'action religieuse." *Mission et charité.*- La Spiritualité de L'École Française. 29-30 (1968): 26-47.

Guillon, Clément, c.j.m. "Christocentrisme." *Mission et charité.*- La Spiritualité de L'École Française. 29-30 (1968): 95-102.

——————————. "Sens du péché et de la croix." *Mission et charité.*- La Spiritualité de L'École Française. 29-30 (1968): 122-129.

Milcent, Paul, c.j.m. "Une spiritualité 'contemplative'." *Mission et charité.*-La Spiritualité de L'École Française. 29-30 (1968): 113-121.

4. Related Studies and Articles

Francis de Sales, Jane de Chantal: Letters of Spiritual Direction - The Classics of Western Spirituality. Translated by Péronne Marie Thibert, V.H.M. Selected and Introduced by Wendy M. Wright and Joseph F. Power, O.S.F.S. New York: Paulist Press, 1988.

Francis de Sales, St. *Introduction A La Vie Dévote.* 1609, 1619. *Introduction to the Devout Life.* Translated and Edited by John K. Ryan. New York: Image Books Doubleday, 1989.

Francis de Sales, St. *Treatise On The Love of God.* 2 vols. Translated by Rt. Rev. John K. Ryan. Garden City, NY: Image Book by Doubleday & Co., Ltd., 1963. Rockford, Ill.,: Tan Books and Publishers, Inc., 1975.

Ravier, André, S.J. "Saint François de Sales." *Mission et Charité.* 29-30 (janvier-juin,1968): 7-25.

III. Ecclesial Documents

1. Vatican II and Papal Documents

Vatican Council II, The Conciliar and Post Conciliar Documents. Edited by Austin Flannery, O.P. Vol. I. Collegeville: Liturgical Press, 1982, 1992.
   s.v. "Perfectae Caritatis." (1965)
   s.v. "Sacrosanctum Concilium." (1963)
   s.v. "Apostolicam actuositatem." (1965)
   s.v. "Lumen Gentium." (1964)

Paul VI. *Marialis Cultus:* For the Right Ordering and Development of Devotion to the Blessed Virgin Mary. (February 2, 1974). Boston: Daughters of St. Paul, 1974.

——————————. Apostolic Exhortation *Gaudete In Domino.* (May 9, 1975). Rome: Vatican Polyglot Press, 1975.

John Paul II. Encyclical Letter *Redemptor Hominis.* (March 4, 1979). Boston: Daughters of St. Paul, 1979.

——————————. Encyclical Letter *Redemptoris Mater.* (March 25, 1987). London: Catholic Truth Society, 1987.

——————————. Apostolic Exhortation *Christifideles Laici.* On the Vocation and the Mission of the Lay Faithful in the Church and in the World. (30

December, 1988). Vatican City: Polyglot Press, 1988.
————————————. Encyclical Letter *Sollicitudo Rei Socialis.* (December 30, 1987) Boston: St. Paul Publ., 1989.
————————————. Apostolic Letter *Mulieris Dignitatem.* (15 August, 1988). Sherbrooke, QC: Les Éditions Paulines, 1988.
————————————. Encyclical Letter *Redemptoris Missio.* The Mission of Christ the Redeemer. (7 December, 1990) Sherbrooke, QC: Editions Paulines, 1991.
————————————. *Tertio Millennio Adveniente.* Apostolic Letter On Preparation for the Jubilee of the Year 2000. (10 November 1994). Vatican City: Libreria Editrice Vaticana, 1994.
————————————. Encyclical Letter *Evangelium Vitae.* The Gospel of Life. (25 March, 1995). Vatican City: Libreria Editrice Vaticana, 1995.
————————————. "Women: Teachers of Peace, Message of Pope John Paul II for the 1995 World Day of Peace." L'Osservatore Romano, English Edition. N.50. 14 December 1994.
————————————. "Letter of The Holy Father, Pope John Paul II, to Priests for Holy Thursday 1995." Vatican City: Vatican Press, 1995.

2. Other Ecclesial Documents

The Code of Canon Law: A Text and Commentary. Edited by James A. Coriden, Thomas J. Green and Donald E. Heintschel. New York: Paulist Press, 1985.
Catechism of the Catholic Church. Città del Vaticano: Libereria Editrice Vaticana, 1994.
Document de Puebla, IV, 2 *Libertatis Nuntius.* Boston: Daughters of St. Paul, 1984.

IV. Other Books

A Kempis, Thomas. *Imitation of Christ.* William C. Creasy. Notre Dame, In.: Ave Maria Press, 1989.
Aumann, Jordan, O.P. *Spiritual Theology.* London: Sheed & Ward, 1980, 1993.
Battelli, G., mccj. *Religious Life in the light of the new Canon Law.* Africa: St. Paul Publications, 1990, 1993.
Bielecki, Tessa. *Teresa of Avila, Mystical Writings.* New York: Crossroads, 1994.
Blaquiere, Georgette. *The Grace to Be a Woman.* Translated by Robert Wild. New York: Alba House, 1983.
Christian Spirituality: Post-Reformation and Modern. Edited by Louis Dupré and Don E. Saliers. New York: Crossroad, 1991. s.v. "St. John of the Cross." By Kieran Kavanaugh.
Giardini, Fabio, O.P. *The Varieties and Unity of Christian Prayerlife.* Rome: PUST, 1994.
The Holy Bible. New Revised Standard Version:Catholic Edition. Toronto: CBS, 1993.
John Paul II. *Crossing the Threshold of Hope.* Translated by Jenny McPhee and Martha McPhee. Edited by Vittorio Messori. London: Jonathan Cape, 1994.
Julian of Norwich. *Revelations of Divine Love.* Edited by Halcyon Backhouse with Rhona Pipe. London: Hodder and Stoughton, 1987, 1992.
Kavanaugh, Kieran, O.C.D. *John of the Cross, Selected Writings.* The Classics of Western Spirituality. New York: Paulist Press, 1987.
Murray, Paul, O.P. *The Mysticism Debate.* Scotdale, Penn.: Herald Press, 1977.
Muto, Susan A. *Meditation in Motion.* New York: Image Books, 1986.

——————————————. *John Of The Cross For Today: The Ascent.* Notre Dame, Indiana: Ave Maria Press, 1991.

Noffke, Susanne, O.P. *Catherine of Siena: The Dialogue.* New York: Paulist Press, 1980.

O'Driscoll, Mary, O.P. ed. *Catherine of Siena: Passion for the Truth, Compassion for Humanity.* New York: New City Press, 1993.

Poulain, A., S.J. *The Graces of Interior Prayer.* (1910) Translated by Leonora L. Yorke Smith. Westminster, Vt.: Celtic Cross Books, 1950, 1978.

Premm, Matthias. *Dogmatic Theology for the Laity.* Rockford, Ill.: Tan Books and Publishers, Inc., 1977.

Rapley, Elizabeth. *The Dévotes- Women & Church in Seventeenth-Century France.* Montreal & Kingston: McGill-Queen's University Press, 1993.

Sheldrake, Philip, S.J. *Spirituality & History.* London: SPCK, 1991.

Teresa of Avila, St. *Interior Castle.* Translated and Edited by E. Allison Peers. New York: Image Books, 1961.

——————————————. *The Collected Works of St. Teresa of Avila.* Translated by K. Kavanaugh, OCD, and O. Rodriguez, OCD. Washington DC: Institute of Carmelite Studies, 1976.

——————————————. *The Book of Her Life. The Collected Works of St. Teresa of Avila.* Vol. I. Translated by Kieran Kavanaugh, O.C.D. and O. Rodriguez, O.C.D. Washington: ICS Publishers, 1987.

Thérèse of Lisieux, St. *The Autobiography of Saint Thérèse of Lisieux- The Story of A Soul.* Translated by John Beevers. New York: Image, Doubleday, 1957, 1959.

Thomas Aquinas, St. *A Tour of the Summa.* Edited by Msgr. Paul J. Glenn. Rockford, Ill.: Tan Books and Publishers,Inc. 1978.

Thompson, William H. *Christology and Spirituality.* New York: Crossroad Publishing Co., 1991.

van Kamm, Adrian, C.S.Sp., Ph.D. and Muto, Susan, Ph.D. "Becoming Spiritually Mature." A Video Series With Printed Formation Guide. Pittsburgh, PA.: Epiphany Association, 1991.

Also available from New City Press . . .

THE WAY OF VINCENT DE PAUL
A Contemporary Spirituality in Service of the Poor
by Robert P. Maloney, C.M., Superior General

What was the spiritual road that St. Vincent traveled? Why have hundreds of thousands of people been inspired by his example and even followed his way? Robert Maloney addresses these intriguing questions and outlines in helpful, practical terms how to follow Vincent's way in today's world. Whether you follow Vincent's way of charity already or if you are interested as to what it might be, *The Way of Vincent de Paul* will help you discover the heart of this vibrant and modern way of life.

"This book draws principally from Vincent's writings to present a schematic view of his spiritual way. The author looks at the ideals which Vincent presented, how these were modified in their original practice, and how this vision is interpreted in the twentieth century."

SPIRITUAL BOOK NEWS

"Father Robert Maloney offers *The Way of Vincent de Paul* to all who would like to become more acquainted with the spiritual vision of this man whose name immediately conjures up not only the poor but the challenge of serving them."

RICHARD R. MCCULLEN, *C.M.*
*Former Superior General of the Congregation of the Mission
and the Daughters of Charity*

ISBN 1-56548-001-5, **4th print.**
paperback, 5 3/8 x 8 1/2, 176 pp., $9.95

To order phone 1- 800 - 462-5980

And . . .

HE HEARS THE CRY OF THE POOR
On the Spirituality of Vincent de Paul
by Robert P. Maloney, C.M. Superior General

In *He Hears the Cry of the Poor* Robert Maloney addresses vital questions of religious communities today. His vision is filled with hope and promise as he discusses the renewal of community and prayer life, the apostolate, and the growing international character of communities. Throughout the book, Father Maloney puts into active and creative dialogue voices from the past and the present. Vincent and his spiritual friends come alive, not only as a force in seventeenth-century France, but as partners in conversation with men and women of today. This book is an excellent resource and guide for those who follow a Vincentian spiritual life, as well as anyone who takes an active role in their Christian community.

"There is a vital relevance to this book, a creative effort of leadership needed by all groups in the Church. I encourage all men and women in consecrated life to read this timely book. Father Maloney is a voice that needs to be heard."

GERALD L. BROWN, *S.S.*
President of the U.S. Conference of Major Superiors of Men

ISBN 1-56548-034-1, **2d print.**
paperback, 5 3/8 x 8 1/2, 168 pp., $9.95

To order phone 1- 800 - 462-5980

And . . .

VINCENT DE PAUL AND CHARITY
**A *Contemporary Portrait of His Life and Apostolic Spirit*
*by André Dodin, C.M.***

Finally a book for all those in search of St. Vincent's spiritual way. *Vincent de Paul and Charity* will take you on a journey of discovery. Dodin will lead you to an unforgettable encounter with a sharp, vibrant and modern personality, who taught and testified with his life that "human actions become actions of God when they are performed in him and through him." You will examine Vincent's charitable works and learn the power of his spiritual way. Dodin, while mentoring you with his unassuming style, will delicately challenge you to follow this way of faith in the love of God. Enjoy *Vincent de Paul and Charity* in one reading, or taste it in bits and pieces, but don't miss the opportunity to learn and live Vincent's experience.

"A lively portrait of St. Vincent in three parts: the main events of his life and ministry, his spiritual way, and the Vincentian tradition. The book is complemented by sixteen pages of photos, over thirty pages of short quotes from Vincent's writings, and an updated annotated bibliography."

SPIRITUAL BOOK NEWS

ISBN 1-56548-054-6, **2d print.**
paperback, 5 3/8 x 8 1/2, 144 pp., $9.95

To order phone 1- 800 - 462-5980